T o k

RES...
GUIDE

トーキョージャーナル・レストランガイド

Tokyo Journal's

TOKYO
RESTAURANT
GUIDE

トーキョージャーナル・レストランガイド

by John Kennerdell

Yohan Publications, Inc.
Tokyo, Japan

Published by Yohan Publications, Inc.
14-9, Okubo 3-chome
Shinjuku-ku
Tokyo, Japan

ISBN4-89684-246-4 C2026
Printed in Japan

CONTENTS
目次

Foreword

Tokyo is no place for a comprehensive or definitive or enduring restaurant guide. For a start we just have too many restaurants—surely more than any other city—and they open and close, remodel, restaff and mutate faster than anyone could possibly track.

What we can do is give you a selection of current favorites, about one for each day of the year. They represent a careful pick of the several thousand I've visited on and off the job for *Tokyo Journal* over the past decade. Some are well known and loved among the gourmet circles of this food-obsessed city. Others are more personal finds, oddities and secrets finally ready to be shared. Together they can only hint at the culinary resources of Tokyo. Sampled one after another, they would make for a year of eating adventures almost beyond imagination.

Our emphasis here is on good food, but also a few other basic principles: congenial atmosphere, personable service, outdoor seating when possible, freedom from cigarette smoke if that's your preference, decent music or none at all. Mostly we've sought value for money. Tokyo becomes unreal very quickly otherwise.

We concentrate on the areas of town with the most culinary excitement, although we've tried not to neglect the others. Our selection probably demonstrates an unfair prejudice against places in hotels, department stores, underground arcades and eighth stories of 12-story buildings. Conversely, we've made a real effort to find outdoor and other atmospheric dining spots. Our listings are purposely low on big-ticket Japanese and French places: Japanese because they're a limitless dream world of their own (and there are already good guides available in Japanese); French because frankly so many of them are becoming dinosaurs, designed and priced for a disappearing generation of diners.

In fact except for a few splurges, we've restricted ourselves to restaurants where dinner will come to no more than ¥10,000 per head. Most will cost less than half that, and lunches will be cheaper still. It can't be said often enough: eat lots of good lunches in Tokyo.

Above all this book simply attempts to be truly *useful*. We try not to send you across town for a bowl of ramen only marginally better than what you'll find at the end of your own block. We've sought out places that we feel are either really worth a trip or else located near where you're likely to be anyway. Thanks to our multinational advisory panel,

はじめに

この二カ国語版、トーキョージャーナル・レストランガイドを出版するにあたって、大変な喜びを覚えずにはいられないということをまず申し上げておきましょう。

私が世界の料理(食物)を学ぶことを目的とした世界一周旅行の途中で、学生として来日したのは、７０年代中期でした。東京は大都市であるので、そこにあるレストランは、当然ニューヨークやパリのものに匹敵するものと信じていました。ところが、結果は失望に終わったのです。もちろん日本食は素晴しかったのですが、私の大好物、イタリア料理のレベルは、ピッツァか、油でぎとぎととしたスパゲティといった程度だったのです。これに比べるとフランス料理は、まだましだったともいえます。でもフランスにいた時私がよく足を運んだ安くて親切なレストランとは違い、ひどくスノッブで、値段も法外だったのです。中国、インド、メキシコ等々、どの料理も現地のものとは似ても似つかぬものばかり。その上、この(世界一周)旅行中、私が一番興味を持った、タイ、マレーシア、スリランカ、レバノン、ブラジル等の料理は、当時存在すらしていませんでした。

過去２０年の間、初めは単なるグルメとして、続いては英語情報誌の『トーキョージャーナル』のコラムニストとして、東京が国際的なグルメの中心地に成長していくのを目のあたりにできたことは、大変な幸運だったのではないでしょうか。

今日、海外から東京を訪れる人々は、私が来た頃とはまったく違い恵まれたレストラン・シーンを体験できるのだと思うと、羨ましい限りです。そんな中で、本当の意味での国際的レストランガイドが出されるのは、まさに時間の問題であったともいえるでしょう。

本書はその対象が、日本人、外国人に関わらず、むしろ世界の他の主要都市にあるレストランを見る時と同じ目で東京のレストランを見た、つまり、その料理の国籍は問題ではなく、他のグルメ都市と同じ基準で、料理、雰囲気、サービスを評価したガイドであるのです。

こう言ってしまうと、当り前のように聞こえるかもしれませんが、実のところ、日本のレストランガイドでは初めての試みなのです。これまでのガイドは、未だに本格的だの、本場の味だのという表現を使っていますが、基本的に大都市では、良いレストランが本格的なのは当然で、例えばシドニーの場合、中国、イタリア、ギリシャなどのレストランは、一般的にその国の人の為のレストランである場合がほとんどで、本格的でなければ数ヵ月ともたないのが現実といっても過言ではありません。

日本のガイドブックで、これほどまでに本格的という言葉が頻繁に使われた訳は、長い間にわたって本格的でないレストラン、つまりXX風ということを看板にした料理が、本物を経験も理解もしていない調理人たちによって作られてきたからでしょう。そして、料理よりも内装や従業員の服装、BGMなどの方に力を入れた店を選んでしまっていたのです。

また、こういう本の中でしばしば、日本人の口に合うという表現でレストランの料理を褒めています。確かに多くの日本人に好まれる味なのでしょう。では、日本人は世界中のグルメたちが好む味を理解することが出来ないほどに、

we've tried to approach Tokyo from neither an "expat" nor a "Japanese" perspective, but simply as a world city, at last ready for comparison with any other.

So how does it compare? For any given cuisine (including Japanese, some might say) there are still places on this globe where you might objectively eat "better." There may even be a city or two where you might enjoy a finer cross-section of the world's foods. I doubt if there's any place where you would find restaurants of more devotion or energy or antic diversity. Tokyo's great gift is its ability to reconcile blue-suit salaryman normality with the non-normal, the arcane, the totally off-the-wall. For all its culinary frustrations over the years, it has finally become—for me anyway—the most fascinating restaurant city in the world.

The usual caveats apply. I've gone back to almost every place listed here within the months before publication, and have assigned the stars and yen signs subjectively but, I hope, fairly. It's not an exact science. Some familiar names are missing, either because of creeping prices or declining quality or simply failure to keep up with the standards of the times. These things happen to the best of establishments. As do disappearances, new identities, or just changes in operating hours and days. It's never a bad idea to call ahead, especially if you're making a special trip. Note that many of these places don't (yet) receive much non-Japanese business. Japanese language ability will smooth the way, but don't let it worry you if you don't have it.

Please think of this book as a work in progress. Feel free to take part. As long as there is a *Tokyo Journal*, there will be a fax number where your comments, advice, ideas, and information are welcome. This city needs an honest, internationally oriented guide to its food. Provided there's interest and demand, we hope to continue to revise and refine this one.

And now, before I now recede into the first person plural, let me personally thank *Tokyo Journal* staff members Gregory Starr for proposing this book and ushering it through production, Kyoko Matsuda and Michiko Toyama for research and translation, Douglas Gordon for art direction and the cover illustration and Tomomi Shimokawa for layout; Koichiro Ando for Japanese-language editing; our readers for their support and input; founding *TJ* muse and mentor Naoko Tsunoi; Rick Kennedy, with whom I've shared proprietorship of the *TJ* food column since the early years of the magazine; our distinguished advisory panel (Andreas Braem, Wolfgang Bechstein, Godfrey Bull, Peter Evans, John Gauntner, Bryan Harrell, Mac Jeffrey, Kevin McAuliffe, Julia Nolet, Sachiko Otsuka, Tui Ruwhiu, Ken Straiton, Maki Takano, Muneo Wakabayashi, and Bill and Yumi Womack); and, most of all, the innumerable and incomparable chefs of Tokyo.

味覚の幅が狭いのでしょうか。もちろん答えはノーです。現代の日本人はあらゆる種類の料理を食べ、楽しむことを知っています。事実、日本人が大好きな料理の中には、初めて口にするには躊躇するような物も多くあります。チリ、ガーリックに始まって、ありとあらゆるスパイスを探し求めている日本人たちには、もう手加減など必要ないでしょう。

過去１０年間のレストラン・シーンは、食べる側も含め劇的な変化をしています。いまでは、本物でない料理は簡単に見破られてしまうのですが、東京にはそんな偽物の料理を見分けるガイド、つまり本書のような正直で正確で、頼りになる助っ人がまだまだ必要です。私自身が食通かどうかは分かりませんが（実際は'通'でないことを望んでいますが）、本書は、料理に多少こだわりがあるけど、ばかばかしい料金を払うようなことをしたくない普通の人が、優良な東京のレストランを見つけ出すためのガイドです。

結果として毒舌に聞こえてしまう部分がたまにあるかもしれませんが、お気に入りのレストランにでさえ、度々欠点を見つけてしまう私であるということを承知しておいて下さい。

いろいろな場所を回った結果、載せる価値のない場所は削除しました。つまり、この本に載っているどのレストランも、少なくとも一度は行ってみるべきだと私が確信する場所なのです。

人生のほとんどのものがそうであるように、この本も完璧ではないかもしれませんし、その欠点をあえて否定しようとも思っていません。

ただ、レストラン選びの指標としてお使いいただくのが目的です。また本書は日本人読者に理解してもらおうと、世界中のレストランガイドと同様の編集方針を採っております。

ここでは、日本語のレストランガイドには見られなかった幾つかのユニークなテーマ、例えば、スタッフがロボットのようにではなく人間らしく振る舞っているレストラン、屋外スペースのあるレストラン、煙草の煙に邪魔されずに食事のできるレストラン等々も用意してあります。逆に、この町で一般に出回っているガイドと違い、この中華料理店は最高の材料を使っているとか、あるフランス料理店は料理に季節毎の色合いを与えているとか、直輸入された８種のスパイスをブレンドしたカレーを出す店があるなどという当り前で不必要なせりふは省かせてもらいました。

むしろ、私が重点をおいたのは、少なくとも個人のレベルにおいて、こうしたレストランのどこが本当の目玉なのかということで、しいていえば、それが料理ではない場合もあるのです。（一部の日本のガイドは、料理に比重を置き過ぎているような気がします。）

私はこの本に出来る限りの事実、意見、批判をとり混ぜたつもりです。最終的にどのレストランに行きたいのかを決めるのは、もちろんあなた自身です。しかしこの本は、東京外食文化への新スタイルのアプローチを行う、また素晴しい新スポットを探す上で大きな助けとなることでしょう。

どんなご意見でもあればお寄せ下さい。こうした事から反省、発見を繰り返し、東京人のあらゆる要求に答えられる、より良いガイドを作っていくことができると思うのです。

KEY
利用法

 Credit cards accepted
クレジットカード可

 English menu
英語メニュー有

 Non-smoking seating available
禁煙席有

 Outdoor (or open-fronted) seating available
屋外／テラス有

 Reservations required or strongly advised
要予約、または予約したほうがよい店

 Vegetarian/natural food
ベジタリアン料理／自然食

Food Quality

★★★★ Among the best of its type anywhere
大変良い

★★★ Very good
かなり良い

★★ Good
良い

★ Food isn't the main attraction
普通

Price

¥¥¥¥	A major splurge (¥10,000/person and up) かなり高め (ひとり10000円以上)
¥¥¥	A minor splurge (¥6000 to ¥10,000/person) やや高め (ひとり6000円〜10000円)
¥¥	Moderate (¥3000 to ¥6000/person) 普通 (ひとり3000円〜6000円)
¥	Cheap, for Tokyo (¥3000/person or less) 安め (ひとり3000円以下)

RESTAURANT LISTINGS

レストラン・リスト

AJANTA

3-11 Nibancho,
Chiyoda-ku
Tel: 3264-6955
Open: 24 hours a day

Indian
¥¥
★★★

Map 9

アジャンタ

Ajanta sticks to its guns, serving food more faithful to the true Indian tradition than any other restaurant in town. Their standard bread is the humble chappati; their curries, thinner and spicier than the buttery, purée-style Mogul curries standard in Tokyo. Their own favorite curry is their *sambar*, a southern-style dhal, and even they'll admit that lentils have never been a big hit in Japan. "But don't you have *nan*?" ask many first-time Japanese visitors, panicking slightly. Yes they do, *and* tandoori mixed grill *and* chicken masala. But Ajanta's heart is clearly in the more mid- to southern-Indian styles, and we should be thankful for the diversity. Of special note here is the fact they'll serve you a good Indian breakfast any time of day or night.

サモサ、ダール(レンズ豆のカレー)、チャパティ(薄いパン)など、最も典型的なインド料理を出す店。しかし、「チャパティって何？ナンは置いてないの？」「レンズ豆のカレーなんて美味しそうじゃないな。チキンマサラはないの？」なんていう、インド北部の特定の料理に慣れてしまった東京っ子のお客が多いので、ここのスタッフには同情してしまう。本当は現地の大部分のインド人が食べている料理なのに、知らない彼らは二の足を踏んでしまうわけだ。確かに北部の料理は美味しいが、ここの本物の味にもトライして欲しい。

AKAONI

Classic wooden-floor interior, a dedicated if slightly disorganized young staff who work in street clothes, and a general sense that *nihonshu*—saké—is a thing of almost religious importance. Provided you don't get falling-down drunk or light up a "strong" cigarette (they list taboo brands) they'll share with you what may be Tokyo's premier collection of connoisseur-grade saké. Not that it stays the same: the 100 or so kinds here evolve on an almost daily basis.

Recommended to eat: the *maguro* "spareribs" and any of the sashimi. The

2-15-3 Sangenjaya,
Setagaya-ku
Tel: 3410-9918
Open: 5:30pm-12:30am;
closed Sun. & hol.

Izakaya
¥¥
★★★ 1/2

Map 26

rest of the food could be a bit more inspired and the master a little more gracious to nihonshu newcomers, but these are quibbles—Akaoni is one of the greats.

木目調で統一されたクラシックなインテリア、ストリート・ファッションに身を包んだ若いスタッフは、プロとは呼びがたいものの献身的である。この店では「日本酒」を神聖なものとしてとらえていて、泥酔したり、香りの強い煙草を吸う人は敬遠される。銘酒のコレクションはおそらく東京で最も充実していると思われ、常時100前後の銘柄があるが、往々にして新入荷のものがベストである場合が多い。特にお薦めなのは、搾り立て酒か大吟醸濁り酒。また、バラエティーに富んだ居酒屋料理の味は充分に平均を上回っているといえよう。

赤鬼

AKIMOTO

3-4 Kojimachi,
Chiyoda-ku
Tel: 3261-6762
Open: 11:30am-2pm &
5-8pm; closed Sun., hol.
& 2nd Sat.

Unagi (eel)
¥¥
★★★

Map 10

A study in *shitamachi* (the old Tokyo "downtown") contradictions. Expect a crowd and a wait, but it's pleasantly atmospheric and the line moves right along. The service tends toward the brusque, yet always in impeccably polite language. The *unagi* is an exquisite handmade production; the prices, not much more than for a box of chicken wings at the Colonel's down the street. Choose *unadon* (eel over rice in a porcelain bowl) or *unaju* (in the more authentic lacquer box). For either, you specify *matsu* (pine), *take* (bamboo), *ume* (plum) or *tsuru* (crane), an ascending scale of eel thickness and quality where even the lowest will not disappoint.

外国人の目から見ると、ここでの下町体験は驚きの連続だ。いつも行列していて待たされるが、それも雰囲気は悪くなく嫌ではない。また客への対応はそっけないが、言葉遣いは丁寧だ。鰻の蒲焼きはきちんと手焼きをしているのに、値段はケンタッキー・フライド・チキンと大差がない！ 値段のわりには美味しい鰻だ。

秋本

ALLORO

Nice atmosphere!
Not large portions.
Good food though.

Festa Azabu Bldg., 6F,
1-7-5 Azabu Juban,
Minato-ku
Tel: 5474-2106
Open: 6-11pm; closed
Sun. & hol.

French
¥¥ 1/2
★★★

CC 🖊 ⛩ **Map 3**

More reason to be grateful for the bursting of the economic bubble: previously an overpriced Italian restaurant, Alloro decided a couple of years ago that its survival lay in becoming a very reasonably priced, very good French restaurant. So for ¥3800 they now offer a wide choice of starters and main courses, all colossal in size and served in a spacious, high-ceilinged room that was clearly designed to cost a lot more. Reserve at least a day in advance and they'll even let you in for lunch (noon-3pm).

以前は高級なイタリア料理を出していたこの店も、バブル崩壊後は手頃な値段のフランス料理に切り替えて、店の名前はイタリア語だが、フランス料理でサービスしている。天井の高い広々とした店内で食べる3800円のコースは、豊富なメニューから前菜とメインディッシュが選べ、すべてにボリュームがあって申し分ない。ワイングラスを傾けながら窓の外を眺めれば、そこから見える東京タワーもエッフェル塔に見えるかもしれない。通常ランチは営業していないが前日までに予約をすれば、月〜金の午後12時〜3時の間2800円のコースを出してくれる。

アローロ

AL PONTE

2-4-3 Nihonbashi Hamacho,
Chuo-ku
Tel: 3666-4499
Open: 11:30am-3pm & 5:30-11pm; closed Sun. & hol.

Italian
¥¥¥
★★★

CC 🍴 **Map 16**

Highly credible northern Italian food in a quarter better known for traditional Japanese cuisine. The ¥5000 dinner includes appetizer, pasta and main course. There's plenty of each to choose from, with an emphasis on fish. The main problem here is simply getting in: as the last best Italian restaurant between downtown Tokyo and the bay, Al Ponte has all the salaryman, OL and *enkai* (roughly "party," but less fun) business it could ever use.

和食の店が多い日本橋で、イタリア北部の料理を出すこの店では豊富なメニューの中から前菜とパスタ、メインに自慢の魚料理が5000円のコースで味わえる。内装はモダンで、白い壁と高い天井がゆっ

アル・ポンテ

たりとした気分にさせてくれる。しかしこの界隈ではここが唯一の美味しいイタリア料理店で、いつもサラリーマンやOL、そして宴会のグループで満員なので予約は早めにしたほうがよい。

AN AN

3-22-9 Higashi,
Shibuya-ku
Tel: 3498-6863
Open: 5:30-11:15pm;
closed Sun. & hol.

Mukokuseki
¥¥
★★★

CC **Map 5**

No use looking for An An outside of business hours: it's just a peeling black wall and an unmarked door. Then each evening they put their menu out on a stand and it becomes a restaurant. Inside is all tatami but, curiously, with tables and chairs. Seating is communal and fortunately An An attracts the kind of trade that makes it work: young but not juvenile, hip but not overly impressed with the fact. Skilled, imaginative food in a sort of 21st-century Japanese mode: *daikon* salad with scallops, *"negitoro" maki* of raw beef, kimchi gyoza, *yoshoku*-style meat and potato croquettes.

杏庵

毎晩外に出されるメニューで、どうにかここがレストランだと分かるような外観だ。畳の上にテーブルとイスというインテリアの中で、若過ぎない客たちと相席で食べる21世紀ジャポネスク料理は楽しい。ダイコンのサラダ、和牛ネギトロ巻、キムチギョーザ、韓国風豚鍋、手作り荒挽き肉じゃがコロッケなどがお薦め。

いつも日本では様々な形で、肉料理の食べ放題が流行しているように思える。10年前は焼肉であり、現在は巨大な肉の塊から皿に直接切り落としていくというブラジル料理のシュラスコが大流行中。欲深い肉好きなら、サンパウロに本店がある『バルバッコア・グリル』（渋谷区神宮前4-3-24（☎）3796-0571)か、ライブのサンバが楽しめる『スーペル・バッカーナ』（中央区銀座6-8-5（☎）3573-5499)がお薦め。

ANGKOR WAT

1-38-13 Yoyogi,
Shibuya-ku
Tel: 3370-3019
Open: 11am-2pm & 5-11pm

Cambodian
¥¥
★★★

Big, noisy and crowded, and with reason: Angkor Wat is working at the peak of its powers these days. Just say *"Omakase"* ("Give us what you will") and they'll feed you till you beg them to stop. It shouldn't cost more than about ¥3000 a head. Standards here are the spicy salads, beef/vegetable rolls, chicken curry and fried and soup noodles. They've now opened a branch in Shibuya (3477-1010).

✄ **Map 23**

アンコール ワット

以前は小さな寿司屋だった場所に、80年代初頭にカンボジアから来た難民が始めた店。今ではスペースも拡張され、満員の店内にはいつも絶頂期のパワーがみなぎっている。ひとり3000円見当のおまかせ料理を頼めば、食べきれないほどの料理を運んで来てくれる。渋谷店（渋谷区道玄坂1-16-16（☎）3477-1010）もある。

APADANA

4-29-4 Jingu-mae,
Shibuya-ku
Tel: 5474-2524
Open: 11:30am-11pm

Iranian
¥¥
★★

Spacious, friendly and conveniently located on the Harajuku main drag. It's also among the best of Tokyo's new crop of Iranian restaurants, specializing in *chelo* (yogurt-marinated lamb), *jujeb* (chicken) and *mahi* (fish) kebabs. For Tokyoites who find Persian cooking a bit bland after all of our high-octane Indian food, Apadana does a medium-spicy curry. Also healthy salads, saffron rice and unleavened bread.

✈ **Map 6**

原宿のメインストリートに面している、ロケーションが最高のフレンドリーなイラン料理の店。代表的なメニューは子羊をヨーグルトでマリネにしたチェロ、ジュジュブ（チキン）、マヒ（魚）ケバブなど。イラン、ペルシャ料理はちょっと味に刺激が足りないという人にはぴったりの中辛カレーもある。またヘルシーなサラダ、サフランライス、一風変わったパンも味わえる。

アパダナ

APETITO

4-3-24 Jingu-mae,
Shibuya-ku
Tel: 3497-0170
Open: 8am-10pm;
Sun. & hol., 8am-9pm

Italian
¥ 1/2
★

📖 🎋 **Map 2**

アペティート

Well-constructed—if rather miniaturized—sandwiches and salads to take out or eat there, preferably outdoors on the patio. They also have an above-average selection of breads and pastries. Best avoided at noon on weekdays: it's a mob scene.

サイズはやや小さめだが、この店の美味しいサンドイッチとサラダはテイクアウトしてもいいし、店内で食べても、もちろん屋外のパティオで食べてもいい。ちょっと工夫を凝らしたパンやペーストリーも美味しい。平日のランチタイムは混雑するので待たされる覚悟が必要だ。

Cambodian food works by contradiction: it's Thai rich and Vietnamese light. Standards include spicy salads, spring rolls and pancake-type dishes, noodle soups and robust stir-fries. The seafood is always worth a try (lobster is a favorite), and Cambodian curry marks the eastern mainland extreme of this most geographically diverse of all spicing styles. One noteworthy dish not in our listings: "Khmer noodle sauté" at Phnom Penh (1-10-14 Ebisu Nishi, Shibuya-ku, 3461-2769), noodles fried crisp, softened with a spicy, sour sauce, then topped with slivers of red bell peppers, green onions, bean sprouts and bits of sweet pork.

ARABIA

1 6 1 Jinnan,
Shibuya-ku
Tel: 5489-3047
Open: 5-10:30pm; Sun. & hol.
until 10pm; closed Mon.

Middle Eastern
¥¥
★★

Map 19

アラビア

Homey restaurant/antique shop: you dine amid countless old hoes, shovels, pickaxes, bellows, pulleys, water scoops, kerosene lanterns and ox harnesses. Beware of the drab chicken, but the tabuleh, hummus, couscous and shish kebab all pass muster.

家庭的な雰囲気のレストランでアンティーク・ショップも兼ねているから、滑車、提灯、シャベルなどの古い道具類に囲まれて食事をすることになる。鶏肉料理は特筆するほどではないが、タブーリ、ハマス（中東風サラダ／ディップ）、クスクス、シシケバブはなかなかのものだ。

ARGENT

1-25-12 Nakacho, Meguro-ku
Tel: 3792-4445
Open: 6pm-midnight;
closed Sun.

French
¥¥¥
★★★

Map 27

アージェント

The good news: four tables of good family-style eating, cooked by gentle chef Nobu Kawaguchi (he comes from a line of *kappo* and sushi chefs) and served by owner Yuri Sugimoto. The not-so-good news: a not-especially-cheap wine list of only Beaujolais, a debased name if there ever was one. Stick with the house red or white. Recommended: tuna tartare, the pâté of the day, the remarkable seafood salad and any of the stews.

テーブルが四つだけの小さな空間で、割烹、寿司の板前出身のシェフ川口氏が優しくもてなしてくれる家庭的な雰囲気のレストラン。ただ感心できないのは、ボージョレイだけのワインリストで、物珍しさもなくなった割に値段も決して安くないことだ。ハウスワインの赤か白にしておくのが無難だろう。お薦めはタルタルツナ、日変わりのパテ、シチュー各種で、特に、シーフード・サラダは絶品。

ARI'S LAMPLIGHT

7-8-1 Minami Aoyama,
Minato-ku
Tel: 3499-1573
Open: 5:30pm-2am;
closed Sun.

American
¥¥
★★

Map 17

An expat institution, whether for the green beer and Irish songs around the piano on St. Patrick's Day or for the adult-size, charcoal-broiled lamb chops, burgers and other simple American fare anytime. It's at its best on Thursday nights, when local musicians drop in to play swing-era jazz. Ari, in case it isn't obvious, is the Bogartian fellow simultaneously playing piano, talking on the telephone and dangling a cigarette from his lower lip.

セント・パトリックス・デーのグリーンに着色したビールと、ピアノを囲んでみんなで歌うアイルランド民謡のせいか、この店は昔から在日外国人のファンが多い。ビッグサイズの炭火焼きラムチョップ、ハンバーガー、その他のシンプルで飽きのこないアメリカ料理もその所以か

アーリーズ ランプライト

も知れない。地元のミュージシャンたちが
ジャズを演奏する木曜の夜はがぜん外国人
客が増える。店のマスター、アーリー氏は
映画「カサブランカ」のボギーみたいにい
つもタバコをくわえながらピアノを弾いて
いるダンディーな人だ。

ASENA

v.good food.
Belly dancer on
wednesday!

Gojuban Bldg., B1,
5-5-11 Akasaka, Minato-ku
Tel: 3505-5282
Open: 11:30am-2:30pm
& 6-11:30pm; closed Sun.

excellent.

Turkish
¥¥
★★★

Map 1

Currently our favorite Turkish place, which
is praise indeed: Tokyo now has dozens,
and standards are high. Asena has all the
true signs of authenticity, like the four
glasses of herbs and spices on every table:
thyme, peppermint, chili powder and a
lemony red powder that has defied
attempts at translation. Or the middle-aged
Turkish gentlemen lounging around the bar
area, not quite staff but not customers
either. Potent *raki* too, and green plush
snack bar stools in one corner, 1966
Akasaka mirrored walls all around and a
belly dancer every Saturday night

Recommended: *karisik meze* mixed
appetizer plate, *imam bayildi* ("The Imam
Sighed") eggplant, *pide* "pizza" and the
superb *iskender kebab*, a sprawling open-
faced kebab sandwich afloat in tomato
sauce and yogurt.

最も自信を持って推薦できるトルコ料理の
店。東京ではこうした店が増え、その水準
も上がった今、確かな支持者を獲得してい
るのは賞賛ものだ。ここには本物ならでは
のしるしがいくつかあって、そのひとつに
はどのテーブルにもタイムやペパーミン
ト、チリパウダーなどのハーブやスパイス
がほのかな酸味のある香りを放ちながら置
かれている。内装も緑色の豪華なバー・カ
ウンターや60年代の赤坂のクラブ風に鏡を
張り巡らせた壁面など、どこかトルコを彷
彿させる。土曜の夜にはベリーダンスも楽
しめる。お薦めは、カリセクメゼ（前菜の
盛り合わせ）、イマンバイルデイ茄子、ピ
デ（ピッツァ）、イスケンデーケバブ（トマ
トソースとヨーグルトで和えたケバブの
オープンサンド）、ラキ（焼酎に似た薬効性
のあるブドウのブランデー）など。

アセナ

ASHOKA

7-9-18 Ginza,
Chuo-ku
Tel: 3572-2377
Open: 11:30am-10pm;
Sun., noon-8:30pm

Indian
¥¥
★★★

 Map 7

アショカ

The waiters wear tuxes, there's real carpet on the floor and cloth on the tables, and generally a sense of more individual space and service than at the big popular chains. You pay for this, of course—most of the curries are in the ¥1500 to ¥1800 range—but even at these prices, Indian food delivers more cooking skill per yen than any other cuisine in this city. The Ashoka style is rich, refined and low on the heat. In addition to the standard chicken, mutton and fish curries, they do a small but excellent selection of meatless dishes, notably the hearty *malai kofta.* Branches in Nishi Shinjuku (3344-4588) and Omiya (048-646-2372).

古風なスタイルという意味では、東京で一番洗練されたインド料理の店といえるだろう。ウェイターはタキシードを着用し、フロアーには贅沢な絨毯、テーブルにはしゃれたクロスがかかっていて、店内のスペースも広く、サービスも行き届いている。カレー一品の値段が1500円から1800円と値段は高めだが、コックの腕のレベルからいったら決して高くはないだろう。この店の料理はリッチで上品で辛さも控えめだ。スタンダードなチキン、マトン、フィッシュカレーに加え、質の良いベジタリアン向けのメニューもある。

AU MOUTON BLANC

Gone are the roses on the tables and the red drapes on the walls: the miniature Mouton Blanc has stripped down for speed. From its name (no longer the "Auberge") to the spartan decor, this is a lean, clean, French dining machine. Including the menu: dinner is a flat ¥3000 now, including choice of starter (recommended: *salade du fromage*), main course (they're good with lamb) and dessert (make ours the sorbet). Food quality is very much in the **Pas à Pas/ Le Mange-Tout/La Dînette** cheap French mainstream, but the wine list is easily the biggest and best of the bunch.

2-3-13 Ichigaya Daimachi,
Shinjuku-ku
Tel: 3355-3004
Open: 11:30am-2pm
& 6-10pm; closed Sun.

French
¥¥
★★★

Map 28

オー　ムートン
ブラン

『オーバージェ　ムートン　ブラン』とし
て、この店はかつて有名なフランス料理
店だったが、今ではその姿を変えてし
まった。テーブルにはもうバラの花は飾
られていないし、壁の赤いドレープもな
くなってしまった。白を基調にした内装
は整然としていて質素である。しかし幸
運にも料理の味は変わっていない。ディ
ナーは3000円で、前菜（お薦めはチーズ
のサラダ）、メインディッシュ（ラム料理が
得意なようである）、デザート（シャー
ベットが美味しい）がそれぞれ選べる。そ
の質は『パザパ』や『ル・マンジュトゥ』、
『ディネット』などの今や主流となってい
る値段の安いフランス料理店と同格だ
が、ワインリストに関しては質、種類共
に群を抜いている。

AUX SEPT
BONHEURS

3-10-13 Kita Aoyama,
Minato-ku
Tel: 3498-8144
Open: 11:30am-3pm
& 5-11pm; closed Sun.

Chinese
¥¥¥¥
★★★★

CC ☷ **Map 2**

オー・セ・
ボヌール

The ultimate in boutique Chinese, served in
the style of French haute cuisine in a chic
Eurodecor setting. Courses begin at
¥7000, but at this level you might as well
commit yourself for ¥10,000 or ¥15,000 a
head and simply say the magic word:
Omakase. You'll be asked for any specific
likes or dislikes, and then perhaps
consulted between courses—of which there
will be many, small in size but marvelously
varied. Based on Shanghai and Sichuan
styles, but with more than a nod to the
Japanese *kaiseki* tradition. It will be, by any
measure, an unforgettable dining
experience.

フレンチ・ヌーベル・キュイジーヌの雰
囲気を楽しみながら、スタイリッシュな
中華料理の究極の味がヨーロッパ調の
シックなインテリアの中で味わえる。
コースは7000円からだが、ここまできた
ら10000円か15000円のおまかせコースを
お薦めする。あらかじめ好き嫌いを聞い
てくれた上、次のコースに移る前には新
たなリクエストもできる。量は少なめだ
が、バラエティーに富んだこの店の上
海、四川風中華には、懐石料理の影響も
みえ、繊細な味わいだ。

BAMBOO

5-8-8 Jingu-mae,
Shibuya-ku
Tel: 3407-8427
Open: 11am-10pm

Sandwiches
¥
★

◣◥ ✿ **Map 2**

バンブー

Limp salads, misguided sandwiches ("Ethnic Burg," etc.), overpriced drinks and —sigh—one of the most pleasant outdoor terraces in the city, open year-round. Their two **Chao Bamboo** branches (6-1-5 Jingu-mae, Shibuya-ku, 5466-4787 and 5-18-20 Roppongi, Minato-ku, 5563-0075) bring equally low standards to Southeast Asian food, but make a lively evening stop for beers, snacks and streetlife.

一年中屋外のテラスで食事ができる東京でも数少ない貴重な店なのに、悲しいことにパサパサのサラダにエスニックバーガーなんて見当違いの名前をつけたり、高すぎる飲み物を出すのでがっかりする。原宿と六本木にある姉妹店『チャオバンブー』では東南アジア料理が屋外で食べられる。料理の味はイマイチだが、ビールとおつまみで外のテーブルに座れば楽しい時が過ごせるだろう。原宿支店（渋谷区神宮前6-1-5（☎）5466-4787）、六本木支店（港区六本木5-18-20（☎）5563-0075）

BAN-THAI

Time Spark,
1-15-1 Tamagawa,
Setagaya-ku
Tel: 5716-3771
Open: 11:30am-3pm &
5-11pm; Sat., Sun. & hol.,
11:30am-11pm

Thai
¥¥
★★

CC ◣◥ ✿ **Map 29**

Shinjuku's Ban-Thai (3207-0068) led the way in bringing real Thai food to Japan, even back when it meant smuggling the ingredients through Narita in suitcases. Despite a recent, much-needed expansion/renovation, it's coasting these days and no longer anything special even by local Shinjuku standards. Better to come to their branch out here: an enormous Ayutthaya-style wooden palace on the banks of the Cao Phraya North, known locally as the Tama. "Kill the organ player," suggests an advisory panel member. A more practical solution: sit as far as possible from stage and speakers.

ここの新宿店（☎）3207-0068は材料をスーツケースに隠し持って来てまで、本物のタイ料理を出そうと苦心していたこだわりの店で、当時から新宿のリーダー的存在だった。しかし最近になってやむ

を得ず拡張と改装が行われ、少々手抜きになってきてもはや特別の店ではなくなってしまった。そこでこの二子玉川支店をお薦めする。ここはチャオプラヤ北岸（実は多摩川だけど）にそびえ立つアユタヤ王朝の木造宮を模した内装である。オルガンの演奏が耳障りなら、ステージから少し離れて座るのが賢明だ。外のテラスは広くて最高だ。

バンタイ

BELLINI'S PIZZA KITCHEN

3-14-12 Roppongi,
Minato-ku
Tel: 3470-5650
Open: 11:30am-11pm

American Italian
¥
★★

  Map 18

A blatant copy of California Pizza Kitchen, the chain that's sweeping the U.S. west coast. That's progress, considering that these premises once housed the Jack & Betty Club (motto: "We Love Food"). BPK cooks their pizzas in a traditional wood-fired oven, and tradition ends there: varieties include Sichuan-style beef and eggplant, cheeseless BLT, and tandoori chicken calzone. Appetizers and pastas range even further (Caesar salad, Mexican fried fish salad, Vietnamese spring rolls, angel hair with ginger black bean sauce). All in all, it's cheap and cheerful and certainly trying its hardest to be Californian. Just avoid the Denny's-like lunch items and the dry, tasteless bread.

明らかにここは、西海岸で最近大人気のニューウェイブ・ピッツァ・チェーン『カリフォルニア・ピッツァ・キッチン』の物真似をした店。どちらの店もコンセプトは、多種多様でユニークなピッツァが食べられるということがウリで、『スパゴ』の大衆版といったところ。四川風エッグプラントとビーフのピザ、カリカリベーコン、レタス、トマトのピザなどをはじめとした、かなり変わったピッツァが揃っている。こんなことをいうと退屈な人間と思われてしまうかも知れないが、ここではノーマルで保守的なピッツァが無難だ。アペタイザーはシーザーサラダ、メキシカンスタイルのフライドフィッシュサラダ、ベトナム風生春巻、和風ドレッシングのサーモンマリネなど種類は豊富だ。

ベリーニズ ピザキッチン

BE-MI

Hongoku Bldg., 2F,
5-2-25 Hiroo,
Shibuya-ku
Tel: 3446-1175
Open: 11:30am-3pm & 5pm-
11pm; Sun. & hol., 11:30am-
9:30pm

Chinese
¥¥
★★

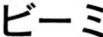 **Map 8**

ビーミ

Big and stylish in a sort of early-'80s disco
mode (monochrome color scheme, pillars
topped with lights, austere high-backed
chairs, etc.), serving *yam cha* and new-
wave Cantonese dishes that would be
acceptable enough anywhere in town. In
Hiroo, where there's still less good food
than meets the eye, it's doubly welcome.

モノトーンを基調にした内装やシンプル
で背もたれの高い椅子など、広くてスタ
イリッシュな、いわば80年代初期のディ
スコ風レストラン。飲茶やニューウェー
ブな広東料理の味は、素晴らしいとまで
はいかないものの、かなりいい線だ。イ
ンターナショナルな雰囲気や高級志向の
街であるのとはうらはらに、なぜかハイ
レベルなレストランが少ない広尾にあっ
て、ここは新しいホープといえよう。

BENGAWAN SOLO

7-18-13 Roppongi,
Minato-ku
Tel: 3408-5698
Open: 11:30am-3pm
& 5-9:45pm

Indonesian
¥¥
★★★

Map 18

ブンガワンソロ

What is there to say? The city's trailblazing
(1954) "ethnic" restaurant, always a sure
bet for its satisfying Javanese food at fair
prices. Beef in hot sauce, shrimp in
coconut cream, satay and *gado-gado* (salad
vegetables with peanut sauce)—Bengawan
Solo's versions, like old friends, may not be
perfect, but after all these years we
wouldn't want them any other way.

1954年創業の文句なしの"エスニック"レ
ストランの老舗。相変わらず良心的な値段
で、美味しいジャワ料理を出し続けてい
る。牛肉の辛いソースあえ、エビのココ
ナッツクリームソース、サテ、ガドガドな
ど、ここの料理は古い友人のようなもの
で、完璧でなくとも、永年の付き合いで粗
探しする気がしないといったところかも知
れない。

BERND'S BAR GERMAN RESTAURANT

Pure Roppongi Bldg., 2F,
5-18-1 Roppongi,
Minato-ku
Tel: 5563-9232
Open: 5pm-2am; closed Sun.

German
¥¥
★★ 1/2
`CC` 💠 ⏩ **Map 18**

バーンズ　バー
ジャーマン
レストラン

To Bernd it's just his mother's recipe for sauerbraten. To our way of thinking it's the definitive version of this meat-and-potatoes classic. For a lighter snack try the steak tartare. To drink he offers good German wine and—after jumping through a series of flaming bureaucratic hoops—Tokyo's first draft Bitburger beer, flown in fresh from Germany. A fine place to begin a Roppongi evening, though it's not easy going back to Japanese beer after the brews here.

オーナーのバーント氏にとっては、彼の母親のレシピに沿って作ったにすぎないザウアーブラーテンも、我々にとってはクラシックな肉とポテトの料理の特別版に思えてしまう。ザウアーとはドイツ語で酸っぱいという意味だが、ザウアーブラーテンという料理もその名の通りある種の酸味があり食欲をそそられる。軽いスナックにはタルタルステーキ（生肉のステーキ）を試してみるのも良い。また良質のドイツワインの他、日本の複雑な輸入規制の壁を乗り越えて樽ごと空輸されるフレッシュなドラフトビールが味わえる。

Hawaiian music, swinging lanterns, mystery food and mugs of beer so big you can barely hoist them? You've found your way into a *rooftop beer garden*, one of Tokyo's perennial rites of summer. Most operate from May till the end of August. They're all pretty similar in feeling, but here are some new and old classics:

● ARK Hills Suntory Beer Patio, 1-3 Roppongi, Minato-ku (5570-9155)

● Kabukicho Beer Garden, 2-1 Kabukicho, Shinjuku-ku (3209-0557)

● Matsuzakaya Dept. Store, 6-10-1 Ginza, Chuo-ku (3572-2431)

● Shinbashi Beer Garden, 2-20-15 Shinbashi, Minato-ku (3574-6409)

● Suntory Bldg., 1-2-3 Moto-Akasaka, Minato-ku (3401-4367)

● Tokyu Dept. Store Honten, 2-24-1 Dogenzaka, Shibuya-ku (3477-3111)

BILLY BAREW'S BEER BAR

1-17-10 Takadanobaba,
Shinjuku-ku
Tel: 3209-0952
Open: 5:30pm-2am; Fri.
& Sat., 5pm-4am; Sun.,
5-11:30pm

Beer
¥
★1/2
 Map 24

ビリー バリューズ ビア　バー

A backstreet bar where loud, defunct pop music is the minus, a hundred or so beers and an unforced cosmopolitan ambiance the plus. Top picks: Timmerman Gueuze and Hoegaarden White. Recommended food: risk their ¥500 "tacos" or, better, go to **Kao Tai** or **La Dînette** first.

世界各地のビールを取り揃えた裏通りのバー。時としてアバの"グレーテスト・ヒット"なんていうびっくりするようなBGMを店内に流して閉口するが、ビールの種類と同じくらい多国籍の客が集まっていて、コスモポリタン東京の雰囲気は満喫できる。お薦めのビールはTimmerman Gueuze、Hoegaarden White。500円のタコスはともかく、ここに来る前に食事は『ディネット』で済ませておいた方が無難だろう。

BINDI

Apartment Aoyama Bldg., B1,
7-10-10 Minami Aoyama,
Minato-ku
Tel: 3409-7114
Open: 11:30am-2pm &
6-10pm

Indian
¥¥
★★
 Map 17

ビンディ

Delightful retro basement decor in the linoleum-floor-yellowing-acoustic-tile-ceiling mode. Delightful owners too: Mr. and Mrs. Mehta aren't about to serve you in anonymous silence. It's also one of the surprisingly few places in town where they're happy to fix up a hot, Southern-style *vindaloo*. And they deliver—this is not a misprint—nationwide.

リノリュウムの床や黄色いタイル貼りの天井など、60年代の東京を思わせるレトロな雰囲気と、オーナーのメータ夫妻との会話が楽しい店。一般に東京のインド料理は北インドのカレーやタンドーリが主流だが、ここでは南インドの辛いヴィンダルーカレーなどが味わえる。また地方発送もしてくれる。

Yam cha (literally, "drink tea," i.e., a meal of tea and dim sum tidbits) is properly served from roving carts, as at Tokyo Daihanten. This allows the dim sum (Japanese: *tenshin*) to be made up en masse, steamed and served fresh. The *yam cha* emporium format, however, requires a larger critical mass of diners than can usually be assembled in Tokyo. So the common solution here is to give you a photo menu and let you order your dim sum piece by piece—which, unfortunately, encourages frozen and otherwise pre-prepared food.

Provided you're willing to risk that, two recommendations: Cox-Top in Azabu Juban (3505-9688) and elsewhere; and Suihan Village in Shinjuku (3342-5758) and Ikebukuro (3986-6410). Old Roppongi favorite Tenshin no Ie (3478-8608) has disappointed lately. For superb, thick-skinned Manchurian-style dim sum (the *real* "gyoza"), look to Shinjuku's Laobian (3348-5810).

BISTRO CAMPAGNARD

6-23-2 Shirokane,
Minato-ku
Tel: 3444-5200
Open: 11:30am-2pm &
6-11pm; closed Sun.

Italian
¥¥
★★★

CC **Map 14**

ごちそう屋 カンパニャール

A.k.a. Gochisoya. One chef, one waiter, five tiny tables and a counter, all packed into a stylish Masami Matsui-designed wood and stone interior. Courses for ¥2200, ¥2500 and ¥3500 (even the cheapest is surprisingly ample) and a redoubtable Chianti Riserva for just ¥3500. They're not above an occasional soupy pasta or oily fish dish, but at these prices all is forgiven. Strangest detail: the free disposable toothbrushes offered in the restroom.

シェフひとり、ウェイターひとりの店で、カウンターと小さな5つのテーブルが、松井雅美デザインによるお洒落な木と石のインテリアの中にある。コースは2200円、2500円、3500円の３種類で、いちばん安いコースでも驚くほどのボリュームがある。また抜群のキャンティ・クラシコ・リゼルヴァがたったの3500円だ。たまに感じられるパスタの水っぽさや、魚料理の脂っこさも、この値段なら目をつぶることができる。細かいことだけど、トイレに使い捨ての歯ブラシが用意されている。

BISTRO D'ARBRE

After years of using the Aoyama Arbre (3407-2257) for inexpensive, spur-of-the-moment bistro fare, we found the Shirokane branch something of a surprise. It's equally cozy, but distinctly upmarket. The stone walls and low lighting offer a sort of medieval intimacy, a bit like a cathedral cloister. Three chefs and two black-suited waiters serve just seven tables.

The food tends toward smallish portions, exquisite presentation and refined flavors—a kind of nouvelle update on classical "Japanese-French" cuisine. The wine list is small but industrious, and while the desserts have disappointed, there always seem to be two or three well-aged cheeses on hand. Unfortunately, this is as good a moment as any to denounce Tokyo's concept of a proper serving of cheese, which is microscopic.

There's more to d'Arbre than meets the eye. Outside, a pleasant garden and some tables they'll let you use any time the weather isn't actively nasty. Upstairs, a charming if not particularly cheap bar, where everyone seems to gravitate after dinner. It feels like a set from *The Avengers*. There's a third Bistro d'Arbre in Shibuya (3476-2239).

5-3-1 Shirokane-dai,
Minato-ku
Tel: 3446-4855
Open: Noon-3pm & 6-11pm;
Sun. & hol., 6-10pm; closed
Mon.

French
¥¥ 1/2
★★★

Map 14

安くて気軽なビストロを求めて何年も『青山アルブル』に足繁く通った後では、この白金店はちょっと異色に映るかもしれない。青山店（☎）3407-2257 同様こぢんまりとはしているものの、あきらかに高級志向である。石造りの壁や低い照明がロマンチックなムードをかもしだす中、3人のシェフと黒いスーツに身を包んだ2人のウェイターが、7つしかないテーブルを受け持つ。料理は上品に凝った盛り付けで、どちらかといえばクラシックな和仏折衷スタイルといえる。東京の店では珍しくデザートには失望させられる。しかし、ワインリストは少ないものの質の良いものを揃えており、デザートの後には2、3種の熟成したチーズも味わえる。屋外にも幾つかテーブルが用意され、2階には、食後の一杯を楽しんで賑わうバーがある。渋谷にも支店（☎）3476-2239 がある。

ビストロ ダルブル

BISTROT DE LA CITÉ

4-2-10 Nishi Azabu,
Minato-ku
Tel: 3406-5475
Open: Noon-2pm & 6-10pm;
closed Mon.

French
¥¥¥
★★★

 **Map 17**

ビストロ・ド・ラ・シテ

For a while it seemed that they'd just keep letting Cité get more and more decrepit, and we mean that as praise. Sadly, they had to go and remodel—the floor's almost level now—and some would say their fish soup has never tasted quite the same. This, of course, could be coincidence. Still uniquely atmospheric, and the kitchen has an undeniable touch with salads and seafood. As usual the real bargain is lunch, currently down to ¥1500.

Equally winning in an even more miniature, jewel-like way is Cité's sister establishment, **Aux Six Arbres** (7-13-10 Roppongi, Minato-ku 3479-2888).

しばらくの間、このレストランの老朽化は意図的に野放しにされているようだった。というのも、それがまた何ともいえない格別なムードをかもしだしていたからだ。しかし悲しいかな改装は免れず、でこぼこの床は修繕され、壁の汚れも落とされてしまった。以来、魚のスープの味が変わってしまったと噂されているのも偶然だろうか。それでもなおユニークな雰囲気やサラダやシーフードの独特な味は昔の面影を残している。

BLUE POINT

4-19-19 Shirokane-dai,
Minato-ku
Tel: 3440-3928
Open: 11:45-1am; Fri. & Sat.
until 2am

Café
¥1/2
★1/2

Map 14

ブルーポイント

As far as we've ever been able to determine, this self-styled "oyster bar" is really a sidewalk café, and, by this city's standards, one of the most picturesque. Strategically positioned along Shirokane's main street, it's a see-and-be-seen scene—arrive if possible by sports car or powerful motorcycle. Recommended: a bowl of café au lait.

自称しているオイスターバーというよりも、サイドウォークカフェと呼ぶのがふさわしいだろう。東京の中では最も眺めの良いカフェのひとつで、白金の目抜き通りに面しており、見ても、また見られても楽しい場所である。高級車やオートバイ、流行のファッション、ペットなどがよく目につく。お薦めはボウルにたっぷり入ったカフェオレ。

BODAIJU

Bunkyo Dendo Center Bldg., 2F,
4-3-14 Shiba,
Minato-ku
Tel: 3456-3257
Open: 11:30am-2:30pm &
5:30-9pm; closed Sun. & hol.

Vegetarian Chinese
¥¥¥
★★★

CC 〰 ▨ **Map 30**

菩提樹

For sheer refinement, no vegetarian cuisine outdoes Chinese temple cooking, that ultimate contradiction of self-denial and sensory gratification. The godhead for this sort of food in Tokyo is Bodaiju. No, it's not inexpensive, and yes, it's easy to find better in Taiwan, but this remains one of Japan's great vegetarian feeds. Lunches from ¥1200; count on at least ¥5000/head for dinner. The Roppongi branch is at 1-1-1 Nishi Azabu, Minato-ku (3423-2388).

グルメにとって自然食の究極といえば精進料理だが、この手の料理を出す店としてここは東京でおそらく最高峰に位置するだろう。人造のエビ、アナゴ、鴨は最高だ。あえて難をいえば、人によっては少々脂っこいと感じる場合があるかもしれない。六本木支店（港区西麻布1-1-1 (☎) 3423-2388）もある。

It's not your imagination: Tokyo still takes a bigger bite out of a diner's wallet than any other city. One recent ranking of average *per person dinner costs* at downtown restaurants frequented by business travelers:

Tokyo	**US$ 69.80**
Rome	**37.25**
Hong Kong	**35.75**
New York	**34.85**
Paris	**32.80**
London	**30.95**
Copenhagen	**28.60**
Frankfurt	**26.70**
Los Angeles	**25.80**
Sydney	**21.50**
Mexico City	**21.35**
Toronto	**17.90**
Barcelona	**17.50**
São Paulo	**15.05**

● **Source:** *New York Times*, July 31, 1994

BOIS CELESTE

2-13-21 Akasaka,
Minato-ku
Tel: 3588-6292
Open: 6pm-2am; closed Sat.,
Sun. & hol.

Beer
¥¥¥
★★1/2

 Map 1

ボア・セレスト

Make that **** if for the cellar of Belgian beers: simply the best. It doesn't come cheaply, though. Few of their brews go for much less than ¥1000 a bottle, and some are almost double that. To eat there's a fine ¥3000 "mini course," or call ahead and order the *tezukuri pasta*, which turns out to be a more than passable *spatzle*.

一本1000円以下のビールは少なく、2000円近くするものもあって安くはないが、4ツ星をつけたくなるほどステキなビアレストランだ。料理は3000円のミニコースが美味しいし、事前に注文が必要だがドイツ風手作りパスタは最高だ。

BOMBAY

1-18-13 Nishi Shinjuku,
Shinjuku-ku
Tel: 3348-3725
Open: 11am-10pm

Indian
¥
★★

  Map 23

ボンベイ

Slightly dingy '60s Shinjuku decor, Japanese cooks, and waitresses in green-and-white pastry shop uniforms. You always half expect some *kare raisu* ("curry rice") abomination until the food arrives and, surprise, it's absolutely okay. Various meat and vegetable curries, generally ¥100 or ¥200 cheaper than the norm. There's a handy branch in the Meguro Station building (3442-4951).

インド料理店といえばインド人コックがいるのが当たり前になってきている中で、日本人コックとパン屋さんのような制服を着たウェイトレスが生真面目に働いているこの店は、妙に懐かしい気分にさせてくれる。店構えは薄汚れていてちょっと昔の新宿といった感じ。いかにもありふれたカレーライスが似合いそうな雰囲気だが、驚いたことに料理は一級のインド料理で、豊富な種類のカレーは他店より割安だ。目黒の駅ビルに支店（☎）3442-4951 がある。

BORDEAUX CELLAR

A whole rambling, split-level house, complete with a big balcony upstairs ideal for parties. Wine crates line the walls and butcher paper covers the tables. There's a funky, slightly temporary feel to the whole operation that reflects their non-elitist approach to wine.

On any given day they'll have at least a dozen wines available by the glass, plus an extensive list of bottles. From France alone are dozens of Bordeaux, Burgundies and Rhônes, as well as regionals like Fitou, Minervois and Madrian; from elsewhere are Kabinett-class German whites, a handful of Spanish bargains, pages of Californians, plenty of sparklers and a few Australian bottles which we always seem to end up drinking. Most are ¥2000 to ¥4000; some actually sell here at or below retail price. At these prices don't expect expert help from the staff.

Recommended food: the house pâté, coq au vin, lamb ribs and the buttery, paella-like *taimeshi*.

3-8-31 Minami Aoyama, Minato-ku
Tel: 5410-4507
Open: 11:30am-3pm & 6-11pm; Sat., 6-11pm; closed Sun. & hol.

Wine
¥¥
★★

Map 2

パーティーに最適な巨大バルコニーのある3層構造になったワインハウス。ワイン樽が壁に沿って並ぶ店内は、ワインに対する気取らないアプローチを反映したファンキーな雰囲気が漂う。常時少なくとも12種のグラスワインと豊富なボトルリストが用意されているが、フランス産だけでもボルドー、バーガンディ、ローヌ、そして珍しい地元ワインが各種揃っている。また、ドイツ、イタリア、スペイン、カリフォルニア、オーストラリアなどのワインの他、スパークリングワインも楽しめる。ほとんどが2000円から4000円で、中には小売価格以下で販売されているものもある。値段が安い分、ワイン選びはスタッフの助けを借りずに自分で探求してみるのがよいだろう。お薦め料理は「おばあさんの作るパテ」、「目の前に広がるブルゴーニュ(鶏の赤ワイン煮込み)」、「ラムチョップ」、こってりしたパエリア風の「口にするたびに感じる海の魔力鯛めし」。

ボルドーセラー

BOTAN

1-15 Kanda Sudacho,
Chiyoda-ku
Tel: 3251-0577
Open: Noon-9pm; closed
Sun. & hol.

Chicken nabe
¥¥¥
★★★

 Map 13

ぼたん

Spared first from the bombing of WWII and then just as miraculously fom the construction frenzy that razed old Kanda in the decades that followed, Botan serves only one dish (a definitive Edo-style chicken nabe, cooked over charcoal at your table) and charges only one price (¥6000). It's a treasure.

Legendary 150-year-old **Isegen** at 1-11-1 Kanda Sugacho, Shiyoda-ku (3251-1229), just around the corner, offers a similar time warp experience with its "angler fish" (*anko*) *nabe*.

この店の建物は第二次大戦の空襲や、古き良き神田界隈を破壊してしまった地上げの嵐からも免れた。料理は「鳥鍋」ただ1種類のみで、目の前で炭を使って作ってくれる。値段も当然6000円均一で実に贅沢な味わい。近所には同じような世界へワープさせてくれる「あんこう鍋」の『いせ源』（千代田区神田須田町1-11-1（☎）3251-1229）がある。

BOUGAINVILLEA

Romane 80 Bldg., 2F,
2-25-9 Dogenzaka,
Shibuya-ku
Tel: 3496-5537
Open: 5-11pm; Sat. & Sun.,
11:30am-3pm & 5-11pm;
closed Mon.

Vietnamese
¥¥
★★

 Map 19

ブーゲンビリア

Not the most cheerful service or decor, but a convenient location and middling good food. Look for the specials posted on the wall, and perhaps try a bottle of white wine (through history or coincidence, Vietnamese food takes to it better than any other Asian cuisine).

特別フレンドリーでもなく、素敵な店構えというわけでもないが、便利なロケーションで、料理もなかなかなのがここ。壁に書かれたお薦め料理と白ワインを試してみよう。ベトナムとフランスの歴史上の関係を考えてみれば、アジアの料理の中ではベトナム料理が最もワインと相性が良いはずだ。

BRASSERIE BERNARD

Nichi-Futsu Gakuin,
15 Ichigaya
Funagawaramachi,
Shinjuku-ku
Tel: 3260-9639
Open: 10am-10pm; closed
Sun. & hol.

French
¥¥
★★ 1/2

 Map 9

ブラスリー ベルナール

Bernard has always cooked the kind of honest, unfussy French food we think Tokyo needs most. In fact his *boudin* (blood sausage), served with potatoes and caramelized apples, has spoiled us for the standard French café version. The problem has been the petit bourgeois decor and atrocious elevator music of his Roppongi headquarters (3405-7877).

Problem solved: lunch on a fine day out on the lawn at his branch here at the Institute Franco-Japonais makes Tokyo's most convincing argument for the Gallic way of life. It's pleasant indoors too, in a garden conservatory sort of way.

素朴で気取らないフランス料理を楽しみたいならここがお薦め。ちょっとブルジョワ趣味のインテリアと六本木店（☎）3405-7877のエレベーター内の音楽はいただけないが、日仏学院にある市ケ谷店の芝生の上で、天気の良い日にランチをすれば、東京にいながらにしてフランス気分は十分味わえる。店内もいい雰囲気だ。

BRASSERIE DE PARIS

3-2-16 Ginza,
Chuo-ku
Tel: 3563-1051
Open: 8am-10:30pm

Café
¥
★

 Map 7

Wonderfully preserved '50s Japanese fantasy of a Parisian café—high ceilings, purple carpet, waiters in shiny black suits. The music is loudish and slightly updated (e.g. orchestral versions of Olivia Newton-John hits); the clientele a mix of salary-people and inexplicably leisured-looking marginals. Third-rate hotel coffeeshop food, which at least is remarkably cheap. Ideal for a hot drink and a newspaper on a cold winter day.

高い天井に紫のカーペットが敷かれ、つやのあるブラックスーツに身を包んだウェイター...という、50年代の日本人が夢に描いたパリの姿が、ここにはある。当時と違

ブラッスリー・ド・パリ

いオリビア・ニュートン・ジョンのヒット曲のオーケストラ版など、多少イマ風でうるさい音楽が流れる店内には、サラリーマン風から時間を持て余し気味に見える謎めいた客たちまでが混じりあっている。三流ホテルのコーヒーショップ並の味だが、安いのがせめてもの救いだ。凍えるような冬の日に、新聞を片手に熱いコーヒーをすするには最適な場所だろう。

BRASSERIE FLO

Convincing, full-scale re-creation of an art nouveau Parisian brasserie (the original Flo is in Montparnasse), owned and operated by—sign of the times—the Skylark family restaurant chain. It's all here, from the wrought iron staircase leading down to the dining level to the parquet floors and mirrors and wood paneled walls. Good food that becomes pretty near irresistible with their breakfast (¥600) and lunch (¥1600) buffets. But it's with dinner that the kitchen really shows its stuff, with regional menus from ¥3800. Their inexpensive "wine of the month" selection offers real value.

Flo has another branch by Gaien-mae Station (3746-0206) and a third in Minato Mirai 21 in Yokohama (045-221-2615).

4-3-3 Jingu-mae, Shibuya-ku
Tel: 5474-0611
Open: 8am-11:30pm; Sat., Sun. & hol., 11:30am-11:30pm

French
¥¥
★★★

 **Map 2**

パリの南西部に位置するモンパルナスにオリジナルの店があり、そのアールヌーボー調ブラッスリーを忠実に再現したと謳ったこの店は、すかいらーくチェーンが経営している。鉄の手摺りの階段を降りて下のダイニングルームへ出ると、寄せ木細工の床と鏡、美しい羽目板の壁とすべてが完璧。600円のブレックファストビュッフェと1600円のランチビュッフェは安くて美味しい。3800円からの地方料理メニューではシェフたちの腕前が発揮されている。月ごとに替わるお薦めワインも値段が手頃で美味しい。外苑前駅すぐそばのFLO南青山店（☎）3746-0206、横浜みなとみらいにあるFLO横浜店（☎）045-221-2615。

FLO 表参道

BRASSERIE LECOMTE

To look at it's just a big coffeehouse in a subterranean arcade. The lights are a bit too bright, the tables much too small. It barely looks like it would have Japanese *kissaten* food, let alone something really edible. Followers of Tokyo French pioneer Andre Lecomte will know better. Whether at noon for the daily ¥2000 lunch or anytime for the salads, soups, Provençale-style scallops, beef filet with Bearnaise sauce, or house specialties couscous and choucroute, Brasserie Lecomte serves up some of the best fast French meals in town. No place is easier to walk into when you're alone or otherwise lack the time or patience for a lot of fancy restaurant folderol.

M. Lecomte's other ventures include an excellent café/patisserie elsewhere in this basement (3475-1770) and another at 7-18-12 Roppongi, Minato-ku (3402-5991).

Aoyama Twin Tower Bldg., B1,
1-1-1 Minami Aoyama,
Minato-ku
Tel: 3479-2838
Open: 11am-10pm; Sat.
until 9pm; closed Sun.

French
¥¥
★★★

CC **Map 31**

明る過ぎる照明と小さなテーブル、一見、地下街にある大型コーヒーショップにしか見えないが、実は素晴らしいフランス料理を出す店である。東京におけるフランス料理の草分け的人物アンドレ・ルコント氏のファンならすでにご存じのはずだが、2000円のランチから、サラダ、スープ、プロヴァンス風帆立、ヒレ肉のビアネーズソース和え、そしてクスクス、ショクルート（豚肉、ソーセージ、ザウワークラウト）などの特別料理に至るまで、彼は最高の味を素早く披露してくれる。ひとりでのランチや、高級店の堅苦しさに費やす時間も忍耐もない時に、ここはぴったりの場所だ。
美味しいカフェとケーキの店（☎）3475-1770はこの同じ地下街と六本木（港区六本木7-18-12（☎）3402-5991）にある。

ブラッスリー ルコント

BRASSERIE PIERROT

Tokyo Design Center, 3F,
5-25-19 Higashi Gotanda,
Shinagawa-ku
Tel: 5420-2223
Open: 11aam-2pm (last
order) & 5:30-9pm (last
order); closed Sun.

French
¥¥¥
★★★ 1/2

Map 14

Not even slightly brasserie-like, and thankfully showing no overt Pierrot motifs. Rather it's clean and bright, with a glimpse of green out the window at one end, and a small patio for alfresco fanatics. We saw people out there on even the hottest days of the infamous summer of '94.

Expect to eat well here: it's run by the same people as **Chez Inno** (3274-2020), generally held to be among the top two or three French places in Tokyo. In our experience Pierrot's chefs show more panache with meat than fish, while starters and desserts have been uniformly excellent. On the wine front they've overcome the chauvinism that afflicts most of our French restaurants, offering wines not only from France but also Italy, Spain and even California. It makes for a list that's more intriguing and affordable (¥3000 to ¥7000) than most. But then you won't go far wrong with the full-bodied house red—a Rioja.

日本のレストランはビール醸造所という意味の「ブラッスリー」や「ピエロ」などという名前を好んで使うが、どうもピンとこない。サーカスのピエロはいいけれど、レストランのインテリアに使われるのはあまり気持ちのいいものではない。幸いなことにこの店は、清潔で明るく、窓からは木々の緑が見えて小さなパティオもあり、平均的なブラッスリーより断然良い。ピエロの絵も目立たなくさりげなく飾ってある。この店は東京のフランス料理店の中ではトップクラスの『チェズ・イノ』と同じ経営だけあって味に定評がある。シェフは魚料理より肉料理のほうが得意のようだが、前菜とデザートはどちらも素晴らしい。ワインはフランス産だけでなく、イタリア、スペイン、カリフォルニア、そしてハウスワインはスペイン産と各種取り揃えているところもこの手の店には珍しい。料金も3000円から7000円と幅広い。

ブラッスリー・ピエロ

BRUSSELS

1-10-23 Jingu-mae,
Shibuya-ku
Tel: 3403-3972
Open: 5:30pm-2am; Sat.
until 11pm; closed Sun.

Beer
¥
★★

Map 6

ブラッセルズ

Tokyo's pioneering Belgian beer bar. The *bierstube*-style Kagurazaka (3235-1890) and cozy Jinbocho (3233-4247) locations almost seem to take pride in serving depressing food, as if to make their ales shine by comparison. This newer Harajuku branch does a little better, particularly with the salads and pita sandwiches. Note that some of their beers emerge from the fridge *way* beyond their expiration dates.

神楽坂と神保町にあるこの店は、まずい料理を出していることに誇りをもっているのではと思ってしまうほどだ。最近、原宿にできた支店のサラダとピタパンのサンドイッチは悪くないが、もちろんここのお薦めはビールで、Hoegaarden White、Hoegaarden Grand Cru、Rodenbach Grand Cruなど、またGueuzeならどれでも。ただ、ラベルにある賞味期限を確認することを忘れずに。

BUNLIN

Hills Shibuya Bldg., B1,
13-13 Shinsencho,
Shibuya-ku
Tel: 3780-6268
Open: Noon-2pm &
6-9:30pm; Sat., 6-9:30pm;
closed Sun. & hol.

Chinese
¥¥¥
★★★ 1/2

Map 19

文琳

Simple, stylish and beautifully lit, Bunlin is the sort of secret Tokyo scene that would inspire Tiger Tanaka to write in his notebook: "Must bring Bond here." Diners sit essentially in the middle of the kitchen, a place as tidy and calm and concentrated on its purpose as a jewelry workshop. There's a token menu, but most everyone just says *"Omakase"* and lets the chef improvise. Bunlin interprets the mainland though a kind of *kaiseki* filter—lots of little plates, miniature bits and seasonal motifs.

お客は小綺麗で落ち着いた雰囲気の、まるで宝石職人の仕事場のような厨房の前に座らされる。一応メニューはあるが、大抵はみな"おまかせ"で、シェフの腕前を見せてもらう。この店は中華料理を"懐石"というフィルターを通して紹介している。季節をモチーフにした数々の小皿料理が、シンプルでスタイリッシュに盛り付けられて出てくる。ランチはかなりお得。

BUNRYU

Fl Bldg., B1,
1-26-5 Takadanobaba,
Shinjuku-ku
Tel: 3208-5447
Open: 11:30am-2pm &
5-10pm; Sun. & hol. until
9:30pm; closed 3rd Mon.

Italian
¥¥
★★ 1/2

CC **Map 24**

文流

Distinctive southernish Italian food in one of the last places anyone would expect: a time-worn basement just across the street from Takadanobaba Station. Between the '50s decor and the retro waiters and clientele, it feels like stepping back into a Yujiro Ishihara movie. All in all a more memorable experience than the other popular Italian place just up the street, **Il Castello** (1-34-14 Takadanobaba, Shinjuku-ku 3208-0432).

東京では数少なくなった独自の味をだしている店で、高田馬場駅向かいのビルの地下にある。50年代風インテリアとレトロなウェイトレスを見ていると、石原裕次郎の映画の世界に引き戻されたようだ。お薦めはカジキマグロ、ブイヤベースとその他の魚料理。

BUON VISO

4-50-7 Yoyogi,
Shibuya-ku
Tel: 3378-2133
Open: 11:30am-4pm &
5-10:30pm; Sun., noon-4pm
& 4:30-10pm;
closed Mon.

Italian
¥¥ 1/2
★★★

CC **Map 32**

ブオン ヴィーゾ

A sleeper. This semi-flashy trattoria looks like it landed on the wrong street—the charmingly dowdy Sangubashi shopping lane—but there's no doubting the knowledge or dedication of the family who runs it. The payoff is skilled northern Italian food at prices noticeably lower than uptown. Good cheap pasta and risotto lunches; tea and cakes in the afternoon; generous dinners from ¥3500.

この店が気に入っているものの、客の少なさに店を閉じてしまうのではないかと心配した、『トーキョージャーナル』の読者が教えてくれたレストランだ。もちろんそうならないことを願うが、参宮橋商店街の中という地味な立地条件の割りには、多少派手すぎる店構えというのが問題なのだろう。豊富な料理の知識と家族経営の親切なサービス、そしてピッツァからフルコースまでの洗練された北イタリア料理が、手頃な値段で食べられて文句なし。

BUONO BUONO

Nishi Ginza Dept., 2F,
4-2-15 Ginza, Chuo-ku
Tel: 3566-4031
Open: 11:30am-11:30pm

Italian
¥¥¥
★★★

CC Map 7

The concept doesn't sound promising: a virtual factory for the production and consumption of Italian food, set above a Hibiya department store arcade and run by the efficiency experts of Mikasa Kaikan. Surprise: the kitchen knows exactly what it's doing, and the size and bustle of the place make it feel more like Milano than Tokyo. Especially useful for business lunches and late dinners. But why do they call it "Vuono Vuono" in Japanese?

大きなレストランより小さなレストランの方が細かいところまで神経が行き届いていて、質がよいと思われがちだが、ここ『ヴォノ・ヴォノ』に来てそれが誤りだと気づくはずだ。この店は本当のイタリア料理を作って食べさせてくれるところだ。厨房はスムーズに回転しているし、その広さと賑やかさは東京というよりむしろミラノにでもいるような気になる。少し遅めのランチには最適だ。

ヴオノ　ヴオノ

CADIZ

3-46-9 Koenji Minami,
Suginami-ku
Tel: 3318-5975
Open: 6pm-midnight;
closed Mon.

Mukokuseki
¥
★★

 **Map 33**

A post-industrial *tapas* bar in the bowels of the Koenji shopping mall. Owner/chef/resident muse Kay Takahashi creates "new soul food and beer from the five continents" and mostly it's healthy, good and unstinting in size. A typical evening might feature a few fresh salads, some big grilled shrimp, *dolmas* (stuffed grape leaves) and—our favorite—fried potatoes dusted in paprika and served with aioli. Casual cosmopolitan atmosphere tending toward wildness as the night wears on.

高円寺の商店街にあるモダンなタパス・バー。オーナーでシェフでもある高橋ケイ氏は創造的な料理と五大陸からのビールを出してくれる。メニューは日替りだが、フレッシュサラダ、大きなエビのグリル、ドルマ、アイオリ（にんにく風味のマヨネーズ）を添えたパプリカのかかったポテトフライなど、料理はボリュームもあって美味しい。厳選されたビールの数々もまたよい。

カディス

CAFÉ DE ROPÉ

6-1-8 Jingu-mae,
Shibuya-ku
Tel: 3406-6845
Open: 11am-11pm;
Sun., 11am-10:30pm

Café
¥
★

◧ ☖ **Map 6**

カフェ・ド・ロペ

The city's sidewalk café par excellence has never made much effort to get its food act together. Currently on offer: passable sandwiches and salads, dubious risottos, gratins and pastas. Recommendation: stick to the French-roast coffee and watch the world go by.

表参道沿いにある原宿の典型的なこのカフェは、料理の面ではほとんど努力が見られない。最近出しているメニューとしてはまずまずのサンドイッチ、リゾット、グラタン、パスタなどがあるが、お薦めはやはりフレンチローストのコーヒーだ。苦めのコーヒーをすすりながら、道行く人々を眺めるのはなかなか楽しいものだ。

CAFÉ DES PRÉS

5-1-27 Minami Azabu,
Minato-ku
Tel: 3448-0039
Open: 11am-midnight

Café
¥
★★

☖ **Map 8**

カフェ・デ・プレ

Tokyo's most ambitious replica of the larger and posher sort of Parisian café. Full-strength, full-price coffee and typical snacks: onion soup, sandwiches, *croque monsieur*, etc. Serious meals are available at ¥¥¥ prices. Downstairs there's **Vinocchio des près**, a high-toned Italian-esque wine bar/restaurant.

Newer, even bigger and quickly becoming the focal point of Tokyo café society is the branch by Omotesando Station (5411-3721).

広くて粋なパリのカフェを、かなりのお金をかけて再現した店。濃さも値段もなかなかのコーヒーとオニオンスープ、サンドイッチ、クロックムッシュなどの典型的なフレンチカフェのスナック、それに本格的な食事が4、5000円から楽しめる。地下に豪華なイタリア風のワイン・バー＆レストランもある。

CAFÉ TANDOOR

2-9-9 Ebisu Nishi,
Shibuya-ku
Tel: 3461-8363
Open: 11:30am-10:30pm;
closed Sun.

Indian
¥
★★

cc 🔲 **Map 5**

カフェ・
タンドール

No burnished brass statuary, no ornamental archways, no Tamil bubblegum music. Simply an open-fronted café that happens to serve some very sincere curries and Indian breads. We especially like their vegetarian and fish curries and the *nan*—thin, flaky, almost crisp. The *masala* tea and other drinks are overpriced even by this city's inflated standards. But buying one entitles you to camp out here all afternoon, and there's no more agreeable sidewalk café scene in all of Ebisu.

真鍮の彫像や装飾的なアーチの門、またインドの映画音楽などはここにはない。ただ店先にテラスのあるカフェがたまたま良心的なカレーとパンを出してくれるといった感じだ。特にベジタリアン・カレーとフィッシュ・カレー、それに薄焼きでかなりカリッとしたナンが美味しい。480円の紅茶はいささか高いが、午後いっぱいかけて、こんな居心地のよいカフェでアフタヌーンティーを楽しめればいいとしよう。

CAHORS

Small. V. good food. Friendly atmos

2-28-8 Uehara,
Shibuya-ku
Tel: 3469-8912
Open: Noon-2:30pm &
6-10pm; closed Sun.

French
¥¥1/2
★★★

cc 🔲 🔳 **Map 34**

カオール

Only in Tokyo: a husband-and-wife operation focusing not just on France, but the tiny region of Cahors in the southwest—home of legendary dark, almost chewy red wines. If the cooking isn't radically different from that at a hundred other Little Tokyo French Places, it's better than most, and where else can you order a Chateau Lagrezette and win a knowing smile from the chef?

フランスびいきのご夫婦が経営しているこの店では、店の名前にもなっている南西部の小さな町、カオール地方の料理にヒントを得たフランス料理を出している。その味は東京に何百とあるフランス料理店の中でも上位にランクされる。また、この地方の伝統的なワインは芳醇な赤で、Chateau Lagrezette をはじめとするカオール地方のワインを注文すれば、彼らが喜ぶに違いない。

CAMBODIA

Yoshino Bldg., 2F,
3-10-14 Takada,
Toshima-ku
Tel: 3209-9320
Open: 11:30am-2pm & 5-
11pm; hol., 5-10pm; closed
Sun.

Cambodian
¥¥
★★★

 Map 24

カンボジア

Smaller, a bit cheaper, and a lot quieter than **Angkor Wat**, and practically as good. Favorites include the raw spring rolls, shrimp *dango* (balls of minced meat), Vietnamese-style *okonomiyaki* ("pancakes" of various vegetables and meats) and the various Khmer-style curries. Beer goes for a bargain ¥500.

前出の『アンコールワット』と比べて、店は小さく混雑もなく、その上値段も安いし、味も負けていない。生春巻、エビ団子、ベトナム風お好み焼きをはじめ、何種類かのカレー料理がお薦め。輸入ビールも500円と安い。

CARMINE

1-19 Saikumachi, Shinjuku-ku
Tel: 3260-5066
Open: Noon-2pm & 6-11pm;
closed Sun.

Italian
¥¥
★★★

Map 9

カルミネ

A decade ago Carmine Cozzolino was one of the first foreign chefs to get the brain wave that our city would respond to honest European cooking at fair prices. He succeeded only too well: it can be hell to get in here, and cramped seating *à la Japonaise* once you do. And worth it nevertheless, with generous courses from ¥3500. Always popular: the *penne* with gorgonzola and the beef filet in green pepper sauce.

カルミネ・コゾリーノ氏は一昔前、東京に手頃な値段の本場イタリア料理を紹介した最初の外国人シェフのひとりであるが、彼の功績は確かなもので、その証拠に店内はいつも満員だ。しかしぎゅうぎゅう詰めの座席も、3500円からのコースは我慢するだけの価値があるほど美味しい。中でもゴルゴンゾーラチーズのペンネと牛フィレ肉のグリーンペッパーソースはこの店一番の人気メニューだ。

CARTHAGO

A one-room medina of books, plants, photographs, flags, maps, crafts, hanging lanterns, Turkish rugs, everything but the caliph's kitchen sink. Self-taught chef Hiroshi Hatanaka (that's him in the fez) recreates dishes from years spent on the southern shores of the Mediterranean.

The Maghreb course focuses on northwestern Africa: *brik* (a fried appetizer of egg and tuna), *kifta* (minced lamb kebab), a cumin/tomato-flavored *soupe de poisson*, ratatouille-like "grilled salad" and a main dish of couscous. The Anatoly (Turkish) course begins with white goat's cheese, olives, stuffed grape leaves, and a chicken noodle soup, then shish kebab, salad and pilaf. Both end with dessert and mint tea or strong Turkish coffee.

3-34-3 Nakano,
Nakano-ku
Tel: 3384-9324
Open: 6-10pm (last order);
closed Wed.

Muslim Mediterranean
¥¥
★★

 **Map 15**

本、植物、写真、旗、地図、工芸品、灯籠、トルコ絨毯などが置かれたこの部屋は、メディーナと呼ばれる北アフリカの普通の住宅地にある家のような雰囲気の店。シェフの畑中博氏はいつもトルコ帽をかぶっていて、地中海の沿岸に何年も住みながら独学で身につけたムスリム料理を披露してくれる。マグレブ（アフリカ北西地方の料理）とアナトリー（トルコ料理）のコースがお薦め。両コースとも仕上げにデザートとミントティーか濃いターキッシュコーヒーがつく。ワインとビールもまた美味しい。

カルタゴ

CASA BELLA

No longer facing the Black Hole S&M lounge (it closed), Casa Bella's location at the wrong end of Kabukicho still doesn't exactly ooze class. Nor will the entranceway—up some dark stairs in a shabby office building—inspire confidence. But the place is packed, and with reason: they've been banging out reliable Spanish food for decades.

Casa Shinjuku Bldg., 2F,
2-42-11 Kabukicho,
Shinjuku-ku
Tel: 3209-6984
Open: 6-11pm; closed Mon.

Spanish
¥¥
★★1/2

Map 22

It's best to concentrate on the tapas and seafood in favor of the less interesting chicken and meat dishes. Recommended main course: paella or the squid ink version of the same, *arroz negro*.

歌舞伎町の無法地帯にあるこの店に行くのは少し恐いかも知れない。その上、店の入り口も老朽化した雑居ビルの薄暗い階段近くにあって、恐怖心を増幅している。ところが、店に一歩入ると、イメージは一新し、中は満員の客で溢れている。それもそのはずで、ここは何十年にもわたり信頼できるスペイン料理を作り続けているからだ。全体に薄暗いのだが、それが粗隠しの効果をしており、実際スペインによくある店のようで良い。チキンや肉料理よりはタパスやシーフードを注文すべきだろう。お薦めは、パエリアもしくはイカスミ入りパエリヤ。

カサ・ベリヤ

CASA DE FUJIMORI

1-25 Aioicho, Naka-ku,
Yokohama-shi,
Kanagawa-ken
Tel: 045-662-9474
Open: 11am-11pm; Sun. &
hol., noon-9:30pm

Spanish
¥¥
★★ 1/2

 Map 35

カサ・デ・フジモリ

One of only two Yokohama restaurants (the other is **Saronikos**) that our 'Hama respondents insisted that we include. Besides, what a wonderful name. Top recommendation: Sevilla-style mushrooms. Caution: The Casa de Fujimori by Meguro Station is eminently avoidable.

浜っ子たちが絶賛する横浜のレストラン。名前もなかなかステキだ。一番のお薦めメニューはセヴィラ風のマッシュルームだが、目黒駅のすぐそばにある支店はお薦めできない。

CASA MONNON

4-2-10 Nishi Azabu,
Minato-ku
Tel: 3499-2559
Open: 7pm-midnight;
closed Sun.

Mexican
¥¥
★★

Map 17

カサ・モンノン

Yes, it's still here. Upstairs, bar-like ambiance and hours, and a history of good, non-mass-produced Mexican food. The epitome of a Nishi Azabu bar/restaurant: relaxed, offbeat, designed for lingering.

東京のメキシコ料理店の中では特に古く、小さくてあまり目立たない存在のこの店は、レストランというよりバーのような雰囲気が漂っているが、メキシコ人シェフによる手作りの美味しいメキシコ料理が味わえる。型にはまらず落ち着いてくつろげる、西麻布の典型的な店だ。

CASA VERDE

2-8-14 Kita Otsuka,
Toshima-ku
Tel: 3916-0182
Open: 11am-10pm

Brazilian
¥
★★

Map 36

カサ・ベルデ

A bit of instant Brazil in the curious environs of Otsuka. Downstairs is a cluttered little shop for Brazilian goods; upstairs a simple restaurant serving distinctly down-home versions of *feijoada*, *picadinho* (stew), *bacalaoada* (cod), Bahian-style shrimp and other Brazilian standards. Portions, even with the ¥1000 weekday lunches, are mammoth. On weekends they do a cheap, all-you-can-eat *churrasco* deal, and there's always a wide range of tropical juices, Brazilian beers and cocktails.

大塚にあるブラジル料理のこの店は、1階がブラジルの雑貨や小物を売っていて2階がレストランとなっている。家庭的な味がするフェジョアーダ、ピカディンニョ（シチュー）、バカリョアーダ（タラ）、ブラジル東部地方の海老料理、その他のスタンダードな料理は素朴で気取らない。平日の1000円のランチを含めどれもがボリュームたっぷり、そして週末は安い値段でシェラスコが食べ放題となる。またトロピカルジュースやブラジルのビール、カクテルの種類も豊富。

CERVEZA

They're dedicated beer people here: glass-fronted refrigerators fill one whole wall and you're given your own card listing about 100 world brews to work your way through. Skip the characterless light lagers and try the likes of Aass (Norway), Pilsner Urquell (Czech Republic), Samuel Smith (U.K.) and the spectacular Ezo Bakushu microbrews from Oregon by way of Hokkaido.

The food spans Japanese, Western and Chinese styles and we reckon it's a match for **Bois Celeste** as the best at any Tokyo beer specialist—and cheaper to boot. One favorite: the *yurinji* Chinese-style chicken.

3-11-10 Roppongi,
Minato-ku
Tel: 3478-0077
Open: 5pm-midnight; closed Sun. & hol.

Mukokuseki
¥ 1/2
★★ 1/2

📷 **Map 18**

セルベザ

ビールファンには絶好の店。壁一面を埋め尽くすほど積まれたビールの産地は約100ヶ国にも及び、注文の際には各ビールの銘柄が書かれたビールカルテが配られる。しかしほとんどのものが日本のラガービールの味と似ているので、変わったものを試したければ、ノルウェーのAass、チェコのPilsner Urquell、イギリスのSamuel Smith、オレゴンの小さなビール工場で日本向けに特別造られた逸品Ezo Bakushuをお薦めする。食事は和、洋、中と何でもあって、東京のビアホールでは最高の『ボア・セレスト』の味にひけをとらず、値段はこちらの方がずっと安い。チキンを中華風にアレンジしたユウリンチは特にお薦め。

ベルギーは世界中のどの国にもないようなユニークなビールを生み出す国だ。そしてここ数年、東京はヨーロッパ以外でこうしたビールを味わえる最高の土地になっている。ただしこれには二つの前提条件を承知しておく必要がある。ひとつは、賞味期限の問題であり、もうひとつは、高い値段のことである。それを知った上で、お薦めはフルーティな香りのGueuze、さっぱりして酸味のあるRodenbach Grand Cru、昔ながらの麦芽を使ったHoegaarden White、強いトラピストエールのChimay、Orval、強力で魅惑的で比類なきDuvel（悪魔という意味）などだ。これらを味わうなら、『ボア・セレスト』、『ブラッセルズ』、『セルベザ』、『海晴亭イースト』だろう。

CEYLON INN

In a warren of little rooms in an old house, owner Ajith Liyanage aims at no less than recreating the entire Ceylonese food experience. That means a massive menu, from vegetable and "green seed" soups and salads to dhals and curries, distinctive Southern breads like *those*, colonialisms like ham and eggs and even that unlikely Sri Lankan standby, the spring roll. This is the place to unravel the mysteries of string hoppers (a kind of rice noodle pancake), *watalappan*, snow pudding and curd (all desserts, not all to everyone's taste). Don't miss the spicy, slightly caramelized eggplant *brinjal mooju*. Lots of intriguing beers, too. It's a measure of this place that the clientele cuts across suburban Tokyo: students, salarymen, pensioners, even the neighborhood Yakult sales ladies on their lunch break.

2-7-8 Kami-Meguro,
Meguro-ku
Tel: 3716-0440
Open: 11am-3pm & 5-11pm;
closed Mon.

Sri Lankan
¥
★★★

 Map 4

小さな部屋が寄せ集まった古い家で、オーナーの アジ・リヤナゲ氏がセイロン島料理のすべてを体験させてくれる。メニューはかなり豊富で、野菜やグリーンシードのスープ、サラダやスリランカ風カレー、南国特有のパン、カツレツやハムと卵といったコロニアル風イギリス料理、そしてなんとスリランカでも人気のある春巻きまである。ライス・ヌードルの一種であるストリングホッパー、万人受けではないがすごく甘いデザートなど、不思議なものに挑戦してみる気があればこの店は最適だ。スパイシーで、ほんの少しカラメル状にしたナスのブリンジャル・ムージュは絶対試すべき。ビールもなかなか美味しい。学生、サラリーマン、お年寄りからランチを楽しむヤクルトレディーまで客層はかなり幅広い。

セイロンイン

*The **Filipino food** scene in Tokyo has gone from bad to worse in recent years. The last couple true restaurants have disappeared (sorry, we don't count **Namin**), leaving to the best of our knowledge only "show" bars and after-hours hostess places. The adventurous might want to try **Barrio** at 1-2-1 Nishi Nippori, Arakawa-ku (3891-1190), but note the weird hours: 5-8pm and midnight-6am.*

CHABLIS-AN

A "wine-deli" that isn't even vaguely deli-like—abandon all hope, ye who seek a real delicatessen in Japan—and with a large, spectacularly poor selection of wine. Come here instead for good big bowls of spinach salad, spaghetti carbonara, *agedashi dofu* and whatever else is on display. Superlative Belgian brews too, including the sinners' delight, Le Fruit Defendu ("The Forbidden Fruit"). We list Chablis-An mainly as our state-of-the-art example of that Japanese perennial, the department store restaurant. They still honor the great tradition of wax food models, but otherwise it's as stylish and atmospheric as any real Tokyo restaurant of ten years ago. Also worth a look: **Ninnikuya Goemon** (3477-8333), one floor down.

One-Oh-Nine 30s Bldg., 6F,
33-5 Udagawacho,
Shibuya-ku
Tel: 3780-2009
Open: 11:30am-2pm & 5-11pm

Mukokuseki

¥ 1/2
★★

 **Map 19**

ワイン・デリを自称している割に、ワインは量は多いが、そのセレクトの幅は狭いし、料理も本物の"デリ"には程遠い。とはいっても、デパートにあるレストランとしてはお洒落な雰囲気で高い水準にあるといえる。料理はサラダ、パスタから揚げ出し豆腐まである無国籍風で、ビールもベルギー産のHoegaarden が全種類揃っている。このビールを、軽くて爽やかな口当たりのホワイトからスタートして、ちょっと強いGrand Cru に進み、最後はコリアンダー風味で最強のLe Fruit Defendu（禁断の果実）で終わるコースにトライしてみると良い。階下には、人気の店『にんにく屋五右衛門』があるので、ついでに立ち寄ることも出来る。

シャブリ・アン

CHARLIE HOUSE

1-15-11 Jinnan, Shibuya-ku
Tel: 3464-5552
Open: 11:30am-2:30pm &
5-8:30pm; closed Sun. & hol.

Cantonese noodles
¥
★★

◆ **Map 19**

チャーリー・
ハウス

While there's certainly nothing wrong with Japanese-style *ramen*, it's so predominant that it can be hard to find a bowl of unadulterated Chinese noodles. This little counter joint is our pick, whether for *chashumen* (with pieces of succulent "five-flavored" pork) *tebasakimen* (with chicken wings) or the excellent daily *teishoku*, which isn't noodles at all but a fine little meal set.

日本風のラーメンが悪いというのではないが、これがあまりにも主流になってしまっているので、本格的な中華麺を食べさせてくれる場所を見つけ出すのは大変だ。そんな中でやっと見つけたこの店の、チャーシュー麺、手羽先麺や、麺類ではないが日変わり定食はお薦め。麺は抜群で、普通のラーメンに比べ細く、歯応えがある。

CHEZ PIERRE

Exc. food & informal atmosphere.
Chotto takai though

1-23-10 Minami Aoyama, Minato-ku
Tel: 3475-1400
Open: 11:30am-2:30pm (last order) & 6-10pm (last order); closed Mon.

~¥16,000/hd.

French
¥¥¥¥
★★★★

cc ◆ ✕ ⇄ **Map 37**

シェ・ピエール

Dinner at Pierre's will quickly explode our ¥10,000/person budget, but here at least you're paying not for the trappings but the essentials—traditional food of unimpeachable quality and effortlessly professional service. They fly in their seafood from France, which might seem like coals to Newcastle unless you've been on a search for, say, true Dover sole. Portions are a touch smaller than in France, which is to say just about ideal. The compact, high-performance wine list features Pierre's own private-label Bordeaux and Burgundy.

完璧な古典的フランス料理の店。ディナーはひとり軽く10000円を超えてしまう高さだが、その味とプロフェッショナルなサービスには納得がいくだろう。魚は贅沢にもわざわざフランスから空輸している。ドーバー海峡で捕れた舌平目の美味しさはこの店のファンいわく国産のものとは大違いで、一度食べてみる価値がある。センスの良いワインリストから、この店独自のレーベルがついたボルドーとバーガンディーまで色々と楽しめる。

CHEZ PRISI

Eiraku Bldg., B1, 2-12-33
Akasaka, Minato-ku
Tel: 3224-9877
Open: 11:30am-2:30pm
& 5:30-11pm; Sat.,
5:30-11pm; closed Sun.

Swiss
¥¥¥
★★ 1/2
CC ◈ ⊞ **Map 1**

シェ・プリシィ

If Monsieur Prisi is getting tired of being characterized as "jovial" he's showing no signs of it. In fact he's the perfect host. It's all very professional here, with emphasis on quality ingredients and straight-ahead cooking over flash or fad. Recommended: steak tartare, fondue, any of the veal and the incredible diet-busting desserts.

流行にとらわれず、素材や味にこだわる
保守的なところがとてもスイス流で良心
的な店といえよう。オーナーのムッ
シュ・プリシィも人の好いスイス主人の
イメージそのもの。お薦めはフォンデュ
と子牛の料理、それにステーキ・タルタ
ルだ。

CHIANTI

Nakamura Bldg., B1,
2-9-15 Jiyugaoka,
Meguro-ku
Tel: 3717-6200
Open: 11:30am-11:30pm

Italian
¥¥¥
★★★
CC ◈ ⊞ **Map 12**

The impressive thing isn't that Chianti is still good. It's that they've kept pace with the revolution in northern Italian food that they launched 35 years ago (est. 1960), and now are better than ever. And if it tends to cost a couple thousand yen more than the new Italian sensation of the month, it has almost always been worth it. Original shop in Iikura (3583-7546); various other locations around Roppongi and Nishi Azabu. This new Jiyugaoka branch is particularly welcome, at the price of occasionally twerpish waiters.

オープンと同時に日本の北イタリア料理
に新風を巻き起こしたこの店は、1960年
代当時の味を、35年経った今も持ち続け
ているだけでなく、むしろ今も向上して
いて驚きだ。ちょっと評判になるといい
気になる、その辺りのイタリア料理屋に
比べたら何千円かは高いが、それだけの
価値は十分にある。ランチは1800円、
2500円、3500円（ウィークデーのみ）。
飯倉の本店（☎）3583-7546 の他に六本
木、西麻布周辺にはいくつかの支店があ
る。新しくできた自由が丘支店もお薦め
だが、ウェイターの態度には多少問題が
ある。

キャンティ

CHICKEN'S

Sets a new standard in low-ball decor: long, communal tables made out of scaffolding tubes and clamps; chairs of the kind you had in elementary school; walls of unfinished concrete and lights hung on bare wires strung along the ceiling. It feels like a food-stall with roof and walls.

The culinary theme, to risk stating the obvious, is chicken. Their biggest seller seems to be the big plate of fried chicken legs and potatoes, but poking about the menu will reveal more interesting foods. We've enjoyed the chicken, tomato and blue cheese salad, the deep-fried eggplant with salsa and the daily pizzas. Draft beer and functional wine are available at very low prices.

3-1-6 Azabu-dai,
Minato-ku
Tel: 3586-5554
Open: 11:30am-3pm &
5:30-11pm

Western
¥1/2
★★ 1/2

 **Map 18**

建築用の足場パイプで造られた長いテーブルと小学校時代を思い出させる木の椅子、壁はコンクリートの打ち放しで、剥き出しの電線に電球が吊り下げられている、そんなユニークな内装のこの店はまるで室内にある屋台のようだ。料理は店の名の通りチキンがメインで、ボリュームたっぷりのフライドチキンとポテトが人気メニュー。他にはトマトとブルーチーズのサラダ、ナスのフライとサルサ、ピッツァもなかなか美味しい。ドラフトビールとワインも安い価格で楽しめる。

チキンズ

CLUB KREISEL

A seasoned chef equally at home in German, Austrian and French kitchens, Hiroshi Noda was drafted by Germany's OAG Haus to spread the gospel of Teutonic cuisine. If this sounds like an impossible mission, give him a chance: sashimi-fresh herring in a sublime sour cream, salads, soups (green pea, liver dumpling, goulash), Alsatian trout meuniere, Berlin-style veal liver, rolled beef, roast duck, Eisbein and some of the best of Germany's wurst.

OAG Haus, 1F,
7-5-56 Akasaka,
Minato-ku
Tel: 3583-9487
Open: 11:30am-10pm; Sat.,
10am-2pm; closed Sun.,
hol. & 3rd Sat.

German
¥¥
★★★

 **Map 1**

Wine snobs put down Germany's bubbly Sekt, but we say that for ¥3000 it's great quaffing. And here's a nomination for the Rote Grütze of custard and berries for the Tokyo dessert hall of fame.

クラブ
クライゼル

ドイツ政府出資の文化施設であるドイツ文化会館が、最高のドイツ料理を出すこのレストランを始める時にシェフとして選んだのが、ドイツ、オーストリア、フランスで長年経験を積んだ野田浩資氏だ。ドイツ料理というとあまり洗練された感じがしないが、その中でも高級料理といわれるものは別格で、野田氏はその達人だ。お薦めは最高の酢づけニシンのサワークリームソース、サラダ、グリーン豆・レバー団子・グラーシュのスープ、ニジマスのムニエルアーモンド風味、ベルリン風子牛のレバー、牛肉のロール巻、鴨のロースト、アイスパイン、そしてもちろんソーセージ。飲み物は炭酸入りSekt、リーズナブルなシャンパンのようなもので、ボトルでたったの3000円。カスタードとベリーのデザート、ロートグルッツも格別だ。

東京の自然食、菜食レストランはなぜ多くが中央線沿線に集中しているのだろうか。『グルッペ』、『香林坊』、『パタパタ』から、便利だがまるで病院の食堂みたいな『グリーンハウス』（中野区中野2-13-26 ☎ 3380-8022）や居酒屋の『がぶり』（杉並区高円寺南3-58-3 ☎ 3314-6060）、古くからの自然食ファンが集まる『すみれ家分庵』（杉並区荻窪4-27-14 ☎ 3393-0688）、教会が運営している『エリム』（杉並区天沼3-7-14 ☎ 3220-0550）、人気の高い『でめてる』（国分寺市本町2-14-5 ☎ 0423-23-9924）などがある。

Time to confess: We seldom get to Tokyo's *big traditional Chinese restaurants.* The best (like the **/¥¥¥¥ Yang Yuan Zhai at the Four Seasons Hotel Chinzan-so Tokyo, 3943-2222) are unquestionably superb, but really need a party of at least five or six to be done right. The mid-level ones—there are hundreds—look and act the part, but too often the food seems lightened and simplified (the nice word is *sappari*) to suit a historical idea of Japanese tastes. It's at Tokyo's smaller, newer and less conventional Chinese places that, in our opinion, you're most likely to find food that begins to approach the real Taipei and Hong Kong article.**

COCA RESTAURANT HAKKEIJIMA

If a food book may be permitted an entertainment recommendation, we'll vote for Hakkeijima Sea Paradise as the best "amusement park" (the term hardly does it justice) in Japan. It also has some of the best eating of any of them, notably at this 220-seat branch of Thailand's most successful restaurant chain. Coca pioneered the new dip-and-swish style of *Thai suki*, and to have it here on their big terrace looking out to sea is a thoroughly un-Tokyo-like pleasure.

Closer to home, Coca's first branch in Japan (5-16-47 Roppongi, 5562-9807) offers the same food, unfortunately served by robotic waiters prone to run amok.

A-1-03 Hakkeijima,
Kanazawa-ku, Yokohama-shi,
Kanagawa-ken
Tel: 045-788-9682
Open: 11am-10pm

Thai suki
¥¥
★★★

Map 38

もしこの本の中でも、行楽地の採点をすることが許されるなら、八景島シーパラダイスは日本一の遊園地だろう。この園内の数あるレストランの中でも、群を抜いているのが、タイスキ（タイ風しゃぶしゃぶ）の元祖であり、タイで最も成功しているレストランチェーンとして知られ

コカ
レストラン
八景島

るこの店だ。海を見渡せる220度の大きな
テラスで食べるタイスキは、その味もさる
ことながら、ちょっとしたバカンス気分を
満喫させてくれる。遠出が億劫なら、東京
にある日本一号店（☎）5562-9807 でも同
じ料理が食べられるが、サービスはあまり
期待しない方が良い。

DA' HONG
YUN TIANTIAN

Redecorate one of those big auto show-
rooms way out on Meguro-dori, hire a couple
dozen mainland cooks and waiters and
busboys, let them cook the way they want
and don't force them to pinch pennies on
the ingredients. Position the whole thing as
a deluxe Cantonese restaurant for the
carriage trade, but cover the highlights of a
few other Chinese cuisines as well, and offer
¥850 lunches and dinners from ¥4500. So
far, Da' Hong Yun Tiantian is keeping to top
Hong Kong standards, and at prices that
would get you laughed out of this class of
restaurant anywhere in mid-town.

Lu Chun Fang Ri Yue (3704-3591),
DHYT's sister establishment a few kilo-
meters further out on the same road,
specializes in dull imitation Sichuan food,
but can be inspirational with the more
Cantonese dishes.

1-1-7 Takaban,
Meguro-ku
Tel: 5721-8866
Open: 11:30am-3pm &
5:30pm-2am

Cantonese
¥¥¥
★★★★

Map 39

大鴻運天天酒楼

かつて目黒通りにあった自動車のショー
ルームをレストランに改装、本場中国か
らやって来た沢山のコックやウェイター
が働いている魅力的な店。メインは広東
料理で、値段は山手線の内側にしては安
い。お薦めは850円のランチと4500円か
らのディナーコースだ。中２階から見え
る１階、２階の風景は1920年代の上海に
あったダンスホールのようだ。

DING HAO

As our sample of a neighborhood *chuka* (Japanese-style Chinese) place, Ding Hao qualifies on convenience (a minute from Yutenji Station), atmosphere (a sunny second-floor corner) and flavor (a grade above average, as are prices). What really sets it apart is an insistence on natural ingredients and a refusal to use any seasonings manufactured by industrial processes. The big food companies won't want to hear this, but diners here seem fully satisfied with rice that's less than cosmetically perfect and foods that lack the chemical "savor" of monosodium glutamate. Recommended: the house specials (eggplant and unagi stir-fry, spicy *mongo-ika* squid, etc.) and the *tantanmen* noodles—always a good standby at these places.

Koekisha Bldg., 2F,
2-12-2 Yutenji,
Meguro-ku
Tel: 3710-5496
Open: 11:30am-2:45pm
& 5-10pm; closed Mon.

Chinese
¥1/2
★★

Map 40

祐天寺駅のすぐ近くという便利さ、日当たりの良い角地の２階という明るい雰囲気、平均点以上の味と安い値段など、どこから見ても文句の付け所がない近所の中華料理店だ。料理はどれをオーダーしても失敗しないが、ナスとウナギの炒め物や、辛く味付けした紋甲イカは特にお薦めだ。もちろん定番の四川風タンメンなどの麺類も揃っていて美味しい。ここでは材料の米や野菜はだいたい無農薬で、化学調味料も一切使用しないという。ほとんどの中華料理店とは一線を画している。化学調味料を製造している会社の人たちは耳にしたくない話だろうが、味は十分満足できる。

頂好

Three ¥90 stamps to the Bun'en Shakai o Mezasu Kai (3-28-12-2B Kamiya, Kita-ku, Tokyo 115) will bring you a copy of their latest Kuuki no Oishii Resutoran *Japanese-language guide to about 600 Tokyo-area eating places that are partly or all **non-smoking**. They've even managed to smoke out a few clean-air pachinko parlors, beauticians, pensions and, incredibly, a bar (**Barbican**, 3565-4111).*

DJ'S PIZZERIA

6-4-5 Roppongi,
Minato-ku
Tel: 3479-5711
Open: 11am-11pm

Italian
¥
★★ 1/2
Map 18

An unexpected pleasure: good pizza, pasta
(try the fettucine), and even main dishes
and desserts, at the lowest of prices in one
of the city's most agreeable spaces—the
old Metropole premises on TV Asahi-dori.
They open the front on fine days and it
becomes a sidewalk café.

DJ'S ピッツェリア

期待した以上の美味しさで嬉しくなるよ
うな、ピッツァ、パスタ、メインディッ
シュからデザートまでを、都内でも最高
の雰囲気の中で、安く食べさせてくれる
店。場所はテレビ朝日通りの、かつて『メ
トロポール』があったところ。天気の良い
日には店の正面を開け、テラスカフェに
変身する。

DOMANI

4-37-7 Ikejiri,
Setagaya-ku
Tel: 3412-4011
Open: 5:30-11pm; Sat.,
Sun. & hol., 5-10.30pm

Mediterranean
¥¥1/2
★★1/2
Map 41

The fount whence so much of it came.
There was a time in the early '80s when it
seemed as if half the young chefs in
Tokyo's new Italian places had apprenticed
at Domani (est. 1966). The southern European food scene has expanded beyond
recognition since then, but the well-worn
Domani remains relaxed, reliable and—
shucks—romantic.

ド・マーニ

1966年の開店当時は、カジュアルで値段
も安く、味も本場のイタリア、フランス
料理を出す新しいタイプの店だった。80
年代前半までは日本各地に広がったイタ
リア料理店のシェフの多くがこの店で修
業をしたほどだった。今もなお残してい
る信頼感に溢れたゆったりとした雰囲気
とロマンティックなムードは、さすが貫
禄十分の老舗である。

DONCHACA

3-9-10 Shinjuku,
Shinjuku-ku
Tel: 3341-2497
Open: 5pm-6am

Izakaya
¥ 1/2
★ 1/2
Map 22

呑者家

Three minor reasons for coming here: inexpensive, satisfying izakaya food, a spirited young crowd, and the assurance you won't be booted out till you're ready to go, even if that means waiting for the first train in the morning. One major reason: a couple dozen first-class *jizake* (regional sakés), generously poured and priced as low as any in the city—typically about ¥550 for an overflowing glass.

Unmissable in the food department: *maguro kimuchi yukke*, a tuna steak tartare with kimchi and an egg yolk.

安くて旨くて、若者たちの熱気でムンムンしている居酒屋。朝6時まで営業しているのも魅力だが、人気の秘密はなんといっても何十種類もある地酒だろう。550円でコップに溢れるほどついでくれる。つまみにマグロのキムチユッケが最高。

DOUTOR

Everywhere
Tel: 3455-6320 (head office)
Open: 7:30am-9pm

Cafés
¥
★★★

ドトール

No pallid roasts, antique beans or chemistry-set "siphon" foolishness here. Just real coffee (pretty fair sandwiches, too), at half the price of traditional places and better quality than its many imitators. Seeing as how Doutor singlehandedly brought coffee out of the Meiji Era we won't complain about the Muzak and the Euro-Plastik decor. And they'd make even more friends if they set aside no-smoking sections. Recommended: Café latte turbo (you make it yourself by ordering a café latte and an espresso and combining the two).

他のどのチェーン店よりも、日本でヨーロッパスタイルの美味しいコーヒーが安く飲めるようになったのはこの店のお陰である。看板までコピーする物真似店が増えた今でも、ここのコーヒーとサンドイッチの人気は依然として王座を譲らない。欲をいえばダサイBGMと内装のプラスチック、そして禁煙席が少ないことを何とかして欲しい。

EDOGIN

4-5-1 Tsukiji,
Chuo-ku
Tel: 3543-4401
Open: 11am-9:30pm;
closed Sun.

Sushi
¥¥
★★ 1/2

 Map 42

The Grand Central Station of sushi. Between this main shop and the neighboring annexes they seat almost 800, a synchronized free-for-all served by a hundred or more chefs. Received wisdom says that being down here by the city's wholesale fish market assures Edogin and its neighbors of better ingredients than shops in the effete suburbs. Reality says otherwise: many of Tokyo's finest sushiya are halfway across town. But there's no doubt that location (along with sheer size and corporate clout) helps Edogin offer enviable value—the slices are still among the largest anywhere.

江戸銀

外国からの旅行者の間でも有名な江戸前の寿司屋。この本店とそれに隣接する新館、別館を合わせると客席はざっと800席、100人ほどの板前が寿司をにぎっている。築地にある寿司屋は旨いと定評があるが、さすが築地市場のすぐそばというロケーションと店の規模の大きさも手伝ってか、ここの寿司ネタの大きさはどこにも引けを取らない。

多少運が良ければ、日本ビール界の退屈な日々も終焉を迎えるかも知れない。日本の4大メーカーは、世界のどの製造業者たちにも負けないだけの技術と施設を持っている。しかし残念なことに、新発売はパッケージが変わっても中身はいつも同じラガー風ばかり。ドライ、アイス、ローカロリー、冬用、夏用と言ったって、味に大した違いはない。時代遅れの法律によって、世界的なブームにもなっている自家醸造が妨げられているが、こんな規制が撤廃されるのも、時間の問題だろう。今のところは『サンクト・ガーレン』や『セルベザ』の情報に注目し、オレゴンの自家醸造会社が日本向けに造った Ezo Bakushu を見つけ出し、トライすることを薦める。

EL CASTELLANO

2-9-11 Shibuya, Shibuya-ku
Tel: 3407-7197
Open: 6-11pm; closed Sun.

Spanish
¥¥
★★

 Map 20

エル・
カステリャーノ

The Castilean of the name is Sr. Garcia, who was turning out good, straightforward tapas and paella here on Aoyama-dori long before the late-'80s Spanish food boom. He's still doing it today, and the walls are covered with words of appreciation from his customers. Top recommendation: rabbit in garlic sauce.

マスターのガルシア氏は"カステェリャーノ"（カスティレアン人）で、スペイン料理が今ほどポピュラーになるずっと前から、この青山通りで美味しいパスタとパエリアを作り続けている。そんな店内の壁はお客からの賞賛の言葉で埋め尽くされている。他のスペイン料理店ではめったにない兎のガーリックソースがお薦めだ。

EL MOCAMBO

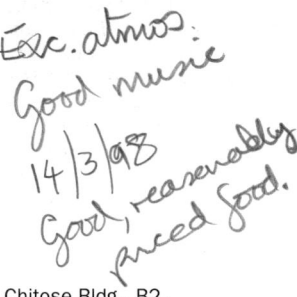

Chitose Bldg., B2,
1-4-38 Nishi Azabu,
Minato-ku
Tel: 5410-0468
Open: 6pm-midnight; Fri. &
Sat. until 2am; closed Sun.

Latin American
¥¥
★★ 1/2

 **Map 17**

"Homesickness begins with food," according to Che Guevara, the celebrated Argentinean expat. Serve the right kind of food and drink, thought El Mocambo founder Shingo Yoshino, and Tokyo's growing Latin American community would finally have a home of its own. So to drink there's Bohemia, Dos Equis and caipirinhas; to snack on, guacamole with chips, *pastelitos* (deep-fried pastries filled with cheese or, better, shrimp), clams in jalapeño broth, and various soft-shell tacos (recommended: pork and onion). Main dishes range from Peruvian pork *adobado* to Brazilian-style cod. Ultimately it's the atmosphere that wins you at El Mocambo—the dramatic underground entrance, the sofas back in their little grottos, the Ruben Blades and Gal Costa on the stereo, the overall sense of space and relaxation.

ラテンアメリカのイベントプロモーター、吉野信吾氏の長年の夢は、拡大し続ける東京のラテンアメリカ・コミュニティのために故郷を造ることだった。そ

して出来たのがこの店だ。酒を飲むなら
Bohemia、Dos Equis、caipirinhasがあ
り、スナック類はワカモレチップス、チー
ズ、または、エビ、パイを揚げたパステリ
トス、あさりのメキシカーナ、柔らかいタ
コス（ポークと玉ねぎがお薦め）などがあ
る。また食事をするならアナト風味の豚肉
の煮込みやタラとタマゴのグラタンなどを
はじめ、バラエティ豊かに揃っている。そ
れにしても、この店が好きな理由は、料理
もさることながら、ここの雰囲気、例えば
ドラマチックな感じの地下の入り口や内装
から、サルサ、サンバ、ボサノバなどの音
楽などによって、リラックスできるからだ
ろう。

エル・モカンボ

EL TORITO

2-6-14 Izumi,
Suginami-ku
Tel: 5376-7611
Open: 11am-midnight

Mexican
¥
★ 1/2

Map 43

Slightly Japanized version of a highly
Americanized version of northern Mexican
food in an ethnic Denny's decor. Those of
you who need regular doses of it know who
you are.

Best in our experience are the meatier
things: *fajitas* (grilled at your own table),
carne asada, *pollo asada* and even the
hamburguesas. The tacos . . . well, they
come in little plastic taco stands and the
fish variety is built around a deep-fried
fishstick, but at least they use lettuce
instead of shredded cabbage. Enter the
enchilada and burrito zone at your own risk.

Branches can be found over Omotesando Station in Aoyama (5466-7917) and
in Nishi Kasai (5696-7488).

アメリカ人が好むメキシコ北部の料理を日
本人向けにアレンジしている店。内装はエ
スニック版ファミリーレストランのようだ
が、鉄板で出されるファヒータやカルネア
サダ（グリルドビーフ）、ポロアサダ（グリ
ルドチキン）、メキシコ風ハンバーガーは
本格的な味。しかしお馴染みのエンチラー
ダやブリトー、タコスはあまりお薦めでき
ない。表参道支店（☎）5466-7917 は大人
気で、西葛西にある第一号支店（☎）5696-
7488 も人気上昇中。

エル・トリート

ENJUU

1-48-13 Minami Otsuka,
Toshima-ku
Tel: 3944-1007
Open: 11:30am-2pm &
5:30-10pm; closed Sun.

Tofu
¥¥1/2
★★★

[CC] **Map 44**

ゑん重

A polished, urban contrast to the rustic style of the famed **Goemon** and **Sasa no Yuki**. At five years old, Enjuu is the youngest tofu restaurant we know of in Tokyo (though the family has been making tofu for generations) and they aren't afraid of innovation—how about a "cheese" cake made of soy milk for dessert? Their *kaiseki*-influenced dinners run ¥3500 to ¥5500; lunches from ¥1000.

この豆腐専門店は有名な『五右エ門』や『笹の雪』の素朴な雰囲気とは対照的に洗練された都会的な店。家が代々続いた豆腐屋なので、古典的な豆腐から豆乳で作ったチーズケーキまで、豊富なバリエーションが楽しめる。ランチは1000円より、ディナーセットは3500円から。

ENOTECA

5-14-15 Minami Azabu,
Minato-ku
Tel: 3280-3636
Open: 11:30am-2:30pm &
5:30-9:30pm; closed Sun.
& hol.

French
¥¥¥
★★★

▨ ⚑ ☎ **Map 8**

エノテカ

Lunch under a blue sky and big white parasols, a glass of Taillevent Chablis in hand—if this is life in the Gaijin Ghetto, sign us up. Orthodox French cooking of quality, if not stunning creativity. Lunches run a bargain ¥1200 to ¥2800; dinners from ¥4800. The attached wine shop comes up with some intriguing French and Italian bottles, often of better value than the neighborhood would suggest.

外国人居住者たちからはしばしば"外人ゲットー"と冗談まじりにいわれる広尾にあるこの店では、青空の下、真っ白で大きなパラソルの蔭で、Taillevent Chablisのグラスを片手にランチを楽しむ...なんてことが誰でもできる。お得なランチは1200円〜2800円、ディナーは4800円から。隣接したワインショップでは毎日6、7種類の試飲をさせてくれ、ここのような高級住宅地では考えられないような安い値段で、フランスやイタリア産のボトルワインが買えるのも嬉しい。

*Summertime is **cold noodle** time. We like **Sodoten** for
hiyashi chuka (cold ramen topped with sliced cucumber,
meats, egg, etc.); **Matsuya** for zaru soba (buckwheat noodles
sprinkled with dried nori seaweed); **Hosenka** for reimen
(Korean style: light, spicy, refreshing).*

ERAWAN

Mixed atmosphere
Good food.

Roi Bldg., 13F,
5-5-1 Roppongi,
Minato-ku
Tel: 3404-5741
Open: 5-11:30pm

Thai
¥¥
★★1/2

Map 18

Long a beacon of sleaze, Roppongi's Roi Building appears to be cleaning up its act even as the rest of the neighborhood heads down the tubes. That was our reaction anyway upon discovering Erawan. It feels like acres of teak up here, luxurious yet (has this word ever been used before in connection with this building?) tasteful. Best of all is the picture-window view of the city from almost anywhere in the house. All too good a view from the women's restroom, or so we're told.

While the food could do with less sugar and more spice, it rates as reasonably good mainstream Tokyo Thai, and is not as pricey as it looks. Three dishes to get you started: *yam pla duk foo* (deep-fried catfish salad), *panaeng gai* (a rich, medium-hot chicken curry) and *kai haw bai toi* (leaf-wrapped chicken). Miss their dull Shinjuku and Ikebukuro branches, but don't miss this one.

六本木のロアビル最上階にあるこの店は、広々とした豪華な雰囲気の中にセンスの良さが伺えるが、何といっても圧巻なのは壁一面のガラス窓から眺める夜景のパノラマだ。女性トイレの個室の中でさえガラス窓になっていて眺望が楽しめる。料理は少し甘さを控えて辛めにしたら言うことはないが、全般に値段も手頃で美味しい。ヤムプラドゥックフー（なまずのサラダ）、パナエングガイ（コクがあってやや辛めのチキンカレー）、ガイホーバイトーイ（鶏肉のバイトーイ葉包み揚げ）などから始めるのがお薦め。新宿と池袋に支店があるが、やはりここがベストだろう。

エラワン

EX

7-7-6 Roppongi,
Minato-ku
Tel: 3408-5487
Open: 5pm-2am; closed
Sun. & hol.

German
¥¥
★★★
Map 18

エックス

A single horseshoe-shaped bar that's more of a club for its regulars than a proper restaurant, but for the heartier sort of German fare, this is as good as it gets. Horst has his own sources for pork and sausages, and there's simply no comparison with the standard Japanese commercial product. He'll even put together a good vegetarian plate if you ask. Fine, fresh beer and a friendly crew, though familiarity with craps and German drinking songs will aid assimilation.

馬蹄形をしたここは、レストランというよりはドイツ人仲間のクラブと呼ぶ方が相応しい。でもだからといって、ポーク料理、ソーセージ、野菜盛り合わせなどのドイツ料理は、本場にひけを取らない旨さだ。新鮮なビールにフレンドリーな従業員、ダイスゲームをしながらドイツの酒盛り歌を合唱しているうちに、いつのまにかこの店にとけ込んでしまう。

FLAGS ANNEX

3-6-7 Ebisu Minami,
Shibuya-ku
Tel: 3715-9071
Open: Noon-2pm & 6-11pm;
Sat. & Sun., 5:30-10:30pm

Mediterranean
¥¥
★★★
CC 🔲 **Map 4**

フラッグス別館

The original Flags near Daikanyama Station has mysteriously disappeared, but this "Annex" remains the perfect time capsule: the same tiny crowded tables and yellowing walls and submarine galley kitchen. The same full-strength Mediterranean cooking too, featuring spicy seafood and what could well be Tokyo's best garlic toast. Their **Cucina Flags** at 2-19-18 Komazawa, Setagaya-ku (3701-6731) focuses on Italian food at similarly low prices.

代官山駅の近くにあった元の店はいつの間にか姿を消してしまったが、所狭しと並んだ小さなテーブルや黄色がかった壁、見渡せるキッチンなど、ここには以前と同じ雰囲気が再現されている。料理も変わらずフルパワーで、スパイシーなシーフードや東京一のガーリックトーストがお薦めである。

7025 FRANKLIN AVE.

3-15-18 Higashi Gotanda,
Shinagawa-ku
Tel: 3441-5028
Open: 11am-9pm;
Sun., 11am-7:30pm

American
¥
★★ 1/2

 Map 14

7025 フランクリン・アベニュ

One of our stars is purely for atmosphere: it's a delight. Bright and spacious even inside, when they open the glass doors onto the patio and the garden beyond, Franklin Ave. proves that Tokyo—Gotanda, for heaven's sake—can accommodate indoor/outdoor restaurants as airy and pleasant as most anything in California.

The burgers and accompaniments here are at least as good as at **Homework's** (in fact probably better), and a bottle of wine can usually be rustled up to give you an excuse for lingering. There's a less scenic branch at 2-24-9 Nishi Azabu (5466-1667).

時にはパーッと明るい気分になりたかったらここに来ない手はない。店内は明るく広々としていて、しかも中庭に向かったガラスのドアを開けると、そこはまるでカリフォルニア。東京でもこんな屋外のスペースをうまく使ったレストランができるのかと驚かされる。ハンバーガー、フレンチフライ、オニオンリングなどは少なくともホームワークスと並ぶほどの美味しさで、気分次第ではシャンパンも飲める。新しくオープンした西麻布店（港区西麻布2-24-9（☎）5466-1667）にも屋外スペースはあるが、景色はいまひとつだ。

*If you're in search of the real **Tsukiji**, and **Edogin** looks like too much of a world tourist attraction, try one of the local sushi shops favored by the fish dealers themselves. Best known are **Daiwazushi** (3542-1111) and **Ryuzushi** (3541-9517), both located inside the fish market. Note that these are open from dawn till early afternoon; best bet for the evening would be **Hamashige Sushi** (3541-9206).*

FUJII

3-25 Higashi,
Shibuya-ku
Tel: 3486-1939
Open: 11:30am-8:30pm

Udon
¥
★★★
 Map 5

Udon to make a believer of anyone. What's interesting here is that it's not tied to any family tradition. The master quit his day job years ago to devote himself to the art of the noodle. He apprenticed at a couple different places and eventually settled on a highly textured Kansai style with a lively sauce that's prepared daily (many places do it up in big batches).

Like most proper udon shops, Fujii does tempura and various other side dishes as well.

自ら店を始めた料理人というのは興味深い存在だ。最初は興味からこの仕事を選ぶ人が多いので、伝統に縛られることがない。結局自分のやりたいように料理を工夫し作り出している。この店を経営する脱サラの店長もそんなタイプで、彼の作る腰の強い関西風のうどんは非常に美味しい。天ぷらや各種のおつまみ類があり、どれも旨い。

藤井

FUKUTOMI

5-8-2 Haneda,
Ota-ku
Tel: 3745-1649
Open: 5-11pm; closed Sun.

Izakaya
¥¥
★★★
Map 45

Fukutomi could be straight out of a *Tora-san* movie set: spacious in a rambling, country-side way, *zashiki* rooms wandering off toward the back, a color TV presiding loudly from one corner. Everything centers on a vast, multi-level counter, heaped with more food than seems feasible. Portions are immense and flavors are sweet and rich in the old Edo tradition, a distinctly different style from the lighter, saltier, more polished "Japanese" cuisine that dominates Tokyo even a kilometer or two inland.

Recommended: *asari* clams, grilled prawns, scallops, *ebi* gyoza (a garlicky, out-sized gyoza enveloping a whole large prawn) and *kama* (fishhead stew).

寅さん映画のセットから抜け出してきたようなこの店は、だだっ広いスペースの中に座敷が迷路のように続いていて、部屋の隅に置かれたカラーテレビがいつもがなりたてている。店の中心にある何段

にも重なっている棚には、次から次へと料理が運ばれてくる。ここからは、古き良き江戸の伝統を思わせる甘くて濃厚な香りが立っていて、ライトだという割には塩辛いだけの現代の和食とは違う。都心からたった1、2キロ離れただけなのに、ここには別世界がある。お薦めは、あさり、海老、帆立、海老餃子と魚のカマだ。

福富

FUKUZUSHI

Sushi snobs—the breed who frequent Ginza's **Kiyota** (3572-4854) or **Jiro** (3535-3600)—may turn up their noses at Fukuzushi, unrepentant purveyor of "international" sushi. It's directly below Spago, and attracts a similarly flashy clientele: cosmopolitan business types, touring rock stars, landed gentry, ordinary folks on a splurge. It has a European cocktail lounge. They give you a napkin, for god's sake, and the fish is actually *on display*.

All of this means there's nothing effete or arcane about the sushi: it's good and generous, and at these prices so it should be. Plus they're better than *gaijin*-friendly here—they've seen it all.

5-7-8 Roppongi,
Minato-ku
Tel: 3402-4116
Open: 11:30am-2pm & 5:30-11pm; hol., 5:30-10pm; closed Sun.

Sushi
¥¥¥1/2
★★★ 1/2

Map 18

銀座の『きよ田』（☎）3572-4854 とか『次郎』（☎）3535-3600 に行くような本当の寿司通にとっては、インターナショナルな寿司屋であるここを軽蔑するかも知れないが、六本木らしい楽しい店だ。来日中のロックスター、国際ビジネスマン、成金、話題づくりに訪れる一般人など、階上の『スパゴ』と客層はよく似ている。布製のナプキンを使ったり、ヨーロッパスタイルのカクテルラウンジがあって、値段も安くはないが、寿司ネタは大きく新鮮だ。

福鮨

GAIA

BEAM Bldg., 7F,
31-2 Udagawacho,
Shibuya-ku
Tel: 5458-4520
Open: 11:30am-2pm &
5-11pm; Sun. & hol.,
5-10:30pm

Mukokuseki
¥
★ 1/2
CC **Map 19**

ガイア

Take the elevator to the 7th floor and voilà, the nose cone of Spaceship Earth—a couple of stories high, all glass, pointed straight up into the Shibuya sky. It's one of the more amusing '90s reincarnations of the beer company-sponsored beer hall (in this case, by Kirin). Gastronauts can choose from a predictably offbeat mix of only slightly institutional food: Provençale-style fish, oyster sauce beef, assorted sausages, chili con carne, etc. Even dinner prices are rock bottom; lunch is a giveaway.

７階でエレベーターを降りると、突然ロケットのノーズコーン（先端部）に踏み込んだような気分になれる、ここは90年代版ビアホールである。数階分が吹き抜けになり、全面ガラス張りという空に向かってそびえ立つ円錐形のこの店は、キリンビールがスポンサーになって作られた。料理に面白みは欠けるものの幅広いチョイスの中には、南仏風の魚料理、牛肉のオイスターソース炒め、ソーセージの盛り合わせ、チリコンカーンなどがあり、値段も相当安い。

GOEMON

1-1-26 Hon-Komagome,
Bunkyo-ku
Tel: 3811-2015
Open: 5-10pm (last order
8pm); Sun. & hol., 3-8pm
(last order 6pm); closed Mon.

Tofu
¥¥¥
★★★
Map 46

Back about the time that Charles Dickens and the London literati were hobnobbing at Ye Olde Cheshire Cheese, their Edo counterparts were congregating at Goemon. And frankly this is the more civilized scene of the two: there's a traditional garden and a carp pond, and with a group of four or so you can reserve one of the open rooms around the water.

Courses range from ¥5500 to ¥7500. There's tofu in just about everything, typically including *agedashidofu* (deep-fried) and *yudofu* (tofu hotpot) in winter; *hiyakko* (cold tofu with toppings) and *gomadofu* (which isn't tofu at all—see **Jugemu**) in summer.

五右ヱ門

『笹の雪』同様、昔から有名な豆腐料理の
専門店として人気がある。古典的な庭園
には鯉を放った池があり、4名以上揃えば池
のすぐそばのテーブルを予約できる。コー
ス料理は5500円から7500円までで、すべ
てに豆腐が使われている。揚げ出し豆腐や
湯豆腐、胡麻豆腐などをはじめ、豆腐料理
のバリエーションが楽しめる。

GOKOKU

A spacious, luminous underground grotto.
You sit at a carved blue lacquer counter and
order from a long menu hand-written by
brush for today and today alone. A sample
¥5000 course: big meaty *tsubugai* shellfish
on skewers. *Satsuma age* (fried fish cakes)
so sweet and juicy they don't need sauce. A
bowl of *kakuni* stewed pork. *Maguro no
kamayaki*, an immense head of tuna broiled
in traditional *shitamachi* ("downtown") style.
Gyutan (beef tongue) pounded thin, not unlike the veal upstairs at their sister restaurant,
La Gola. And, for a finale, *miso shiru* soup with
the good, deep tang of Edo miso.

Don't be fooled by the waiters in their
embroidered Burmese vests or their patter
about "new Pan-Asian cuisine": at heart, this
is Tokyo home cooking of the old school. It
would make a high-impact introduction for
any visitor, both to our city's food and its
new idea of affordable luxury.

Inagaki Bldg., B1,
7-4-5 Roppongi,
Minato-ku
Tel: 3796-3356
Open: Noon-2pm & 5:30pm-
4am; Sat., 5:30pm-midnight;
closed Sun.

Japanese
¥¥¥
★★★
cu **Map 18**

実際の値段よりはずっと高級なイメージ
を持つ、地下にあるしゃれた洞窟風レス
トラン。毎日筆で書き替えられる長いメ
ニューもあるが、最もお得なのは5000円
のディナーコース。内容は盛りだくさん
で例えば、焼きツブ貝、さつま揚げ、大
盛の角煮、下町風マグロのかま焼き、階
上にある姉妹店のイタリアンレストラ
ン、『ラ・ゴラ』の子牛を思わせる、薄切
りの牛タン、そして美味しい味噌汁など
である。

五穀

GOLD LEAF

The Front Bldg., B1,
2-17-6 Jiyugaoka,
Meguro-ku
Tel: 3724-1212
Open: Noon-3pm &
6-10:30pm; Sun. & hol.,
6-9pm

Thai
¥¥¥
★★★

 Map 12

ゴールド
リーフ

Stakes out the high ground in Thai food: chi-chi decor, waiters sweeping through like opera stars, celadon right down to the ashtrays. Over-the-top for daily Thai eating, but a worthwhile splurge, and the brunch (¥1100 for women, ¥1300 for men; ¥2000 on weekends) is a major deal. Their original shop is in Hiroo (3447-1212) and there's a branch in the Hilton Hotel in Shinjuku (3348-1212).

贅沢なインテリアやオペラのスターを思わせるようなウェイターたち、それに美しい器や銀製品と、美しくカットして盛られたフルーツや野菜。ここには、東京で最も豪華なタイ料理店と呼ぶに相応しい雰囲気がある。ちょっとかるくタイ料理でもというには、大げさ過ぎるかも知れないが、話題づくりのために一度は行ってみる価値がある店だろう。男性1300円、女性1100円のビュッフェ式ランチ（週末は2000円）は超お得。広尾の本店（☎）3447-1212 の他に新宿ヒルトンホテル内にも支店がある。

GORGER
JACKPOT

5-36-13 Daizawa,
Shibuya-ku
Tel: 3414-5206
Open: 5:30-11pm; Sun.
from 5pm; closed Tue.

French
¥¥
★★

 Map 21

We'd like to like the Shimo-Kitazawa/Ebisu/Machida Jackpot chain more. They try hard to make French-style food an everyday affair, keeping the prices down and the decorative French off the menu. Alas, at most of their nine locations both the kitchen and the cellar are just too erratic to recommend. Gorger, despite its gag-inducing name, is an exception: cozy in a well-worn, almost *izakaya*-like way, with good daily specials on the blackboard and cheap, non-toxic red and white Côtes-du-Rhône.

気軽に食べられるフランス風料理のチェーン店のひとつ。値段は低めで、メニューも日本語でしか書かれていないが、こうした店のメニューのフランス語はたいがい飾りにしか過ぎないのでこれはかえって良い傾

ゴージェ
ジャックポット

向だ。このチェーンの９つの支店の大部分は、残念ながらキッチンが散漫過ぎる気がしてならないが、その点ここは居酒屋に近い心地よい雰囲気を持っていて落ち着ける。黒板に書かれた日替わりメニューのほか、安価なワイン、特に **Côtes-du-Rhône** の赤か白がお薦め。

GRACE

Samgetang or "clay pot chicken," the specialty here, will come as a surprise to anyone expecting the usual Korean garlic and fire. It's simply a whole young chicken in a mild ginseng broth with rice, pine nuts, and dried *nasume* fruit. The ¥4000 course includes kimchi, *namul* vegetables, ginger tea, and ice cream.

While aficionados caution that Korea's magical root requires steady use for any real effect, a single bowl of *samgetang* warms and soothes, and even seems to help ward off incipient colds and depression. It is, after all, chicken soup. Also recommended: *yaki bibimba*, a sizzling stone bowl filled with spiced minced-meat, vegetables, and rice, to which you mix in some hot, sweet Korean-style miso.

1-7-2 Azabu Juban,
Minato-ku
Tel: 3475-6972
Open: 11:30am-2pm &
5pm-midnight; Sun. & hol.
until 11pm;
closed 3rd Sun.

Korean
¥¥
★★★

Map 3

この店の特製料理サンゲタン（またの名をチキンの土瓶蒸し）は、若鶏を朝鮮人参のだし汁に入れ、米、松の実、乾燥ナツメと一緒に煮込んだものだが、韓国料理は辛く、ニンニク臭いという概念とはずいぶん違い驚くだろう。4000円のコースにはキムチ、ナムル、生姜茶、アイスクリームがついてくる。専門家にいわせると、朝鮮人参は長期間服用しなければ効果がでないそうだが、一杯のサンゲタンは身体を温めてくれ、ひき始めの風邪に良く効くような気がする。焼きビビンバも美味しい。

グレース

GU

Cony Bldg., 2F,
2-26-8 Kitazawa,
Setagaya-ku
Tel: 3485-2187
Open: 6pm-2am; closed Wed.

Japanese
¥
★★

 Map 21

Gu takes a countercultural '60s approach to health food: they stay open about six hours later than most vegetarian places; there's a considerable selection of booze; and the staff isn't adverse to smoking on the job. Classic Shimo decor too, from the mismatched, old wooden tables and chairs to the piles of Rastafarian tracts by the door. Try the ¥980 *genmai teishoku*: a main dish like a curry, a couple of salad-like side dishes, brown rice and pickles. Recommended non-alcoholic drink: ginger juice.

60年代調のカジュアルな雰囲気を持ったヘルスフードの店。よくあるこういうタイプの店とは違い、閉店時間がかなり遅く、アルコール、喫煙も大丈夫だ。下北沢らしい雑然とした内装で、寄せ集めの古い木のテーブルと椅子、入り口の傍らに置かれた不思議なイベントのチラシなど、いってみれば60年代の学生寮風だ。カレーなどのメインにサラダ風おかず、玄米、漬け物がついて980円の玄米定食と生姜ジュースがお薦めだ。

GURUPPE

5-27-5 Ogikubo,
Suginami-ku
Tel: 3393-1224
Open: 11:30am-2pm &
5-9:30pm; Sat. & hol.,
11:30am-3pm & 5-9:30pm;
closed Sun.

Japanese
¥
★★

 **Map 47**

Located over a bustling vegetable stand beside Ogikubo Station, Guruppe looks the perfect part for a Chuo Line natural food restaurant: slightly worn and anything but fashionable (remember those hokey half-timbered walls from the '70s?), yet airy and inviting. It's clearly a place that inspires loyalty: you get the impression that everyone here comes everyday. À la carte dishes are available, but regulars tend to stick with the lunch and dinner sets, mostly based around a vegetarian or fish main dish. The brown rice has real character, more than can be said of the *miso shiru* or *tsukemono*. (Not to pick on Guruppe: watery soup and dull pickles are a failing at many of our natural food restaurants, and "low sodium" is no excuse.) They offer lots of juices and other healthy drinks, including *nihonshu* and *genmaishu* from organically grown brown rice.

グルッペ

荻窪駅のすぐそばの八百屋の上にあるこの店は、ちょっと古くさい70年代調の、いかにも荻窪らしい雰囲気を残したレストランだ。お客はみな常連のようで、野菜と魚を中心としたメニューのランチとディナーに人気がある。味噌汁と漬物はごく普通だが、玄米ご飯は格別美味しい。ヘルシードリンクを含む飲み物の種類も豊富で、日本酒と玄米酒は有機米で作られた逸品を揃えている。

GYE NYAME

1-3-10 Nakazato,
Kita-ku
Tel: 5814-2721
Open: 4:30-11pm, Sat. &
Sun. from 3pm

Ghanaian
¥¥
★★

 Map 48

Apart from the cooking, ably handled by his wife Beatrice, ex-soccer pro Sampson Odei plays all positions these days—owner, *maître d'*, waiter and busboy. He'll also tell you about Ghanaian food, which has enjoyed a long give-and-take with other cuisines in Africa and even the Middle East and India. Our favorite dish here, the fish in palaver sauce, works along the lines of a *sag* curry, but with whole spinach instead of purée. The palm nut chicken curry offers another contrast with India: milder, thicker and laden with the tropical flavor of palm oil. The ¥2500 set of Ghanaian curries and stews provides a good introduction.

元プロのサッカー選手だったサンプソン・オデイ氏がオーナー兼、支配人兼、ウェイター兼、皿洗いとして忙しく動き回っているガーナ料理の店。夫人のベアトリスさんもキッチンに立っている。ここのお薦めは、Palaverソースで和えた魚料理で、インドのサグカレーを思わせるが、ホウレン草はピューレにせず丸ごと使っている。ヤシの実風味のチキンカレーもまたインド料理の雰囲気だが、よりマイルドでとろみがあり、ヤシ油による強い南国風の香りがする。初めての人にはガーナカレーとシチューの2500円のセットがお薦め。また、時々、日曜日に行われているオムツー（餅のようなもの）とビールの会に立ち寄ってもいいだろう。何を意味するかは分からないが、ナンパやフフという面白い名前の料理もつまみとして美味しい。

ジ ニャメ

HALLELUJAH BUSSAN

1-5-6 Hyakunincho,
Shinjuku-ku
Tel: 3200-0112
Open: 24 hours a day

Korean
¥
★★★

📧 **Map 22**

A Korean mini-mart that manages to squeeze four tables into the back area and serve the real Korean food that Japan is finally discovering for itself. Industrial-strength kimchi and wonderfully authentic *kejan* (raw chili crab), *yukke* (Korean steak tartare), *bibimba* (sizzling rice with toppings in a hot stone bowl) and noodles. Recommended grog: smooth, milky *makkoli*, Korean "rice beer." Date warning: this place has all the atmosphere of a broom closet.

24時間営業の韓国食料品店で、奥にテーブルが4つだけあり、激辛のキムチや本式のケジャン（唐辛子で和えた生のカニ）など、ここの家族が食べているものと同じ料理が食べられる。ユッケ、ビビンバ、麺類なども美味しいが、是非試して欲しいのは乳白色をした口あたりの良い韓国の濁り酒マッコリ。気に入れば持ち帰り用に買うこともできる。店内は質素で、デートコースにはちょっと不向きである。

ハレルヤ物産

THE HAMBURGER INN

3-15-22 Roppongi, Minato-ku
Tel: 3405-8980
Open: 11:30-5am; Fri. & Sat. until 6am; closed Sun.

Burgers
¥
★ 1/2

🗞 **Map 18**

Quick, before our gourmet credentials are revoked: 1) Because it has a picture-window view of the Roppongi street scene; 2) Because it's open till the sun comes up; and 3) Because it has been here forever and has never tried to change its name, tablecloths, burgers or clientele. Long live the Inn.

グルメの本でこの店を選んだら、笑われてしまうかもしれないが、これには3つの理由がある。第一に六本木に展開するストリートシーンが窓越しに見えること。第二に深夜営業していること。そして第三には長年の歴史を持ち、店の名前や客層、ハンバーガーの味をかたくなに守り続けていることである。これからも変わらずにずっと続けて欲しい店である。

ハンバーガー・イン

HANEZAWA GARDENS

3-12-15 Hiroo,
Shibuya-ku
Tel: 3400-2013
Open: 5-9:30pm,
roughly Apr.-Sept.

¥
★

 Map 8

羽澤ガーデン

First-timers always goggle a little. This can't be here, not in the middle of Hiroo. Towering trees, swaying lanterns, picnic tables, endless beer and traditional (c. 1960s) beer garden food so bad it's almost good. A summer must. Note, however, that reservations are required.

Other atmospheric garden-type (as opposed to rooftop) summer beer scenes can be found at **Happoen Beer Garden** (1-1-1 Shirokane-dai, Minato-ku, 3443-3111) and **Meiji Kinen Kaikan Beer Terrace** (2-2 Moto-Akasaka, Minato-ku, 3403-1171).

広尾の真ん中にこんなゆったりしたスペースがあるなんて、初めて訪れる誰もが驚いてしまうビアガーデンである。高くそびえる木々と揺れる提灯を背景に、ビールと懐かしい味のする典型的なおつまみが楽しめる。夏になると毎年足を運びたくなる場所である。

HANTEI

2-12-15 Nezu,
Bunkyo-ku
Tel: 3828-1440
Open: 5-10:30pm; hol.,
4-9:30pm; closed Sun.

Kushiage
¥¥
★★★

Map 49

はん亭

Kushiage (deep-fried things on sticks) raised to artistry. There's no ordering: they just start bringing skewers, stopping after every six to ask if you want to go on. Only monster appetites will make it through all 36. The master reportedly had his eye on this century-old building for years before he finally secured it for his shop. It was worth the wait—as is the line to Hantei, which begins in the tea room next door. Branch in Kanda Sudacho (3254-2638).

美しい古風なビルの中にある、質の高い串揚げ料理を出す店。メニューはなく、勝手に串揚げを出し続け、6本毎にそれ以上続けるかどうかを聞いてくれる。怪物的な食欲の持ち主であれば全種類36本を制覇することができる。千代田区神田須田町（☎）3254-2638 に支店がある。

HARD ROCK CAFE

5-4-20 Roppongi,
Minato-ku
Tel: 3408-7018
Open: 11:30am-2am; Fri. &
Sat. until 4am; Sun. until
11:30pm

American
¥
★ 1/2

  Map 18

ハード　ロック
カフェ

Rock 'n' roll and burgers 'n' beer and a giant gorilla peering in the window at you. We'll assume that anybody from anywhere knows the format—a Hard Rock Cafe has just opened in western China, for heaven's sake—so in a nutshell: it's loud, lively, cheap and at the very epicenter of Roppongi nightlife. Did we mention it was loud?

巨大なゴリラの人形が窓越しにのぞき込んでいることで有名なこの店を一言でいうなら、ロックンロールとバーガー、ビールの店ということだろう。ロンドン、ニューヨーク、そして中国にまで進出しているここを今更説明する必要はないだろうが、あえていえば、安くて活気があって、六本木ナイトライフの中心地だといえる。

HEALTHY-KAN

Asahi Rokubancho Mansion,
2F, 4 Rokubancho,
Chiyoda-ku
Tel: 3263-4023
Open: 11am-3pm & 4:30-
9pm; Sat. until 8pm; closed
Sun. & hol.

Japanese
¥
★★

 Map 10

Apart from the occasional overstewed flavor (a common hazard at our natural food places, if truth be told), the food is just fine. In fact this could be the archetypal Tokyo "health" restaurant: comfortably cluttered, a bit dilapidated, run by a staff that's not unfriendly but too busy with their chores to stop long and chat. Try the daily ¥1200 *bento* and the *tempe* "steak." It's also a relaxing afternoon refuge for herbal teas and carrot cake.

市ヶ谷駅から数分のマンション２階にあるここで出される料理は、自然食レストランによくある欠点、料理がたまに煮過ぎではと感じることを除けば、なかなかだ。多くの自然食ファンの間では、東京でベストという1200円の日替わり弁当の他、豆腐から作ったてんぺステーキがお薦めだ。午後のお茶に、ハーブティとキャロットケーキのために立ち寄るのも良い。

ヘルシー館

HOKKAIEN

Not even a quarter-century old, Hokkaien already looks and feels the part of an Asian classic: fluorescent lights, linoleum floor, wall-to-wall Oriental bric-a-brac. It's decor as afterthought, as at so many of the finest Chinese restaurants around the world, yet so few in Tokyo.

In the best Chinese tradition, too, is the vast menu. Everyone seems to have their own approach. *Tokyo Dining Out*'s Clint Hall recommends the Beijing-style appetizers (chicken with hot sesame sauce, sliced fish sauté, braised eggplants with pork) and the imperial dishes like quick-fried lamb with sesame. *Good Tokyo Restaurants*' Rick Kennedy likes to order the Peking duck, an *o-koge* (scorched rice) dish and whatever else the waiter recommends (which usually isn't on the menu at all). *Bungei Shunju*'s self-styled "Japanese Michelin" guide approves of the sharkfin, tofu and seasonal fried vegetable dishes. We can vouch for the *nira manju* and even the dim sum. In short: it's a place to return to, to explore, to make your own.

2-12-1 Nishi Azabu,
Minato-ku
Tel: 3407-8507
Open: 11:30am-2:30pm &
5-10pm

Chinese
¥¥¥
★★★ 1/2

 **Map 17**

開店から四半世紀も経っていないのに、蛍光灯、リノリュウムの床、壁を埋めた東洋のガラクタ類などの醸し出す空気によって、この店は台北やクアラルンプールにある古い中華料理店に紛れ込んだような錯覚を起こさせる。
中華料理の魅力のひとつは膨大なメニューだ。ここここの客はそれぞれに気に入った料理があるようだが、私は北京料理の前菜（鶏肉の辛い胡麻ソース和え、魚のソテー、茄子と豚肉の炒め物）、胡麻で和えたマトンの揚げ物、北京ダック、オコゲ料理、フカヒレ、豆腐、季節の野菜の炒め物などの宮廷風マンダリン料理が好きだ。また、にら饅頭や飲茶はお薦めだ。これでもまだ不足というのなら、ウェイターに言ってメニューにない料理を教えてもらうと良い。こういう店には何度も通い、メニューを試していくと、いつかは自分だけの料理に会えるだろう。

北海園

HOMEWORK'S

5-1-20 Hiroo,
Shibuya-ku
Tel: 3444-4510
Open: 11am-9pm; Sun. &
hol., 11am-6pm

Burgers
¥
★★

▨ ✈ **Map 8**

The degree of Japan's culinary deprivation struck home the day we saw a Japanese food magazine lauding Homework's as a gourmet revelation—which it probably is, after enough fast-food burgers. But really now—these are just good, honest, home-made American burgers. And so they should be, at about quadruple the Golden Arches' price.

In fact, the nicest thing here is the row of tables along the front, facing out on Tokyo's most effortlessly cosmopolitan promenade. Second nicest is the avocado burger. There's a branch at 1-5-8 Azabu Juban, Minato-ku (3405-9884).

大好きな『7025フランクリン・アベニュ』のハンバーガーに勝るとも劣らないバーガーショップ。様々な人種が集まる活気のある店で、広尾商店街に面している。お薦めはアボカドバーガー。麻布十番支店（港区麻布十番1-5-8 ☎ 3405-9884）

ホームワークス

HONG PHAT

Suki Bldg., 2F, 4-9-10
Takadanobaba, Shinjuku-ku
Tel: 3366-1371
Open: 11:30am-2pm &
5-11pm; Sun. & hol., noon-
10pm; closed Mon.

Vietnamese
¥1/2
★★

▨ ➤ **Map 24**

A simple Vietnamese place, much like the dozen or so others that have sprung up around town in the past couple years. Two notable features at this one: it's just around the corner from Takadanobaba Station, and they have the excellent export version of Vietnam's 333 Beer (ask for *ba-ba-ba*). Recommended: beef noodles, chicken salad and Vietnamese-style *okonomiyaki* and curry.

Set dinner ¥3500+
Not impressive

高田馬場駅のすぐ近くにあるこの店も、ここ2、3年の間に急増した素朴なベトナム料理店のひとつだ。ベトナムのビール333（バ・バ・バと発音する）があり、ベトナム風牛肉うどん、蒸し鶏のサラダ、ベトナム風お好み焼き、カレーなどがお薦め。

ホング
ファット

HOSENKA

2-21-12 Azabu Juban,
Minato-ku
Tel: 3452-0320
Open: 5pm-3am; Sun. & hol.
until midnight; closed Mon.

Korean
¥¥
★★★
Map 3

鳳仙花

Kankoku katei ryori (literally "Korean family cooking") is code for real Korean food, as opposed to *yakiniku*, the more Japanized style of grill-it-yourself meat. Hosenka is one of the best and best-known of the former, specializing in various kimchi, *reimen* (Korean-style cold noodles), *pajon* (like *okonomiyaki*, but with more character) and hearty stews and other main dishes—and no *yakiniku* at all.

いわゆる焼肉も悪くはないのだが、韓国料理といえば家庭料理の方に魅力を感じていた。そして嬉しいことに近年、日本にもこういう店が増えて来た。ここのキムチ、冷麺、パジョン（日本のお好み焼きよりスパイシーで、何度食べても飽きない独特の味）は、有名店の名に恥じない美味しさだ。ちなみに、焼肉はメニューにない。

---

*"Shimokita" in the vernacular, simply "Shimo" to its foreign friends—call **Shimo-Kitazawa** what you will, just choose your restaurants with care. Along those bohemian alleys await countless gristly ¥800 "steaks," leaden "pastas," and "ethnic" travesties for the local student population. Thankfully, in the past few years it has developed a new breed of more quality-conscious restaurant that still offers unequaled value for money. Not in our listings but worthwhile: wildly popular yakitori at **Jindaiko** (3467-0725), the excellent sakés of **Echigo** (3467-4602), nouveau Sino-Japanese **Tokutoku Light** (3468-5210), dirt-cheap French **Copain Copain** (3466-5533) and over-the-top Americana at **Rock'n'Roll Diner** (3411-6565).*

ICHI

Outside, the only sign is embedded in the ground. Inside there's an improbably high ceiling, a big communal table, an adult clientele and a staff that fields questions without tooth-sucking or running off to ask the cooks. Ichi radiates the kind of quiet confidence that promises a good meal.

Fairly traditional at first glance, the menu begins to reveal some intriguing oddities once the food arrives. The *nikujaga* (meat and potato stew) has become a light curry. The salmon comes with mustard sauce, like a visitor from France. The tofu is in teriyaki burger form and the gyoza are filled with shark fin. There is garlic rice, and Japanese-style roast beef, and sardine croquettes with terrific tartar sauce. And no lack of straightfoward nomiya fare, like stewed *daikon* (Japan's giant white radish), or *kani miso* made from crab eggs, or various grilled skewers of vegetables or chicken (don't miss the *tsukune*).

Here, if nowhere else, ask for *nihon-shu*—an open earthenware bowl filled with a cool liquid more viscous and amber-colored than anything the West knows as "saké."

3-5-8 Ebisu Minami,
Shibuya-ku
Tel: 3715-0291
Open: 5:30-11:30pm; closed Sun. & hol.

Mukokuseki
¥¥
★★★

Map 4

店にある唯一のサインは地面に埋め込まれていて、入り口は目立たないが、中に入ると信じられないほど高い天井に巨大な相席テーブルがあって、なかなかしゃれた感じのする無国籍料理の店だ。この界隈にしてはお客の年齢層は高く、知識豊かなウェイターはどんな質問にもその場で答えてくれる。彼らは自分たち独自の料理を心得ていて、一見保守的に見えるメニューも実はユニークなアイデアで作られている。例えば、軽くカレー味を効かせた肉じゃが、フレンチマスタードを添えた鮭、テリヤキバーガーに変身している豆腐、そしてフカヒレ入りのギョーザなどである。また、ガーリック

ライスや和風ローストビーフ、イワシのコロッケのタルタルソース添え、ダイコンの煮物、カニ味噌、串焼き（つくねは絶品）などの飾り気のない居酒屋料理も揃っている。たくさんある焼きものの器の中から自分で選ぶことができ、それに入れて出してくれる日本酒も美味しい。

壹

ICHINOCHAYA

Nihonshu scholar and author Isao Sakuragi spreads the faith at Ichinochaya, Tokyo's ground zero for connoisseur-grade *ginjoshu*. Typically, he features three of these super-sakés per month, plus another 20 or so regular favorites. Shown on the menu for each are region of origin, rice variety, polishing percentage (expressed as the weight of the remaining rice), *nihonshudo* (minus figures are sweet *amakuchi*; plus means increasingly drier *karakuchi*) and *sando*, a measure of organic acids that corresponds to body. This type of information is beginning to appear on saké labels, so if you notice any pattern to your preferences you can actually look knowledgeable the next time you walk into a saké shop.

2-21-10 Kanda Awajicho,
Chiyoda-ku
Tel: 3251-8517
Open: 5-11pm;
closed Sat. & Sun.

Izakaya
¥¥¥
★★★★

 Map 13

Recommended food: sashimi (the classic foil to really good *nihonshu*); fish in grilled, fried or *nimono* form; and raw oysters and a different cook-it-yourself *nabe* stewpot each week in the winter.

酒の専門家で作家の桜木氏はこの店から吟醸酒信仰を広めているといってもいいだろう。ここの酒は独自のメニューを作っていて、彼はこの店で毎月変わる3種のお薦め吟醸酒について細かく解説している。また、20数種の酒についての産地、米の種類、精米歩号、日本酒度、酸度などに関しても詳しく分析している。お薦め料理は、刺し身の盛り合わせ、生ガキ、焼き魚、煮魚、そして冬には鍋物もある。

一ノ茶屋

ICHIOKU

4-4-5 Roppongi,
Minato-ku
Tel: 3405-9891
Open: 5pm-3am; Sun. & hol.
until 11pm

Mukokuseki
¥
★★

 Map 18

一億

Inimitably off-the-wall pioneer of mukokuseki cuisine—not that they'd admit or probably even realize it. Delicate palates may find the food greasy; others will enjoy every bite. We love the tables in the crawl space below the ceiling; it's like being a kid again, hiding in the closet.

Ichioku makes no fuss about it, so even regulars may not realize that the policy here has always been health-oriented: organically grown vegetables, free-range chickens and no MSG. Favorite orders: the tofu steak on its sizzling hot metal plate and the "Western-style" cheese gyoza.

無国籍料理の草分け的存在だった店。料理は少し脂っこいと感じる人もあるかもしれないが、ほとんどは何を頼んでも安くて美味しい。天井裏のスペースに置かれたテーブルに座ると、押し入れに隠れて遊んだ子供の頃を思い出すようで楽しい。お薦めは、豆腐ステーキとチーズが入った洋風ギョーザ。

IIDAYA

3-3-2 Nishi Asakusa,
Taito-ku
Tel: 3843-0881
Open: 11:30am-9pm; closed
Wed.

Dojo (loach)
¥
★★

Map 50

Here we'll part company with just about every other guidebook and recommend that if you have *dojo* (loach) only once in Tokyo, it not be at the wonderfully ancient (est. 1801) **Komagata Dojo** (1-7-12 Komagata, Taito-ku, 3842-4001). The second time, certainly, but for your first experience with this most humble of fish, we suggest a place that isn't quite so oppressively famous. Iidaya is perfectly atmospheric in its own right, and many cognoscenti actually prefer the sweeter, stronger seasoning style here.

Recommended: *dojo honenuki nabe* (a stew of boned dojo prepared at your table) and *namazu* (catfish) *nabe*.

東京でどじょう料理の老舗といえば、1801年創業の『駒形どぜう』（台東区駒形1-7-12（☎）3842-4001）だが、ここはあ

飯田屋

まりにも有名すぎて常に混んでいるので
もっとリラックスして食べたい時にはこ
の店がいいだろう。味付けは濃いめだ
が、どじょうじたいに甘さがあって美味
しい。どじょう骨抜き鍋となまず鍋がお
薦め。

IL BIANCO

Relaxed and accommodating, Il Bianco
would be a pleasure even without Tokyo's
most enlightened wine policy. It works four
ways: 1) With the ¥500 cover charge
comes a bottomless glass of their ordinary
house Bardolino. 2) For ¥500 more a head
(worth it) they'll be equally forthcoming with
their Chianti. 3) All wines in their sizable
cellar go for actual retail price. 4) Bring
your own—they'll open and serve it for free.

To eat we recommend the ¥8000
course for two, including assorted anti-
pasti, pasta, main dish, dessert and
coffee. Food is served family-style, and
something about the abundance of it, the
free-flowing wine and the classic, white-
linen tablecloths and wooden parquet floor
makes Il Bianco feel like the epitome of an
Italian restaurant.

Nichiei Bldg., 2F,
4-8-3 Roppongi,
Minato-ku
Tel: 3470-5678
Open: 11:30am-3:30pm
& 5-11pm

Italian
¥¥
★★ 1/2

Map 18

東京で最も進んだワインポリシーを抜き
にしても、この店のゆっくり出来て肩の
凝らない雰囲気は評価できる。このワイ
ンポリシーとは、1）500円のカバー
チャージで、ごく平凡なハウスワインが
飲み放題、2）さらに500円追加するだけ
で、かなり得する"キャンティ"飲み放
題、3）この店の巨大なワイン貯蔵庫にあ
るワインを全て小売値段で飲める、4）自
分の好きなワインの持ち込み可、開栓と
お匂は無料サービスというものだ。前菜
盛り合わせ、パスタ、メインディッ
シュ、デザート、コーヒーで二人前8000
円のコースが良心的だ。

イル　ビアンコ

ILE DE FRANCE

Andre Pachon's Ile de France had become such a trusted Roppongi fixture that we feared the worst when he left and the restaurant moved to new quarters in Aoyama a couple years back. Not to worry: the cooking remains sound, solid and firmly rooted somewhere between Périgord and the Midi. It's the sort of place where they bring you a pot of rillettes with the bread, where the smallest pichet of wine is half a liter and where if you ask the chef for his best dish, he's likely to recommend the humble, wonderful cassoulet. In a city divided between temples to haute cuisine and cheap bistros, it's a welcome middle ground, and the least self-conscious and most French of them all. The new room makes a sunny, pleasant haven for lunch (courses for ¥2900 and ¥4500).

Daihan Bldg., 2F,
3-6-23 Kita Aoyama,
Minato-ku
Tel: 5485-2931
Open: Noon-2pm
& 6-10:30pm

French
¥¥¥
★★★

📷➡ **Map 2**

東京在住のフランス人に、この街のお気に入りのフランス料理店はどこかと聞いたら、この店を選ぶ人がかなり多いだろう。でもそれは、ここの料理が最高に美味しい訳でも、雰囲気がお洒落だということでもなく、またどこにもなく、ここだけに最高の何かがあるわけでもない。それはただ、フランスの何処の町にでもある、正真正銘のブルジョワ趣味のレストランだからだ。ここは高級料理ではなく、多くのフランス人が故郷を離れて懐かしく思う田舎料理の数々を食べさせてくれる。例えば、魚のスープ、ポトフ、鴨のコンフィ、ステーキや、シェフのアンドレ・パション氏自慢の白豆、豚肉、ソーセージ、ガチョウを煮込んだシチュー、キャスレーなどだ。
このようなタイプの店の中で、最も信頼されていたここが、数年前に六本木の地下から、青山通りの日当たりの良い現在の場所に移った時には、どうなるかと心配された。でも心配は杞憂に終わり、店の雰囲気（特にランチ時）、料理の味も以前に増して良くなった。

イル　ド
フランス

*Pizza is a highly personal subject
(we remember the American girl on the
ferry from Brindisi complaining about
"that stuff they call pizza in Italy"),
so here are four picks for different tastes:
Pizzeria Sabatini for the streetwise Roman
version, **La Baracca** for a more rustic style,
Ponte Vecchio for a wonderful
paper-thin adaptation and
Spago for the outer limits.*

IL FORNO

Consistently unimaginative "Santa Monica-style" pizza and pasta, but in a lively atmosphere and at what are known as "popular" prices. It's one of those places that seldom excites but always does the job. There's an equally crowded branch just above Omotesando Station (3400-0518).

Tokyoites who happen to visit California's original Il Forno (2901 Ocean Park Blvd., Santa Monica) may be surprised to find that it's an altogether more adult production. But then this wouldn't be the first time that an overseas restaurant concept has been watered down for local consumption.

Piramide Bldg., 3F,
6-6-9 Roppongi,
Minato-ku
Tel: 3796-2641
Open: 11:30am-3pm
& 5:30-11pm

Italian
¥¥
★★

  Map 18

個人的にはここで出されるカリフォルニアスタイルのピッツァやパスタより、本場イタリアの料理の方が好きなのだが、活気ある雰囲気や手頃な値段からか人気がある。安くて良質のワインもあり、特に赤のCorvoがお薦め。いつ行ってもまず失望させられることのない店である。表参道駅のすぐ上に人気の支店 (☎) 3400-0518 がある。

イル・フォルノ

IL PRIMO

If every train line radiating from Tokyo has its own culinary character, the Chuo Line's is resolutely early-'70s retro. That's certainly the look at the pocket-sized Il Primo, but the food has little in common with the student-oriented fodder usually dished out at these places. Owner/chef Shin Yamamoto studied his craft in Italy, and it has made a difference. Even when he wings it, as he does on many of the seafood pastas and risottos here, it works. A good example: his crab and tomato linguini. It's dense and rich and thoroughly Italian in spirit, if not in the details.

Other pluses: some good Piemonte wines (the Dolcetto is worth a try), a counter brimming with handsome desserts and enjoyably corny Italian pop music of the "Volare" vintage. One minus (or have we just been unlucky?): rather glum service from a pair of waiters who look like they'd rather be elsewhere.

5-46-5 Chuo,
Nakano-ku
Tel: 3384-3981
Open: 11:30am-2:30pm
& 5-10pm; closed Wed.

Italian
¥¥
★★ 1/2

 **Map 15**

70年代の中央線沿線にかつてあった、学生向けの安いレストランのような雰囲気が残るポケットサイズのこの店の味は、その印象とは違ってなかなかのものだ。オーナーシェフの山本信氏は本場イタリアで修行した料理に、彼独自の工夫をつけ加えている。それは魚介類のパスタやリゾット、例えばカニとトマトのリングイーニなどのオリジナル料理によく現れている。あまりディテールにこだわらなければ、これはもう十分にイタリア料理の精神を継承しているといえる。イタリアのポップミュージックが流れる中で、北イタリアのピエモンテ地方のワインや美味しいデザートを楽しむのも良い。ただ、問題（たまたま私の運が悪かっただけかも知れないが）はウェイターのふてくされたサービス態度でいただけない。

イル・プリモ

INAKAYA

Mandeni farewell.

7-8-4 Roppongi,
Minato-ku
Tel: 3405-9866
Open: 5pm-11pm

Robatayaki
¥¥¥
★★★

[cc] **Map 18**

田舎家

Overpriced, overly famous and undeniably one of the best at what it does: top-end *robatayaki* prepared and served with gusto. It's a non-stop, six-hour performance of culinary hustle. Everyone loves it, and they can get practically ecstatic if they're not paying. Branches nearby in Roppongi (3408-5040) and Akasaka (3586-3054).

最近はちょっと有名になりすぎたし、値段も高いが、炉端焼きの店としては、味、サービス共に最高の店のひとつだと認めざるを得ない。日本人、外国人を問わず多くの人に愛されていて（特に支払いをするとき以外は）、6時間フル回転だ。六本木にもう一軒（☎）3408-5040 と、赤坂（☎）3586-3054 に支店がある。

ISTANBUL

3-10-7 Shinjuku,
Shinjuku-ku
Tel: 3226-5929
Open: 5-11:30pm; closed
Sun.

Turkish
¥¥
★★

[cc] ◪ 🔁 **Map 22**

イスタンブール

Tokyo Turkish pioneer Istanbul may not have the range of magnificent vegetable dips found at **Asena** or **Topkapi**, but for the meatier sort of Anatolian fare it's still a well-respected contender. Tiny and crowded, with an atmospheric Shinjuku backstreet setting. Recommended: *doner kebabs* to eat, *raki* to drink.

『アセナ』や、残念ながら閉店してしまった『バルバロス』には及ばないが、それでも充分に美味しいトルコ料理を出す店。トルコ料理は世界のどこでもなぜか軽視され過ぎているような気がするが、ここは確かな味と独自の雰囲気を持った個性的な店である。新宿裏通りにあり、小さいせいかいつも混み合っている。お薦め料理はケバブ、飲み物はトルコ式ブランデーの raki がいい。

ITCHO

4-10-3 Nishi Azabu,
Minato-ku
Tel: 3409-9646
Open: 6pm-midnight

Mukokuseki
¥¥
★★ 1/2

Map 17

一兆

One of the more intimate interpretations of the *mukokuseki* ("no-nationality") theme. They do about 40 dishes per evening, a touch more Japanese in style than the norm for this kind of food, and mostly displayed on the counter in front of you. There's passable wine by the carafe and Mexican beer, but saké might be the way to go. Itcho attracts a relaxed, adult crowd, but then so does the whole Nishi Azabu area.

数多くある無国籍料理店の中で、ここを比較的親しみやすく感じるのは、こぢんまりした店内と、毎晩カウンターに並べられる40種類ほどの料理が日本料理に近いからなのだろう。デキャンターに入ったワインやメキシカンビールもあるが、ここではやはり日本酒がぴったりくる。西麻布全体に言えることだが、ここもお客は大人が多く落ちついた雰囲気だ。料理の善し悪しはともかく、私がこの辺りのレストランを好むのは、それが最大の要因かも知れない。

IWASHIYA

7-2-12 Ginza,
Chuo-ku
Tel: 3571-3000
Open: Noon-2pm & 5-9pm;
closed Sun. & hol.

Japanese
¥¥ 1/2
★★ 1/2

 Map 7

We first heard of this place from John Wilcock's 1968 edition of *Japan on $5 and $10 a Day*. Imagine, Doris, a restaurant serving nothing but *sardines*!

It's true, though some of their dozens of sardine dishes work better than others. In general, the less ground up and otherwise altered, the better—it turns out that sardine meat achieves as much of its appeal from texture as taste. For lunch, it may be best to avoid the ¥1200 *teishoku* (it's prepared ahead of time and can taste a little cafeteria-ish) and invest a couple hundred yen more for one of the other sets. Dinner courses from ¥6000; or do it cheaper à la carte. Despite the Ginza address, there's a comfortable *shitamachi* feeling to the communal seating and service.

Sardine lovers partial to high-grade saké can skip Iwashiya and head straight for **Ryuma** (3-21-4 Shinjuku, 3354-7956), a friendly, salt-of-the-earth *iwashi* specialist with some superb rice wines—keep an eye out for the Tengumai *yamahai*.

この店は『一日を5～10ドルで暮らす日本』という本の68年版で見つけた。今ではいちばん安いものでも10ドル位するが、メニューの中身は当時とほとんど変わらない。10数種類ある鰯料理の中には味のばらつきもあるが、経験からいって、あまり手間をかけていない鰯の姿をとどめた料理に美味しいものが多いようだ。昼食時には1200円の定食を避け（作り置きをしてあり、特に新鮮なわけではないので）、もう数百円奮発して定食以外のセットをオーダーするのが正解。6000円からのディナーコースの他、一品料理もある。銀座という場所にありながら、サービスや長いテーブルでの相席など、下町情緒を感じさせる。鰯好きで、なおかつ酒にもうるさい人には、新宿の『流馬』（新宿区新宿3-21-4 (☎) 3354-7956) もお薦めだ。

いわしや

JEMBATAN MERAH

1-3 Maruyamacho,
Shibuya-ku
Tel: 3476-6424
Open: 11am-11pm

Indonesian
¥¥
★★★

  **Map 19**

ジュンバタン・メラ

A Bengawan Solo spin-off, more innovative with their menu if perhaps a touch less reliable in their cooking. On a good night there's no other Indonesian food in Tokyo to touch it. Handy for a late-ish dinner after shows at Bunkamura and other Shibuya venues. Recommended: any of the specials. Note the new branch in Akasaka (3588-0794).

古くて有名なインドネシアレストラン、『ブンガワンソロ』に長くいた従業員が始めた店で、メニューの内容は革新的だ。料理の味は時にムラがあるものの、良い日に当たれば東京一のインドネシア料理を楽しむことができる。東急文化村などでショウを見た後の遅いディナーに最適だ。お薦めは特別料理のどれでも。赤坂に支店 (☎) 3588-0794 がある。

JIGOKU RAMEN HYOTTOKO

1-8-4 Ebisu Minami,
Shibuya-ku
Tel: 3791-7376
Open: 11am-2pm & 5-10pm;
closed Sun. & hol.

Noodles
¥
★★
Map 5

地獄ラーメン・ひょっとこ

Recognizable by the fire-breathing demons
out front. Specialty of the house is the
triple X-rated ¥1300 *akaike jigoku* ("Red
Lake of Hell") *ramen*; fail to choke it all
down and you have to go into the kitchen
and wash ten dishes. Their other noodles
are saner both in spice and price.

この店の自慢料理は1300円の激辛、赤池
地獄ラーメンで、もしこの料理が食べ切
れなかったら、キッチンで皿洗い10枚の
罰が与えられる。しかし、これ以外の
ラーメンは値段も辛さも正常である。

JUGEMU

2-44-10 Tomigaya,
Shibuya-ku
Tel: 3465-6913
Open: Noon-2pm; dinner by
reservation only; closed Sun.

Gomadofu
¥¥
★★★★

 Map 5

Jugemu falls somewhere between *kaiseki*
house and mom-and-pop diner. Meals
range from a basic lunch set (the "o-
bento") for ¥1200 to custom-built, nine-
course dinners for ten times that. Almost
all the dishes here derive from the Buddhist
vegetarian tradition, and perhaps about
half use *gomadofu*, the house specialty, in
one form or another. Following an old
temple custom, the menus change com-
pletely each month.

What you should also know is that this
modest-looking shop is gomadofu purveyor
to the Emperor and his father before him.
Whichever level you choose to approach it
on, this is food of the highest integrity.
Note that they're open for dinner by reservation only, and that you'll need a party of
at least three.

懐石料理と家庭料理の中間といった感じ
の胡麻豆腐料理屋。料理は1200円で食べ
られるランチのお弁当から、その10倍は
する9品の特製ディナーコースまでバラ

寿限無

エティーに富んでいる。また、昭和天皇以来、宮内庁御用達の店でもある。メニューは古寺の習慣に従って毎月変えられる。夜は3人以上のグループで予約をした時のみ開けてくれる。

*Gomadofu only looks like tofu. The texture and flavor are its own, and the words used to describe them begin where "rich," "smooth" and "ethereal" leave off. Painstakingly made from sesame seeds, it was traditionally served to visiting VIPs at Buddhist temples. Apart from kaiseki palaces and the rare specialty shop (**Jugemu**), it most often appears these days at tofu restaurants like **Goemon**.*

JUNGLE

More mischief along the Aoyama Cemetery strip: loud music, hallucinogenic pink lighting, uninspired vaguely Jamaican food and a hot sauce that could wake the dead. The staff inhabits a world of its own, but occasionally can be roused to bring you something. Best used for its outdoor tables, say for a late-night beer after dinner at nearby **Rice Terrace** or **Monsoon Café**.

2-5-3 Nishi Azabu,
Minato-ku
Tel: 3797-1949
Open: 11-5am

Caribbean
¥
★

  **Map 17**

青山墓地の反対側の外苑西通りには新しいレストランやバーが増えているが、そんな中でも際立っているのがここ。派手な音楽にピンクのライト、屋外にはテーブルもあって、スタッフたちは自分たちが作る世界を楽しんでいるように見える。料理はジャマイカ料理といっているが、普通のバーのスナック類とほとんど変わらない。ただしソースはかなり辛め。近くの『ライステラス』や『モンスーンカフェ』で食事をした後ここに立ち寄り、外のテーブルでお酒を楽しむには便利なスポットだ。

ジャングル

KEAWJAI

Teak and gold decor, pink marble tabletops, Regency chairs, discreet Sukhothai court music piping in on the speakers—this is not your standard Thai curry truckstop. The food also ranks well above the Tokyo norm, if a little more enthusiastic with the carved fruits and vegetables than totally necessary. The ¥1800 buffet lunch is a favorite with the staff of the nearby Thai Embassy. And probably because of the heavily Thai clientele, the cooks are amenable to whipping up any favorite recipes you may have, whether or not it's on the menu (which itself runs to well over 200 dishes).

On the east side of town find Keawjai near Kinshicho Station at 4-9-4 Kinshi, Sumida-ku (3626-6256).

Meguro Kowa Bldg., B1,
2-14-9 Kami-Osaki,
Shinagawa-ku
Tel: 5420-7727
Open: 11am-10pm

Thai
¥¥
★★★

Map 14

チーク材とゴールドの内装、ピンク大理石のテーブルと宮殿の椅子、そして控えめなタイの宮廷音楽と、ここはまさに高級志向のタイレストラン。しかし、それだけに料理も値段も東京の標準をやや上回っている。特に1800円のビュッフェ式ランチは近くのタイ大使館のスタッフたちに人気がある。

ゲウチャイ

KAISEITEI EAST

The owner started this place because he felt that Brussels charged too much (arguable) and didn't try hard enough with its food (hard to argue). The result is a friendly little bar-restaurant featuring some 50 Belgian and other premium beers, and at the best prices in town. And good food, as promised, notably the garlic cheese *yaki*: great big slices of garlic, grilled brown on his teppan and then dripped with melted cheese. The house specialty is *okonomiyaki*, sufficiently new-wave in style to possibly win over even those of us who have our doubts about this curious Japanese snack food. Recommended beers: Budvar, Duvel, Kwak. Worth a visit too is the original **Kaiseitei** (5376-1955) in Takaido, Suginami-ku, featuring *teppanyaki* and good Niigata saké.

3-1-10 Kitazawa,
Setagaya-ku
Tel: 3469-0801
Open: 6pm-1am; closed Mon.

Okonomiyaki and beer
¥¥
★★ 1/2

Map 52

オーナーがブリュッセルで経験した、高い食事の値段（私も同感）、不味さ（これには異議あり）が、ここをオープンさせるきっかけになったという。結果としてこの親しみやすい雰囲気のバー＆レストランでは、ベルギー産をはじめとして50種類の旨いビールが安く飲める。また料理はどれも美味しく、特に、大粒のガーリックを鉄板でキツネ色に焼き、その上に溶けたチーズをかけた「ニンニクのチーズ焼き」や、「特製お好み焼き」、ビールではBudvar（本物のチェコ産 Budweiserで、アメリカ産コピーよりコクがあって美味）とDuvel（英語でdevil）がお薦め。鉄板焼や新潟産の酒が売り物の高井戸支店（☎) 5376-1955 にも行ってみる価値がある。

海晴亭イースト

KANTIPUR

3-2-6 Nishi Azabu,
Minato-ku
Tel: 3470-1288
Open: 11:30am-11pm;
closed Sun.

Nepalese
¥¥
★★ 1/2

 **Map 18**

What the original Shibuya basement Kantipur (3770-5358) lacks in atmosphere has always been made up for in good cooking and fair prices. This newer branch adds to those virtues a bright, spacious room with a picture-window view onto TV Asahi-dori. Beginners can edge into this food via two set dinners (¥2800 and ¥3500), either of which will fill to bursting anyone but a Himalayan herdsman.

Favorites: *momo* (mutton dumplings with spicy yogurt dip), *bhuteko bhatmas* (soy beans stir-fried with mustard oil and lemon) and fiery hot "mutton chili." Bargain-hunters should come for lunch, which here lasts until a leisurely 4pm.

手頃な値段で美味しい料理が食べられる代わりに、雰囲気に欠ける渋谷地下の本店に比べて、このテレビ朝日通りが見渡せる支店は明るく広々としていて文句ない。ネパール料理の初心者でも満足させてくれる、2800円と3500円の２種類のセットディナーから試してみると良い。その他のお薦め料理はモモ（辛いヨーグルトソースにつけて食べる羊肉入りギョーザ）、マスタード油とレモンで炒めた大豆、激辛のマトンのチリなど。午後４時までやっているランチは何といってもお得だ。

カンティプール

KAO TAI

2-14-6 Takadanobaba,
Shinjuku-ku
Tel: 3204-5806
Open: 11am-2pm & 5-11pm;
Sun., 5-11pm

Thai
¥
★★ 1/2

CC **Map 24**

カオ　タイ

Picture a short-order *chuka* (Japanized-Chinese) joint with portions and prices for the Takadanobaba student crowd. Now make it Thai and make it authentic—hot enough that the uninitiated have to fan their mouths and hiss "*Karai!*" But they come back, and you can see that soon they won't be satisfied with anything less. Useful for full meals at rock-bottom prices or just a spicy snack and cold beer before exploring the many other new places in the neighborhood.

一見中華料理屋だが、本場に近いタイ料理を出している店。量も値段も高田馬場の学生たちにぴったりだ。思わず「辛い!」と叫びたくなる料理もあるが、この味が忘れられなくて足を運ぶファンも多い。食事はもちろんのこと、ちょっとしたおやつやビールだけで立ち寄ってもいい。

KAOTAN RAMEN

2-34-30 Aoyama,
Minato-ku
Tel: 3475-6337
Open: 11am-5am;
closed Sun.

Noodles
¥
★★

Map 17

かおたんラーメン

Why people would line up outdoors in all weather for a bowl of ramen in a tumble-down shack begs questions that go beyond the culinary. Worth a trip for sociological interest alone, never mind the (admittedly pretty good) "noodles in deluxe Fukkien soup stock." Dress warmly.

行列ができる店は東京では珍しくもないし、ニューヨークだったらもっとあるかもしれない。でも真冬の凍てつく夜に550円のラーメンを求めて掘立小屋の前に並ぶ輩がいるとは? 受ける秘訣はスープか、手頃な価格か。もしかしたらそこに列があるからかも!? 結構イケるラーメンではあるが...。

KENBOKKE

4-11-28 Nishi Azabu,
Minato-ku
Tel: 3498-7080
Open: 11:30am-2pm &
5:30-11pm; closed Sun.

Indian
¥ 1/2
★★ 1/2
 Map 17

ケンボッケ

A one-man Indian operation with a difference. It's pleasantly café-like, with a view of the Shuto Expressway to delight any structural engineer. The stereo is more likely to be playing Art Tatum than Indian film themes, and sensible little touches show up everywhere. How many of our other Indian restaurants, for example, provide a decent-sized glass of water? Fine curries, too, which become more interesting if you venture beyond the standard meat and chicken offerings.

インド人の主人がひとりで賄っているこの店は、よくある普通のインド料理店とはひと味違う。シタールの代わりにジャズを流し、大きなグラスにたっぷりと水を注いでくれて、店のところどころに光るセンスの良さは気持ちのいいカフェのような雰囲気だ。スタンダードなマトンやチキンカレーも美味しいが、それ以外のカレーも試してみる価値がある。

KEYAKI GRILL

Capitol Tokyu Hotel, B1,
2-10-3 Nagatacho,
Chiyoda-ku
Tel: 3581-4511
Open: Noon-3pm
& 5:30-10:30pm

Grill
¥¥¥¥
★★★
 **Map 1**

欅グリル

No doubt there are other worthy hotel grills in this city, but the one our respondents keep going back to is Chef Karl Hörmann's Keyaki at the Capitol Tokyu. Hörmann is the consummate veteran, and his no-holds-barred Sunday/holiday buffets are the stuff of Tokyo expat legend. They range from French and Italian to American, but Hörmann saves his best efforts for his home country audiences—Swiss, German, and especially Austrian. There are no surprises to this food, nor would Keyaki fans want there to be.

都内の数あるホテル内グリルの中で、ついつい何度も足を運んでしまうのが、カール・ハーマン氏がシェフをしているここだ。料理の達人として知られる彼の、日曜、祭日のビュッフェは、今や伝説になっている。レパートリーはフランス、イタリア、アメリカ料理と幅広いが、スイス、ドイツ、そして彼の故郷オーストリア料理には一層腕の冴えが感じられる。

KINO KÜCHE

2-11-32 Nishi,
Kunitachi-shi,
Tokyo
Tel: 0425-77-5971
Open: 5pm-midnight;
closed Mon. & 3rd Sun.

Izakaya
¥¥
★★★

📅 **Map 53**

Owner/chef/Eastern European cinema buff Ken Sasaki combines hobby and work in an izakaya as far out on the culinary scale as it is on the Chuo Line. Prepare for exotica such as *ikagoro ruibe* (that's Ainu), a squid liver sorbet that literally melts in the mouth. Or *gonbafairaantora* (that's Hungarian in *katakana*), a mammoth mushroom stuffed with liverwurst, breaded, deep-fried and served with tartar sauce. Or a different quiche every evening.

There's more typical izakaya fare too, cooked atypically well: *agetori* (deep-fried chicken) of supreme tenderness and an assertive *negi* (green onion) sauce of not-quite Yamato origin; *jaga bataa* (buttered baked potato), various *nabe* stewpots (try the kimchi), heavenly *yaki o-nigiri* (grilled rice balls) made of *haigamai* (unpolished rice), and homemade *o-shinko* pickles of the highest standard. Saké is the obvious drink for all this, either the nightly special or one of their regular selections.

東ヨーロッパ映画のファンであるオーナー兼シェフの佐々木健氏は、その趣味と仕事をこの居酒屋でうまく融合させ発揮している。口の中でとろけるイカの胆のシャーベット、イカゴロルイベ（アイヌ語）や、レバーのパテを詰めた巨大なキノコにパン粉をつけて揚げ、タルタルソースで食べるゴンバファイ・ラーントヴ（ハンガリー語）などどれも料理は凝っている。また、毎晩変わるキッシュなどのおしゃれなメニューの他、ネギのタレで食べる柔らかい鶏の唐揚げやジャガバター、鍋物（キムチ鍋が美味）、胚芽米で作った焼きおにぎり、特製おしんこなどの典型的な居酒屋料理もお袋の味そのもの。ここの料理にはやはり日本酒が合うが、日替わりスペシャルか、常時用意されているセレクションの中から選べる。趣味として佐々木さんは料理と映画の情報を満載した新聞「木乃久兵衛通信」を発行している。

木乃久兵衛

KIRIN YOKOHAMA BEER VILLAGE

1-17-1 Namamugi,
Tsurumi-ku, Yokohama-shi,
Kanagawa-ken
Tel: 045-503-8250
Open: 11am-9:30pm;
closed Mon.

Beer
¥
★★

📶🏯 **Map 54**

キリン横浜
ビアビレッジ

Not the most convenient location—25 minutes on the Keihin Kyuko Line from Shinagawa to Namamugi Station, and ten minutes' walk from there—but for a taste of the beers Japan's brewers could offer us if they wanted, this is the place. Their custom brews (¥330 to ¥700/glass) typically run from lager to wheat beer to stout styles. Assorted snacks for ¥600 to ¥800 (try the *tartine*). If real hunger strikes, there's a Kirin-run restaurant next door.

京浜急行で品川から生麦まで約25分、そこから徒歩10分あまりという、決して便利とは言えない場所にある。でも日本の醸造所だって、その気になればこれだけのビールが作れるということを知るには、最適のところだ。特製のビールが一杯330円から700円で、非常に新鮮で、かなりの品揃えのラガー、麦芽、スタウトがある。おつまみの盛り合わせは600円から800円（タルティーンがお薦め）で、どうしてもお腹が空いて物足りなければ、隣にはキリン直営のレストランもある。

There's actually a successful Japanese-language guide to
restaurants with lines of people waiting outside.
Lines aren't unique to Japan, of course,
but their psychology may be—the "I don't know exactly
what it's for, but if I don't get in line
I might be missing out on something" phenomenon.
Consistently longest lines of any Tokyo-area restaurant
(one recent TV survey counted 137 people):
Midori Zushi, *1-20-7 Umegaoka, Setagaya-ku*
(3429-0066). It's good, but as at most of these places,
the original attraction appears to have been
less sheer quality than value for money—they simply
serve huge pieces.

KLEINES WIEN

Kleines Wien ("Little Vienna") couldn't be much smaller if it tried. The decor is authentic Tokyo *sunakku* ("snack bar"), right down to the spotlights, low tables and tiny plush stools. The food is the work of Vienna-trained Shigeo Tanaka: meaty goulash, white pork sausage with sauerkraut, homemade bread filled with bacon and onion and local color in the form of chicken *teriyaki* and *yoshoku* croquettes.

The real motivation to come here is Tokyo's best selection of Austrian wines—pungent, fruity and fragrant—available by the glass or bottle. For white we're partial to the dry Muscat; for red, the dark, almond-bitter Pinôt Noir.

3-6-26 Kita Aoyama,
Minato-ku
Tel: 3499-3488
Open: 6pm-midnight;
closed Sun.

Austrian
¥¥
★★

Map 2

クライネス・ウィーン

どう頑張ってもこれ以上小さくはできないようなミニサイズの店だが、内装はスポットライトから低いテーブル、カウンター用のスツールまで一通り揃ったスナック風である。料理はウィーンで修行を積んだ田中氏が腕をふるっていて、彼の得意料理の中には、具だくさんのグーラッシュ、ホワイトソーセージのザウアークラウト添え、ベーコンと玉ねぎを詰めたホームメードのパン、それにコロッケやチキンのテリヤキなどの日本の洋食風もあって親しみやすい。

KOBE 77

Benihana notwithstanding, teppanyaki doesn't require circus stunts with knives and fire. All it really takes is a cook and a hot steel table. Kobe 77 operates with a bare minimum of fuss (decor, too) just a few steps from the Roppongi crossing. Mix and match appetizers like *yasai itame* (grilled mixed vegetables) and garlic sprouts with beef, a ¥2800 sirloin or two (everything is designed for sharing), the heroic garlic rice and their patented "ice cream steak" for dessert.

Oda Bldg., B1,
6-1-3 Roppongi,
Minato-ku
Tel: 3479-3689
Open: 5pm-5am

Teppanyaki
¥¥
★★★

[CC] [◆] **Map 18**

神戸77

『紅花』や、ここに類した店のおかげで、西洋人の多くが鉄板焼というものを知るようになった。でもこれで、鉄板焼にはまるでサーカスのようなナイフと火の曲芸が付き物だと信じさせてしまった。こういう先入観を持った人たちは、六本木交差点近くにあるこの店にはがっかりするかも知れない。店内の装飾、そして料理法もシンプルだからだ。野菜炒めや牛肉のニンニクの芽和えなどの前菜から、サーロインステーキ、ガーリックライス（大量のニンニクを使っている割には臭いが気にならない）、自慢のアイスクリーム・ステーキのデザートがお薦め。

KOMAHACHI

A mid-town après-office eating and drinking scene that stands out from the norm. For one thing there's the inventive food, like the pumpkin fried with almonds and the *mochigome shumai*. They have an expert selection of saké too, and—this can make all the difference—a master who is thoroughly at ease with customers of the non-Japanese persuasion.

5-16-1 Shiba,
Minato-ku
Tel: 3453-2530
Open: 5-11:30pm;
closed Sun. & hol.

Izakaya
¥¥
★★★

[CC] **Map 55**

オフィス街の真ん中、アフターファイブの寄り道コースにある店として、ここは飛び抜けた存在だ。その理由のひとつは、料理が工夫されていることで、例えば、アーモンドをまぶして揚げたカボチャや、餅米シュウマイなどだ。また、お酒の種類も多く、充実している。そして何より私がここを気に入っている訳は、外国人の客でも歓迎してくれることだ。一見日本人には関係ないことのようだが、客層が多岐にわたっている店ほど、様々な点で優れている店が多いような気がする。

駒八

KORINBO

Nakano Broadway, 2F,
5-52-15 Nakano,
Nakano-ku
Tel: 3385-7005
Open: 11:30am-3:30pm
& 5-8pm; closed Sun.

Vegetarian Chinese
¥
★★

Map 15

香林坊

The other end of the luxury spectrum from **Bodaiju**: a couple of Chinese ladies, a few woks and a crowded counter where the main draw is a daily ¥900 tray of decent vegetarian eats. Just finding this place (allow some time) will take you back decades, to a Tokyo of linoleum floors, fluorescent lights and bead curtains. The food is not entirely ungreasy, but for anyone on a meatless diet it makes a welcome break from the endless *konnyaku* and *hijiki* of Tokyo's many Japanese-style vegetarian restaurants.

2、3人の中国女性スタッフが働くこぢんまりとしたノスタルジックな店。料理の種類は少ないが、カウンター席は混み合っている。目玉は900円のベジタリアンセット。

KOTCHAN

1-11-11 Kabukicho,
Shinjuku-ku
Tel: 3200-9566
Open: 6pm-3am

Korean
¥¥
★★★
Map 22

こっちゃん

It looks awfully temporary, but they assure us they'll still be around by publication date. And these makeshift buildings are good fun: you half feel you're on a camping trip. The culinary interest here lies in seeing what a purely Korean kitchen can do working in the Japanese-Korean *motsu nabe* and *yakiniku* tradition. Their grill-it-yourself *kalbi* is just about our favorite in Tokyo. Recommended drink: a big bowl of milky white *makkoli* rice beer.

東京の仮設レストランは、まるでキャンプにでもきたような気分にさせてくれて楽しい。韓国人ばかりが働くキッチンの中で、モツ鍋や焼肉が調理され、出来上がっていく様子を見るのも面白い。自分で焼くカルビは抜群。大きなボウルに満たされた乳白色の韓国風濁り酒、マッコリがお薦め。

KRI-KRI

One of Tokyo's true mukokuseki pioneers. Owner/chef Honma-san and his wife traveled the world for years before starting this place, and it shows in the remarkable range of foods: ratatouille and mille-feuille from France, couscous and kebabs from the Middle East, Egyptian soup, gyoza-like Nepalese *momo*, etc. Typical of the place are the herbs and spices: they're grown on the roof of the building. It's also a good long walk from the nearest station, which means that it tends to select its own clientele: artistes, ex-hippies, adventurous *Hanako* readers and just neighbors.

3-38-12 Yoyogi, Shibuya-ku
Tel: 5388-9376
Open: 5pm-midnight;
closed Sun. & Tue.

Mukokuseki
¥¥
★★

CC **Map 23**

クリクリ

東京の無国籍料理のパイオニア。オーナーシェフの本間さん夫妻は長い間世界中を旅行したあとこの店をオープンした。料理の種類は豊富でフランスのラタトゥイユとミルフィーユ、中近東のクスクスとケバブ、エジプトのスープにモモと呼ばれるネパールのギョーザなどがあり、それらには彼等が旅行で得た経験が伺える。また料理に使うハーブやスパイスはビルの屋上で栽培しているものなのだ。駅からちょっと不便なここは本当に好きな人たちだけが集まる店だ。

長年に渡るニンニク好きで、世界一のニンニク都市、カリフォルニア州ギルロイ周辺に居住していた経験もある者として、80年代中頃の日本でもあったニンニクブームには感激していた。そんな中で最初に人気が出た『にんにくや』のパワーは今も衰えない。また最近では、『にんにくむら』や、『にんにく屋五右衛門』（港区六本木7-4-10 誠志堂ビル5F（┓）3475-6173）も気になる存在だ。

KUIMONOYA RAKU

A groundbreaker in the mukokuseki movement, more in terms of presentation—big platters of food out for your inspection on the counter—than cuisine, mainly Japanese with Chinese and European overtones. Mostly it's just good, cheap eating in a pleasantly rough-hewn, communal sort of atmosphere. Expect things like *daikon* or pumpkin salads, stews of pork or fish, stir fries and spicy tofu dishes.

7-14-2 Roppongi,
Minato-ku
Tel: 3403-0869
Open: 5:30-11:30pm

Mukokuseki
¥¥
★★
Map 18

The Harajuku branch (4-36-2 Jingumae, Shibuya-ku, 3423-3759) is also recommendable; the one in Shimo-Kitazawa (3795-3724) is just too cramped for comfort.

料理を見せるという意味では、ここは無国籍料理の革新派といえるだろう。カウンターに並んだ大皿に盛られた料理は、中国やヨーロッパの影響を受けた和食が中心になっている。安くて美味しい食事のひとときが楽しめる。原宿店（渋谷区神宮前4-36-2（☎）3423-3759）と下北沢店（世田谷区北沢2-20-14（☎）3795-3724）もある。

くいものや楽

LA BARACCA

Like a comet across the gastronomic heavens, **Il Boccalone** (3449-1430) enlightened Tokyoites to the pleasures of quality Italian countryside cooking and ambiance. But even its greatest fans—and there were many—admit that the spark went out of the place when ex-don Borroni Silvano called it quits.

Silvano is now to be found at the gracious Baracca out here in Toritsu Daigaku, serving up a familiar range of pasta and pizzas, grilled meats and fish and daily specials not on the menu (and if you don't ask they may not tell you). Portions remain generous, the wines overpriced and the atmosphere spirited.

Tachikawa Bldg., 2F,
2-11-4 Nakane,
Meguro-ku
Tel: 5701-4020
Open: 5:30pm-midnight;
Sun. until 11pm; closed Mon.

Italian
¥¥¥
★★★ 1/2
 **Map 25**

ラ　バラッカ

If you like the style, take note of Silvano's even newer **Il Buttero** (5-13-3 Hiroo, Shibuya-ku, 3445-9565). Similarly ebullient service, cooking and prices.

開店から数年間、良質なイタリア田舎料理と雰囲気の良さで東京人を楽しませていた『 イル・ボッカローネ 』（┐）3449-1430 の経営陣から ボローニ・シルヴァーノ氏が退いてから、ここが一時の輝きを失ってしまったことは、多くの顧客が認めるところだ。現在彼は都立大学にある、この新天地で腕を振っている。パスタ、ピッツァ、肉、魚料理や、メニューにないその日のお薦めなど、かつての彼の料理に再会できる。多めの料理の量から、高いワインの値段、店の雰囲気まで、古巣を彷彿とさせてくれる。

LA BLANCHE

2-3-1 Shibuya,
Shibuya-ku
Tel: 3499-0824
Open: 11:30am-2pm (last order) & 6-9:15pm (last order); closed Wed.

French
¥¥¥
★★★

 **Map 20**

ラ・ブランシュ

Cozy and narrow and somehow a lot like a Parisian suburb around, say, 1970. One does occasionally feel not quite up to the refined standards of one's neighboring tables—Aoyama Gakuin *o-josan* (young women of means) dress up and bring their moms here—but the feeling passes. Chef Tashiro is one of Tokyo's old pros; trust his course menu or work out something with him.

居心地が良く、こぢんまりと細長い形のこの店は、70年代のパリ郊外にあったレストランのような雰囲気。青山学院のお嬢様とその母親という、ちょっと上品な感じの人たちがお客の中心だが、落ち着ける場所である。シェフの田代氏は一級のプロで、彼が吟味した材料で作られるコースはもちろん信頼できるが、シェフと一緒にメニューを決めてオリジナルのコース料理を考えるのも楽しい。

LA BODEGUITA

1-7-3 Ebisu Minami,
Shibuya-ku
Tel: 3715-7721
Open: 6pm-midnight;
closed Sun. & hol.

Cuban
¥1/2
★ 1/2

[cc] **Map 5**

ボデギータ

Judging La Bodeguita by its food is beside the point: it's a salsa dancing scene and a good one, which is to say hot, crowded and sweaty every weekend. For our purposes it's also Tokyo's only Cuban restaurant, offering beans and rice, chorizo sausages, banana fritters, and plenty of cold beer and even colder *mojitos*.

東京で唯一のキューバンレストラン。料理よりも、サルサのダンスと店内の熱気に人々が集まって来て、週末は特に満員ですごい迫力。チョリソー、豆の煮込みがかかったライスとバナナフリッター、キリキリに冷やしたビールに大人気のモヒートス（ラムベースのカクテル）などがある。

LA BOHÈME

16-2 Daikanyamacho,
Shibuya-ku
Tel: 3476-4799
Open: 11:30am-5am

Café
¥ 1/2
★ 1/2

[cc] ◆ ✖ 🎌 **Map 4**

ラ・ボエム

Nominally Italian food so mediocre it must be willful, offset by late hours and two very pleasant places to sit: the open-air front on the main Daikanyama drag and warm winter seating by the fireplace downstairs. It's cheap, comfortable and almost always open when you want it to be.

Other atmospheric Bohèmes can be found in Ikejiri (5486-1021) and Yokohama (045-662-0901). Beware that service can be quirky, and they sometimes enforce a strange ban on shorts and "sandals without heels."

特別美味しくもまずくもない名ばかりのイタリア料理だが、朝5時まで開いていて、ゆっくりくつろげるのが良い。夏は涼しい外の大通りに面したテーブル、冬は地下にある暖炉近くの席がお薦め。気取った店ではないが、時々服装チェックがあり、短パンとサンダル履きでは入店を断られる場合もあるので注意が必要。

LA CASITA

13-4 Daikanyamacho,
Shibuya-ku
Tel: 3496-1850
Open: 11am-10pm; Wed.,
5-10pm

Mexican
¥¥
★★

◈ 🏯 **Map 4**

ラ・カシータ

Authenticity be damned—we've always had a sneaking fondness for the food here. Marvelous *chilaquiles* and good-enough tacos, enchiladas, etc., though portions could be a little less stingy. A bit of luck will get you a table on their balcony, overlooking the old Daikanyama Station area.

これぞ本場のメキシコ料理とはいわないま
でも、多くのファンを持つレストラン。極
上のチラキリスをはじめタコス、エンチラ
ダスなどは文句なく美味しい。量がもう少
し多ければ申し分ないのだが...。バルコ
ニーには2、3のテーブルが出ていて、こ
こでも食事ができる。

LA DÎNETTE

2-6-10 Takadanobaba,
Shinjuku-ku
Tel: 3200-6571
Open: 11:30am-1:30pm
& 6-9pm; closed Sun.

French
¥ 1/2
★★★

🔁 **Map 24**

The delightfully low-rent La Dînette has no illusions of grandeur. Their stock in trade is hefty portions, full flavors and no silliness. Entrées ("appetizers" in American) include niçoise and seafood salads, *terrine*, *rillettes* and hot or cold soups depending on season. Main dishes ("entrees" in American) feature lamb, chicken, duck and fish, all with better than average vegetable garnishes. At ¥1000 for lunch and ¥2500 for dinner it's superb value. Alas, one pays in other ways: reservations are a must, and they like to make you promise that you'll leave within 90 minutes. The wines are unreliable (except the house wine: reliably bad) and even the cheapest costs practically as much as two dinners. For fast-eating non-drinkers, it's paradise. For the rest of us, still worth an occasional trip.

フランス人が本当にいつも食べているフラ
ンス料理を出しているレストラン。ボ
リューム、香りたっぷりのランチ1000円
とディナー2500円は上等。ワインは料理
の値段に比べて高く質もあまり良くないの
でお酒を飲まない軽食派にとっては最適の
店といえるだろう。しかし、それ以外の人
にも一度は足を運ぶ価値が充分にある。予
約は必要。混雑するので1時間半以上の長
居はダメ。

ディネット

LA ESCONDIDA

Okabe Bldg., B1,
2-24-12 Nishi Azabu,
Minato-ku
Tel: 3486-0330
Open: 6-11:30pm

Mexican
¥¥¥
★★★

 **Map 17**

エスコンディーダ

Rustic stone interior (which can feel a little cavernous), strolling mariachi musicians (who can be a little loud) and regional Mexican cooking so authentic that burrito and taco lovers may feel lost. La Escondida tries a bit too hard—and the prices reflect it—but it's still a strong contender for the best of the Mex. Recommended: any of the Yucatan specialties.

近くにある『エル・モカンボ』の姉妹店。洞窟を思わせる石を使ったインテリア、各テーブルを回って演奏してくれるメキシコ版“流し”マリアッチ、そしていろいろな地方の特色を生かしたメキシコ料理の数々は一流で、ブリトーとタコスしか知らない人達は当惑してしまうかも。値段も一流並でちょっと高めだが、東京のメキシコ料理レストランの中で上位にランクされることは間違いない。ユカタンの地方料理がお薦め。

L'AFFRESCO

Hibiya Chanter, B2,
1-2-2 Yurakucho,
Chiyoda-ku
Tel: 3581-7421
Open: 11am-5pm
& 5:30-10pm

Italian
¥¥¥
★★★

Map 7

リストランテ・アフレスコ

Superior Venetian-style cooking, strong on the seafood, polenta and risotto. Best values are the ¥3000 lunches and the seasonal dinner courses for about ¥4800 (¥1500 more for all the wine you can drink). What really brings in the punters, though, is the over-the-top decor, a riot of chandeliers, statues, *faux*-marble pillars, dried flowers, and frescos on every wall. It looks like a Toontown version of a Lido palazzo, but it works: you almost forget that you're in what, after all, is the sub-basement of a Hibiya department store.

ベニス風料理のこの店は魚介類、とうもろこしの粉で作ったポレンタ、リゾットが特に美味しい。店内はシャンデリアやブロンズ像、人造大理石の柱にドライフラワー、そしてフレスコ画などでいっぱい。しかし、この少しこり過ぎのインテリアも日比谷の地下街にいることを一瞬忘れさせてくれるのだから、一役買っているといえるだろう。

LA GOLA

7-4-5 Roppongi,
Minato-ku
Tel: 5410-5550
Open: 6pm-midnight;
closed Sun.

Italian
¥¥¥
★★★

 Map 18

Started by a group of food-loving friends, La
Gola feels older, more comfortable and
more assured than its couple of years.
Good regional Italian food, lovely wines by
the glass and a friendly adult atmosphere.
We'd say more except that it's hard enough
to get in as it is.

グルメの仲間同士が集まって始めたこの店
は、開店して2、3年だがもっと古くから
あるような感じがし居心地が良く、味にも
磨きがかかったようだ。上等なイタリア料
理で、ワインもこの上なく美味しい。ボト
ルだけでなくグラスでも注文できるので、
料理を食べながらいろいろなワインを味
わってみるのもいいだろう。冷たい雨の降
る日に暖かく元気づけてくれるような、そ
んな親しみやすい落ち着いた雰囲気が何よ
りの魅力だ。地下は姉妹店の『五穀』。

ラ・ゴラ

LA GRANATA

5-3-3 Akasaka,
Minato-ku
Tel: 3582-3241
Open: 11am-10:30pm

Italian
¥¥¥
★★★

 Map 1

No longer the bargain it once was, nor does
the food seem quite as enticing as it used
to, now that Tokyo is bursting at the seams
with new-wave Italiania. But La Granata
remains what it has been for decades:
utterly reliable and unfailingly pleasant. By
Akasaka standards, that still sets it apart.
And they still do a mean swordfish.
Granata Moderna (3582-5891) next door
is more of the same, and there's a branch
in Ginza (3535-6334).

かつては本格的なイタリア料理が食べられ
る数少ない店のひとつだったが、今ではそ
うしたレストランも増え、ここの値段も随
分上がってしまった。しかし、これまで信
頼できて楽しめるという店の姿勢はずっと
くずしていない。いまだにこれといったイ
タリア料理店のない赤坂で、これは価値あ
ることだ。隣の『グラナータモデルナ』(☎)
3582-5891 も同様の店。銀座にも支店 (☎)
3535-6334 がある。

グラナータ

LA JOLLA

Koyasu Bldg., 2F,
5-16-3 Hiroo,
Shibuya-ku
Tel: 3442-1865
Open: 11am-3pm &
5-10:30pm; Sat., Sun. & hol.,
11am-10:30pm

Mexican
¥
★ 1/2

CC ✕ **Map 8**

ラ　ホイヤ

More highly North Americanized Mexican food: dripping tacos, enchiladas gooey with cheese, fishbowl-size margarita glasses, the works. It's enormously—some would say inexplicably—popular with the Hiroo gaijin community. Smokers have to seek refuge on the staircase outside, and bridge-and-tunnel people from Saitama may feel they've entered another world altogether. There's another La Jolla in Jiyugaoka (5701-1737).

水っぽいタコス、チーズでべとべとになったエンチラーダス、金魚鉢ほど大きいマルガリータのグラスなど、ここはすっかりアメリカナイズされたメキシコ料理店だ。なぜだと理解出来ない人もいるだろうが、広尾のインターナショナル・コミュニティでは絶大な人気がある。ちょっと一服という喫煙者は外の階段に出なくてはならない。自由が丘に支店（☎）5701-1737 がある。

LA MARÉE DE CHAYA

24-2 Horiuchi, Hayamacho,
Miura-gun, Kanagawa-ken
Tel: 0468-75-6683
Open: Noon-2:30pm &
5:30-11pm; closed Mon.

French
¥¥
★★

CC ✕ **Map 56**

ラ・マレー・
ド・チャヤ

A perennial must for fans of the Shonan Beach scene, and even better (i.e. less frantic) just before or after our official six-week summer. Located by Hayama Marina a few minutes' drive from Zushi Station, Marée de Chaya comprises a first-rate ****/¥¥¥¥ French restaurant upstairs and this delightful seaside café terrace below. Ideal for a bottle of chilled white as the sun goes down behind Mt. Fuji across the bay.

湘南海岸のファンであれば、是非知っておくべき店のひとつで、混雑していない夏の前後に行くのが狙い目。逗子駅から車で数分の葉山マリーナのそばにあり、1階がこのシーサイドカフェテラス、2階に一流のフランス料理店がある。相模湾をはさんだ対岸にある富士山に沈む夕日を眺めながら、よく冷えた白ワインのグラスを傾けるには理想的な場所だ。

L'AMPHORE

3-5-4 Jingu-mae,
Shibuya-ku
Tel: 3402-6486
Open: Noon-2pm (last order)
& 6-9:30pm (last order);
closed Wed.

French
¥¥¥¥
★★★★

[cc] **Map 2**

アンフォーレ

For no particular reason—or was it creeping costs?—we've drifted away from Roppongi's still excellent little **Aux Six Arbres** (3479-2888). As it turns out, so has Chef Igarashi, in his case to open the cool, clean L'Amphore here behind Aoyama-dori. It's a place that strikes a fine balance between tolerable cost (count on ¥15,000 for two for lunch, ¥25,000 for dinner, including a good wine) and innovative, meticulously prepared food of the highest quality. It's also just about right in terms of atmosphere: elegant enough for any conceivable occasion but not so intimidating that first-timers or solo diners need shy away.

六本木で人気のレストラン『オーシザーブル』(☎) 3479-2888 の元シェフ五十嵐氏が独立して青山通り裏に出した店。このクールで清潔なレストランでは、カップルで15000円のランチと25000円のディナーは納得のいく美味しさだ。丁寧な調理法と芳醇なワインは十分満足できる。フランス料理にウニやゴボウなどの日本の食材を使ったものもあり、その味は他に類を見ない。エレガントだが気取り過ぎないこの店は、初めてでもひとりでも気軽に入れる雰囲気がある。

90円切手3枚を"分煙社会を目指す会"（〒115 北区神谷3-28-12-2Ｂ）に送ると、東京の禁煙席のあるレストランを600軒も載せた日本語のガイドブック「空気の美味しいレストラン」の最新版が手に入る。これにはパチンコ屋、美容院、ペンションから、驚いたことにバー（『バービカン』(☎) 3565-4111／リッチモンドホテル内）まで掲載されている。

LA PATATA

2-9-11 Jingu-mae,
Shibuya-ku
Tel: 3403-9664
Open: Noon-2pm &
6-11:30pm; Wed.-Sun.,
6-11:30pm

Italian
¥¥¥¥
★★★

 **Map 11**

ラ　パタータ

A sentimental favorite. Dinner prices have crept past ¥10,000/person—too much, given the times and the competition—but La Patata remains as cozy and cordial a little Italian restaurant as any in the city. Credit goes to Chef Tsuchiya, multi-talented cook, host and man of the soil (he grows many of the herbs used here, and a lot else besides). He also puts together a terrific, if not particularly bargain-oriented, wine list. Recommendation: the ¥2500 lunch.

昔と違ってイタリアンレストランがしのぎを削っている中、ディナーがひとり10000円とは高い気もするが、街のまん中にあっても、ゆったりとして気楽な雰囲気で食事ができるのは魅力だ。シェフ土屋氏の、調理人、ホスト、趣味の園芸家（店で使われるハーブの多くは彼が育てたもの）というマルチタレントぶりも賞賛に値する。特に安いというわけではないが、なかなかのワインリストも揃っている。2500円のランチは得だ。

Among the dozens of *Japanese-language* restaurant guides to this city, we can provisionally recommend three:

• *Pia Map Gurume* (Pia): Invaluable maps showing some 10,000 restaurants throughout metro Kanto, but most of the blurbs are pure burble.

• *Tokyo Ii Mise Umai Mise* (Bungei Shunju): A "discriminating" guide, written mostly by and for gentlemen of means and a certain age. Strong on upmarket Japanese and French, highly uneven on others.

• *Tokyo Taberu Chizu* (Shobunsha): Falls between the above two, with maps to about 1,700 places and generally helpful descriptions. Probably the most useful of the lot.

LA PINETA

As insatiable as our city's appetite for Italian food is, in these lean times it takes a certain amount of chutzpah to build a smallish, no-compromise—and not especially cheap—trattoria way out here on Jiyu-dori. It's confidence that finds expression in the kitchen, too: La Pineta isn't content to cook standard dishes in standard ways. They add a skilled little signature to almost everything, from the aniseed in the *grissini* bread sticks before the meal to the hard buttery Castilean flan at its end. Fans of the lusher, more garlicky sort of Italian food may find it all a little austere. Lovers of Tuscany and points north will be in their element.

The wine list aims to please beginners and experts alike, with an especially wide selection of reds (about eight Barolos alone) and a full range of prices (about ¥3500 to ¥15,000). Nothing desultory about the cheaper choices, nothing pointlessly showy about the pricier ones—it's a list built for performance.

3-4-2 Yagumo,
Meguro-ku
Tel: 3723-7098
Open: Noon-2pm & 6-10pm;
closed Sun.

Italian
¥¥¥
★★★ 1/2

 **Map 25**

東京では依然としてイタリア料理の人気が衰えない。とはいえ、こんな都心から外れ人通りも少ない自由通りで、味にも値段にも妥協しないでトラットリアを経営していくには、それ相応に自信があるのだろう。その自信は当然キッチンから伝わってくる。ここでは、当たり前のものを当たり前に調理するのでは満足しないようだ。例えば、ブレッドスティックに入れたアニスの実から作ったカスティリアニ風フランスのデザートのように、熟練の技が隠れたところに使われている。量が多かったり、ガーリックがきいたイタリア料理が好きな人には物足りないかも知れないが、タスカーニ地方より北の料理が好みなら、十分納得できるだろう。バローロだけでも8種類ある赤中心のワインリストも3500～15000円が中心で、安くても厳選されているし、高いものでもその価値は十分にあるから、多くの人に喜ばれるだろう。

ラ・ピネータ

LA RANARITA

Pleasant as its greenhouse-like back room may be, the La Ranarita in the Quest Building in Harajuku (3478-3310) somehow hasn't drawn us away from the many other fine Italian eateries in the area. Here in Asakusa it's different: there's a lot less local competition and prices feel a notch lower. Also, a breathtakingly spacious interior with a high-rise view out over the Sumida River and the endless urban sprawl. For sheer visual impact, the **New York Grill** is the only match we've found in Tokyo.

The food tends toward the lighter side of the northern Italian spectrum, and is frankly more professional than passionate. Lunches start at ¥1500; dinners from ¥6000.

They have an adequate wine list but the real opportunity is to drink the world's freshest Asahi draft. Alas, there are other hints of Asahi corporate culture too, from the anonymous service to the tacky plastic check holder firmly placed on your table at the end of the meal.

Asahi Beer Tower, 22F,
1-23-1 Azumabashi,
Sumida-ku
Tel: 5608-5277
Open: 11:30am-2pm &
5-9pm

Italian
¥¥¥
★★★

 **Map 57**

この店の原宿店（☎）3478-3310には温室風の快適なバックルームがあるにも関わらず、近辺にイタリア料理店が多いのであまり足を運ぶ機会はないのだが、ここ浅草店は事情が違うようだ。地域的に競合する相手は少なく、多少値段も安く、何よりも隅田川や下町を見下ろす、とてつもなく広いスペースは、視覚的なインパクトでいえばこの本に登場するレストランの中で『ニューヨークグリル』に次いでベストだろう。軽めの北イタリア料理にはあまりシェフの情熱は感じられないが、ランチは1500円から、ディナーは6000円から。ワインリストもまあまあだが、ここの目玉は世界で最も新鮮なアサヒのドラフトビールだろう。
ところが残念なことに、サービスはぱっとしないし、請求書を持ってくるのに

ラ・ラナリータ

安っぽいプラスティックのクリップボードに挟んでくる。アサヒビールの文化に対する認識はこの程度かと疑われる。せめて革製のホルダーで持ってくる位の配慮がほしい。

言いにくいことだけど、西洋人の目から見ると、日本には本当のサラダを出す店は少ない。刻んだキャベツ、缶詰のアスパラガス、チューブや瓶入りのマヨネーズというのが三大汚点で、これに味気ないトマト、くどい味のドレッシング、サウザンアイランドが続く。これに加えて、健康的には良い考えなのかも知れないが、朝食にサラダを食べるという習慣も理解に苦しむ。そんな中でも美味しいサラダを出す店として、『ビストロ・ド・ラ・シテ』、『ブラッスリー・ルコント』、『ル・スフレ』、『ソリーソ』、『タブローズ』、『ヴィクトリア・ステーション』を薦めたい。

LAS CHICAS

5-47-6 Jingu-mae,
Shibuya-ku
Tel: 3407-6865
Open: 11:30am-11pm

Café
¥¥
★★

🆑 ◈ 🎌 **Map 2**

A third renovation in as many years has moved Las Chicas slightly upmarket. It also seems to have given some of the staff an attitude, but we're hoping that will pass. Although they've got a real dining room now, there's still plenty of outdoor seating and good '90s café food at only slightly inflated prices. At dinner they move into the ***/¥¥¥ range. Note that the wine list, featuring two of our favorite Antipodean labels (Cape Mentelle and Cloudy Bay), is available all day, inside or out. Now if they'd only stop this creation/destruction cycle for a bit and let us enjoy them as they are.

大通りからちょっとはずれた所にあるフレンドリーなカフェ。今回3度目の改装で、本格的に食事もできるダイニングスペースを設けてグレードアップしたようだ。しかし、店の表には以前と変わらずテーブルが出してあり、気軽に立ち寄れる雰囲気を残している。値段はやや高めだが、現代風にアレンジされた料理の味は逸品。ダイニングでのディナーは￥￥￥から。オーストラリア、ニュージーランドでそれぞれ人気の高いワイン、Cape MentelleとCloudy Bayがこの店のお薦め。

ラス・チカス

LA TERAZZA

The new La Terazza already has too much going for it to ignore: the sidewalk terrace of its name; a choice setting along the road to Azabu Juban; super desserts and real espresso. With luck, by the time you read this, they'll have worked out the kinks: '90s cooking-academy food that careens from pretty good to plain incompetent, grotesque loud music (would you believe Disney cartoon soundtracks?) and a general lack of focus.

5-11-27 Roppongi,
Minato-ku
Tel: 5411-0130
Open: 5:30-11:30pm; Sat.,
noon-2:30pm & 6-11:30pm;
Sun. & hol., noon-2:30pm &
6-10:30pm; closed Mon.

Italian
¥¥
★★

Map 3

麻布十番の一等地にある新装のこの店には、サイドウォークテラスや抜群のデザート、本物のエスプレッソなど、既にいくつもの売り物がある。そこで是非、この本が出るまでに次のことは改善しておいてほしい。ひとつは、メニューによっても、また日によっても味にばらつきがあることだ。もうひとつは、店内の音楽がとても騒々しくグロテスクで、時としてディズニーのアニメのテーマ曲が流れていることまである。経営方針がはっきり定まればかなり期待できる店ではあるのだが。

ラ テラザ

LA TERRASSE

This prime piece of restaurant real estate has been through more recent changes than the LDP. First it was good stylish French (**A Tantot**), then poor stylish Chinese, then, briefly, a branch of **Chez Prisi**. They're independent now, but the Swiss identity seems to have stuck, with fondue, raclette, rosti and even some crisp Swiss wines on offer. Reasonably good salads, pasta, meat dishes (especially veal) and desserts, too. The namesake terrace remains Roppongi's most congenial outdoor eating spot.

Axis Bldg., 3F,
5-17-1 Roppongi,
Minato-ku
Tel: 5570-1991
Open: 11:30am-9:30pm
(last order); closed Mon.

Continental
¥¥
★★

 Map 18

六本木アクシスビルの３階はレストランが入れ替わり立ち代わり変わっている。最初はおしゃれなフレンチレストラン『ア・タント』、次は美味しくない中華料理店、そして短期間ではあったがスイス料理の赤坂『シェ・プリシィ』支店。現在のこの店はコンチネンタル料理のはずだが、フォンデュやスイスワインなどがあり前の店の香りを残している。そして美味しいサラダとパスタ、肉料理（特に子牛）がウケている。デザートもなかなか贅沢な風味だ。店の名の通り、屋外のテーブルで気持ち良く食事ができるスポットだ。

ラ・テラス

LA TERRE

Exactly the same vintage (1981) as *Tokyo Journal*, and just around the corner from our first office. Lunch on the little terrace here has been a rite of spring every year since. We suspect that they keep the portions smallish and the menu unchanging to lure us back for dinner, and we keep meaning to go, if only noontimes weren't so pleasant. Even from inside there's a leafy green view, and the cherry blossom season is sheer beauty (and booked accordingly).

1-19-20 Azabu-dai,
Minato-ku
Tel: 3583-9682
Open: 11:30am-2pm &
6-10pm; closed Sun. & hol.

French
¥¥
★★ 1/2

Map 18

『トーキョージャーナル』創刊と同じ1981年に、かつて編集部のあった場所のすぐそばにオープンした店で、小さなテラスでのスタッフとのランチは毎春恒例の行事になっていた。料理は量が少なく、メニューの中身が変わらないのは、ディナーに来てもらうための作戦なのだろうか。ともかく、味はしっかりしており、決して裏切られることはなく、ここの支配人もまた最高だ。また、テラスからも店内からも見える木々の緑、特に桜の咲く季節の美しさは絶景だ。

ラ・テール

LA VERDE

1-7-2 Jingu-mae,
Shibuya-ku
Tel: 3470-6498
Open:11:30am-11pm

Italian
¥
★★

CC Map 6

ラ・ベルデ

People said La Verde's spaghetti would lose its tang after they moved out of their old grease-encrusted quarters on the other side of Meiji-dori. If so, it has been worth it in saved laundry bills. For about ¥1000 you get a throwaway salad, a gargantuan bowl of excellent spaghetti (recommended: *vongole rosso*) and a cup of standard *kissaten* coffee. Unrivaled bulk/¥ ratio.

安くてボリュームたっぷりの若者に人気のスパゲッティ屋。数年前、明治通りの向かいにあった古くて脂ぎったこの店が、現在の竹下通りに移ってから味が落ちたというウワサもあるが、決してそうは思わない。以前よりも店は広く、きれいで気持ちが良い。およそ1000円でジャイアントサイズのスパゲティにスモールサラダとコーヒーが付いてくる。スパゲッティ・ボンゴレロッソは特にお薦めだが、サラダとコーヒーはイマひとつだ。

LE MANGE-TOUT

22 Nandomachi,
Shinjuku-ku
Tel: 3268-5911
Open: 11:30am-2pm &
6-9:30pm; closed Sun.
& 3rd Mon.

French
¥¥
★★★

✖ Map 9

Think of Mange-Tout as an upmarket **Pas à Pas**: less hectic, noisy and cramped, a bit more polished with its food. They give you even less choice here: you pick one main course of three. Everything else is up to them. And frankly, they know best. One does wish the wine list tried a bit harder, though all of the half-dozen or so bottles on it are textbook examples of their types, and not at all expensive. Mostly they've somehow captured something ineffably French here: not just the minimalist decor and the gauzy curtains in the windows, the Latin-tinged '60s jazz on the stereo, the weird find-us-if-you-can location, not even just the food. It's the total package, and it's obviously from the heart.

『パザパ』の高級版といった感じのこの店は、ゆったりとしたスペースの中を時が静かに流れ、洗練された料理がサービスされる。実際はメニューからの選択肢は少なく、3種類のメインコースから1品

を選んでしまえば、あとはお任せというこ
とになる。それにしても、タイミング良く
料理を出していくこの店の技は卓越してい
る。かなりのうるさがたでも、2番目のデ
ザートが出てくる頃には十分満足するだろ
う。ワインリストがもう少し充実すればと
思わなくもないが、それでもここの6種類
は基本を押さえているし、値段も高くな
い。何となくここにいると本物のフランス
の空気を感じるのは、インテリアや60年
代のラテンジャズ、店が裏通りにあるとい
うだけでなく、これらのこと全てが渾然一
体となっているからだろう。

ル・マンジュトゥ

LE RÉCAMIER

3-2-3 Moto-Azabu,
Minato-ku
Tel: 3408-5044
Open: 11:30-2pm &
5:30-10pm; Closed Mon.

French
¥¥¥
★★★

Map 18

Finding good little cheap French places in
Tokyo these days is no challenge. Finding
expensive lavish ones never has been.
What's hard is what's in between: restaurants that use real linen and silver but
draw the line at crystal chandeliers; where
the service is smooth and professional
without being stiff or pretentious; where
they're not nearly so interested in im-
pressing you as pleasing you. Le Récamier
qualifies on all counts. Occupying a whole
house down a little lane off TV Asahi-dori,
it's a perfect minor splurge. Better than
average, highly seasonal cooking too.

最近の東京では、安くて美味しくてこぢ
んまりしたフランス料理店を見つけ出す
ことはそれほど大変なことではない。ま
た反対に、高くて大げさな店を見つける
ことも容易だ。この両方の良いところだ
けを折衷したのがこの店だ。例えばリネ
ンや本物の銀製品を使っているが、大仰
なガラスのシャンデリアは下げていない
し、サービスは滑らかで手慣れている
が、堅苦しくはなく、丁寧過ぎることも
ない。ここは何よりも、客を驚かすこと
よりは喜ばすことに力を注いでいる店
だ。テレビ朝日通りから少し入った路地
にある一軒家で、一度行けば友達に自慢
したくなる店だ。

ル・レカミエ

L'ESCARGOT

5-63-10 Yoyogi,
Shibuya-ku
Tel: 3460-5770
Open: 11am-2pm & 6-11pm;
closed Mon.

French
¥¥
★★★

CC 🏮 **Map 58**

A neighborhood bistro with a split personality: cozy, triangular-shaped room downstairs below the skylight, open-air stone terrace above. The former tries hard to be Parisian with its red plush and mirrors, while the latter achieves its charm the natural way—it looks out onto a leafy corner of Yoyogi Park. Small lunches of very high quality for ¥1700. Dinner recommendation: the ¥3900 course, with a selection of seven starters and eight main dishes.

代々木公園の緑が見える一角にある気軽なビストロ。空が仰げる三角形の地下の部屋はとてもフランス風で、解放された石造りのテラスがあるが、インテリアは中途半端で感心しない。1700円のランチは量は少ないが質は高い。ディナーのお薦めは3900円のコースで、前菜は7種類、メインディッシュは8種類から選べる。

エスカルゴ

LES DEUX MAGOTS

Bunkamura,
2-24-1 Dogenzaka,
Shibuya-ku
Tel: 3477-9124
Open: 11am-10:30pm

Café
¥¥
★★

🏮 **Map 19**

Yes, it actually is run in cooperation with Café Deux Magots in Paris, though it's hard to see any resemblance beyond the usurious price they both charge for a cup of coffee (¥650 at this one). If anything the food is probably better here—the bread certainly is—and there's a bigger variety of it: salads (including a good *salade niçoise*), soups, sandwiches, cakes (excellent *tarte tatin*) and sorbet *coupes*.

ご存じの通り、ここのパリ店は最も有名なカフェのひとつで、値段も高く、すっかり観光地になっている。2、3日もパリに滞在したら、ここと同じくらい素敵で親切な店は簡単に見つけられるだろう。いずれにしても、東急文化村は自分のところのカフェに一流の名前が欲しかった

カフェ・ドゥ・マゴ

だけなのだろう。結果として、値段以外に両者の共通点はあまりないようだが、料理、特にパンに関してはここ、東京店の方が勝っている。サラダ・ニソワーズなどのサラダ類、スープ、サンドイッチ、ケーキ（リンゴのタルトタタンがお薦め）、シャーベットは結構いける。

LE SOUFFLÉ

To call this genteel—okay, slightly stiff—café Tokyo's only soufflé specialist considerably understates the case. It's one of the few places in any city where you can have a world-class soufflé without first having to order and eat a whole French meal. The dozen or more varieties run from vanilla to coffee to Calvados and apples, but the crowd-pleaser is the framboise.

Should you need the meal, they have that too: small, superb salads (the scallops in the *salade St.-Jacques* are a marvel), and a few main dishes along the lines of *canard rôti à l'orange* and *blanquette de veau*. Prices on these will add up quickly, but the quality is astonishing. Their dry French cider makes a fine drink, and there's good strong coffee afterwards.

Custom Park Side Bldg., 2F,
3-13-10 Nishi Azabu,
Minato-ku
Tel: 5474-0909
Open: Noon-10pm;
closed Mon.

French
¥¥
★★★ 1/2

Map 17

上品で、多少堅苦しい雰囲気のするここは、東京で唯一のスフレ専門店である。世界中探しても気軽にスフレだけを楽しめるところは珍しく、ここはフランス料理も出している。スフレは、バニラ、コーヒー、カルヴァドス、リンゴなど10数種類あり、中でもフランボワーズ（ストロベリー）はお薦め。料理ではサラダ（帆立貝のサラダに入っている帆立は、柔らかく、甘く、風味があって素晴らしい）や、メインディッシュの鴨のロースト・オレンジソース、子牛のブランケットがある。全般に量は少ない割に値段は高いが、質は申し分ない。ドライで爽やかな口当たりのフランスのサイダー（アルコール度5％）や、食事の後に出される強めのコーヒーは美味しい。

ル・スフレ

LILLA DALAARNA

If **Stockholm** feels like too much of a production for a casual Scandinavian meal, drop by here, right up the hill. Petite and unassuming, Lilla Dalarna lets you take an à la carte approach to a similar range of food: Swedish bread and biscuits and pickles and cheese, herring and smoked salmon, sausages and meatballs and steaks. First-timers and budgeteers can enjoy a good sampling via the lunch (¥2800) and dinner (¥4000) courses.

5-9-19 Roppongi,
Minato-ku
Tel: 3478-4690
Open: Noon-3pm & 6-9:30pm

Swedish
¥¥
★★ 1/2

🎴 **Map 18**

もし時間がなく、お腹も『ストックホルム』で食べるほどは空いていない、でも美味しいスカンジナビア料理が食べたい時は、ちょっと丘を上がったところにあるこの店を、試してみてはどうだろうか。店は小さく、控え目だが、栄養満点のスウェーデン料理が何でも揃っている。自家製パン、ビスケットから、漬け物、チーズ、塩漬けのニシン、スモークサーモン、ソーセージ、肉団子、ステーキまで、コースでもアラカルトでも注文できる。初心者や財布の中身が心配な人は2800円のランチコースか、4000円のディナーコースを試してみると良い。

リラ・ダラルナ

L'ORANGERIE DE PARIS

Hanae Mori Bldg., 5F,
3-6-11 Kita Aoyama,
Minato-ku
Tel: 3407-7461
Open: 11:30am-3pm & 5:30-
10:30pm; Sunday brunch:
11am-2:30pm

We don't quite understand the name—surely this is L'Orangerie de Tokyo?—but there's no doubting that it's still the reigning brunch champion. Well, okay: the **New York Grill** now does a great one too, and **Trader Vic's** includes champagne. But from 11am to 2:30pm each Sunday, L'Orangerie lays out what surely has to be one of the most luxurious buffets in town, priced at a very fair ¥3500 per head (plus drinks, service and tax). The rest of the time it reverts to an upscale ***1/2 ¥¥¥¥ French restaurant of the old school.

French
¥¥¥
★★★

🎬 ✈ **Map 2**

オランジェリ・ド・パリス

日本のレストランはどうして外国の都市の名前を付けるのが好きなのだろう。本来なら東京にあるのだから『オランジェリ・ド・トキオ』にすべきでは...？しかし、ここのサンデーブランチの美味しさはさすがだ。毎日曜日の11時から2時30分まで、豪華なビュッフェスタイルのブランチが3500円で楽しめる。それ以外の時間帯はレベルの高い古典的なフランス料理を出している。

LOS REYES MAGOS

After almost ten years in Spain and another ten helming the miniature Los Reyes Magos, owner/chef Mitsuaki Watanabe has the sunny disposition of a man who knows what he loves and finds himself able to make a living doing it. Sit at one of the five tiny tables if you like, but the more sociable scene is at the counter facing his open kitchen.

Recommended: *caracoles* (snails) with hazelnuts, *paella marinera*, swordfish grilled with garlic and any of the nightly specials.

5-55-7 Yoyogi,
Shibuya-ku
Tel: 3469-8231
Open: 5:30-10:30pm (last order); closed Sun. & hol.

Spanish
¥¥
★★ 1/2

🎬 ◈ ✈ **Map 59**

ロス・レイエス・マーゴス

スペインに暮らして10年、この小さなお店を経営し始めて10年というオーナー兼シェフの渡辺光昭氏は、自分の好きなことをして暮らしを立てる達人。陽気な人柄がお客を引き付けているようだ。店内に5つある小さなテーブルに座ってくつろぐのもいいし、キッチンに面しているカウンター席で隣合わせた気の合う仲間と会話を楽しむのもいい。お薦め料理はカラコレス（かたつむり）のヘイゼルナッツ添え、パエリア・マリネーラ、ガーリックを効かせためかじきのグリル、そしてその日のディナー・スペシャルはどれを取っても美味しい。

LUNCHAN AOYAMA

The name confuses everybody ("Is that Chinese for 'luncheon?'"), but there's no mistaking Lunchan's cooking. It's the cutting-edge, all-American item, a free-for-all of Mom food, Wolfgang Puck-ishness, pizzas, pasta and Asian imports. Decent value too, considering the size of the portions. We're still coming to terms with the Denny's-on-steroids decor, and there have been recent reports of declining service and wine selection, but Lunchan remains a major Tokyo resource. Note the fine Sunday brunch.

1-2-5 Shibuya,
Shibuya-ku
Tel: 5466-1398
Open: 11:30am-11pm;
Sun. & hol., 11am-10pm

American
¥¥ 1/2
★★★

🆑 🔲 🔳 **Map 20**

最もポピュラーないまのアメリカ料理が食べたければこの店。一見、ファミリーレストランをちょっとグレードアップさせただけのように見えるけれど、実は食材も調理法もロサンジェルスやニューヨークにあるおしゃれなレストランとほとんど変わらない。ミートローフやコーンビーフとキャベツの"おふくろ"料理、クラムチャウダーやターキーチリなどの地方料理、シーザーサラダなどの古典的なアメリカンサラダ、BLT にクラブサンドイッチ、ハンバーガー、パスタ、ピッツァ、そしてタイ風グリルチキンや韓国風バーベキューなど、アメリカ風にアレンジしたエスニック料理はどれもボリュームがあって値段も手頃。また、デザートもなかなかで、特にこれぞ本物といえるニューヨークスタイルのチーズケーキがお薦め。

ランチャン
バー＆グリル

LYON

One of the city's best values in medium-upscale, medium-classical French food. The only downside is erratic if well-intentioned service by the not-quite-ready-for-prime-time staff. They're allegedly in training to go to Lyon's sister establishment, the legend-in-its-own-dinnertime **Hôtel de Mikuni** (3351-3810)—and better

4-3-27 Kudanshita Kita,
Chiyoda-ku
Tel: 3263-3773
Open: 11:30am-2pm, 5:30-
9pm (last order); closed hol.
lunch & Sun.

French
¥¥¥
★★★
CC 〒 **Map 10**

リヨン

them than us—but some of them have
been here for years.

Recommended: the ¥3900 dinner
menu or the extraordinarily price-effective
¥1200 lunch, accompanied by a bottle of
the ¥3000 house red or white.

サービスも低下し、それほど落ち着ける場
所でもないが、古典的なフランス料理が
リーズナブルな料金で楽しめる店としては
ずせないのがここ。1200円のランチと
3900円のディナーメニューがお薦め。

MADAME
CHANG'S
HOME
KITCHEN

2-26-15 Seijo,
Setagaya-ku
Tel: 3416-7170
Open: 11am-9:30pm;
closed Tue.

Chinese
¥¥
★★
CC ◈ **Map 60**

マダムチャン
ホームキッチン

"You could be in Helsinki," was how one of
our respondents described Madame
Chang's. Or Capetown, or Honolulu, or
most anywhere else. Timeless, generic
"international" Chinese in a perfect setting:
the curiously Westernized old money/
nouveau riche suburb of Seijo Gakuen.
Creative ordering pays: their standards are
pretty standard.

世界のどこの街に行っても、たいていこ
このような中華料理屋が一軒はあるもの
だ。いかにもの内装や丸テーブル、メ
ニュー内容で、一旦店内に足を踏み入れ
ると、自分が一体どこの街にいるのか分
からなくなる。海老のチリソース和え、
野菜のクリーム煮といった基本的な料理
の味はごく平凡だが、シェフの腕に挑戦
するつもりになって、注文に工夫を凝ら
せば、驚かせてくれるかも知れない。ラ
ンチは安くてお薦め。

MAENAM

3-1-20 Nishi Azabu,
Minato-ku
Tel: 3404-4745
Open: 5pm-4am

Thai
¥¥
★★ 1/2
 Map 18

To be honest, we didn't expect much of a flashy, ex-disco Charleston-run Thai restaurant. We were wrong: Maenam has always satisfied, and the prices invariably seem to work out to about a third less than at any comparable place. While *yakiniku* or ramen have long been Roppongi's late-night snack of choice, a *phat thai* or a good spicy Thai soup does the job just as well.

かつてディスコがあった場所で、『チャールストンクラブ』の人が経営しているというので全く期待していなかったというのが本音だろう。ところがこれが大間違いで、料理にはいつも満足するし、値段も他店に比べたらかなり安い気がする。六本木で深夜の腹ごしらえといえば、焼き肉かラーメンが定番だが、これからはパット・タイ（ヌードル）かタイ風ぴり辛スープというのも良いのでは。

メナム

MAENAM NO HOTORI

2-1 Kanda Jinbocho,
Chiyoda-ku
Tel: 3238-9597
Open: 11:30am-2:30pm
& 5:30-11pm;
closed Sun. & hol.

Thai
¥¥
★★★
Map 13

Traditionally one went to Jinbocho to buy books, not to eat well, or even to eat at all. That was until this notably serious Thai restaurant began to draw gourmet trade from all over the city. The interior remains somewhat ascetic and the staff hasn't quite mastered the *mai pen rai* ("No problem!") philosophy, but there are certainly no flies (in any sense) on this food. *Yam* salads, soups or curries, it's pitch perfect.

食事をするというよりは、本を買いに行く場所というイメージが強い神保町で、本格的なタイ料理を出すこの店が都内のグルメたちを集めている。インテリアは多少冷たい感じがし、従業員ももっとリラックスしてほしいが、料理については本物のタイ料理の味で、申し分ない。

メナムのほとり

MAE YAO

21 Shinanomachi,
Shinjuku-ku
Tel: 3355-0280
Open: 11:30am-8pm; Sat.,
11:30am-7pm; closed Sun.,
hol. & 3rd Sat.

Thai curry
¥
★★
Map 61

メー　ヤウ

Miraculously it's still here: just a shack, really, and just meters from the sleek new Shinanomachi Station. Three varieties of rich Thai/Malaysian curry on rice (¥600 each), cheap Singha, and coconut jelly for dessert. Branch in Waseda (5273-3770).

まるで掘っ建て小屋のようなこの店が、タイカレーを始めてすでに10年以上になるが、この場所でよく続いているといつも驚かされる。コクのある3種類のタイ／マレーシアカレーは各600円。安くて美味しいシンハビール、そしてココナッツゼリーはデザートに。早稲田に支店（☎）5273-3770 がある。

MAHARAO

Mitsui Bldg., B1,
1-1-2 Yurakucho,
Chiyoda-ku
Tel: 3580-6423
Open: 11am-10pm

Indian
¥ 1/2
★★★

  **Map 7**

The original Indian assembly-line operation, but the price is right and the food never fails. Classic recommendation is the tandoori mixed grill or the bigger Maharaja Delight combo; our personal favorite is the chicken Afghani. For what it's worth, your author has just computed that he has eaten the latter more times than any other dish at any restaurant in this city.

The same management runs **Maharaja** branches in Shinjuku (3354-0222), Shibuya (3477-5188 and 3770-1778), Ginza (3575-0726 and 3572-7196), Ueno (3835-0818), Yokohama (045-316-3293) and Chiba (043-297-0175).

特別なサービスはないが、料理の味も値段も文句はない。タンドリーミックスグリルやカレー、シシケバブ、タンドリーチキン、ナン、ライスを一皿に盛り合わせマハラジャデライトがお薦め。チキンアフガニは是非トライしてみて欲しい一品。姉妹店の『マハラジャ』新宿店（☎）3354-0222、渋谷店（☎）3477-5188／3770-1778、銀座店（☎）3575-0726／3572-7196、上野店（☎）3835-0818、横浜店（☎）045-316-3293、千葉店（☎）043-297-0175 がある。

マハラオ

MAI-THAI

1-18-16 Ebisu, Shibuya-ku
Tel: 3280-1155
Open: 5:30-11pm

Thai
¥¥
★★★

[cc] [◆] **Map 5**

マイタイ

Compact and friendly, Mai-Thai ranks among Tokyo's best for *yam* (Thai-style salads), *goong pla* (spiced raw shrimp), *larb* (spicy minced meat) and other light dishes, and not far behind with soups and curries. They also put out their own line of canned Thai curries. Branches in Aoyama (5466-6464), Osaka (06-539-1727) and Kyoto (075-641-7243).

タイ風サラダのヤム、辛く味付けした挽き肉ラープ、そしてサラダタイプの料理やスープとカレーが美味しい店。オリジナルのタイカレーの缶詰も売っている。大阪店（☎）06-539-1727、京都店（☎）075-641-7243。

MANDALA

2-17 Kanda Jinbocho,
Chiyoda-ku
Tel: 3265-0498
Open: 11am-11pm;
closed Sun. & hol.

Indian
¥¥
★★

[cc] [◆] **Map 13**

マンダラ

The latest outpost of the **Maenam no Hotori** empire is everything we've come to expect from these people: authentic if rather refined food, a cool clean decor, and none of the usual "ethnic" excesses. Basically northern-style Indian cooking, but with the occasional foray into lesser-known curries. The best bargains are the ¥2200 and ¥2900 "Mini Courses," served from 2pm to 5pm and not particularly miniature. All dishes can be prepared in five logarithmic degrees of spiciness, though the waitress will cringe if you order the hottest.

『メナムのほとり』の経営者が出した最新の店だけあって、ここは洗練された本場のインド料理と"エスニック"しすぎないクールでしゃれた内装がいい。基本的には北部の料理が中心だが、東京ではめったに食べられない珍しい種類のカレーもあり、カレーファンには魅力である。ここの一番のお薦めは午後２時から５時の間に出るミニコース。値段は2200円と2900円で、名前はミニだが量はビッグで、すべての料理に５段階の辛さがあり、いちばん辛いレベルは想像を絶するほど。お店の人のアドバイスに従ったほうが良さそうだ。

MAREICHAN

3-22-6 Nishi Ikebukuro,
Toshima-ku
Tel: 5391-7638
Open: 11am-2:30pm
& 5-10:30pm

Chinese-Malaysian
¥
★★

 Map 62

マレーチャン

Mareichan hasn't quite made up its mind as to whether it's a proper restaurant, a fast-food joint or a bottle-keep snack bar. Good inexpensive food in any event, from noodle and rice dishes (we like the *nasi lemak*) to full-bore Malaysian curries. Not a lot of carefree smiles from the Chinese staff, though.

ここは未だに自分たちの店を本格的なレストランにするのか、ファーストフード店にするのか、それともボトルキープできるスナックにするのか決めかねているようだ。麺類、ご飯類から強烈なマレー風カレーまで安くて美味しい。ただ、中国人の従業員たちの愛想笑いは期待しない方が良いだろう。ココナッツで炊いたご飯に、肉、小魚、辛いサンバルソースを乗せたナシレマックが特にお薦め。

MARUGO

1-8-14 Soto-Kanda,
Chiyoda-ku
Tel: 3255-6595
Open: 11:30am-3pm &
5-8:30pm; closed Thur.
& 3rd Wed

Tonkatsu
¥
★★ 1/2

Map 63

丸五

While generally not a good place to be caught hungry, Akihabara was part of Old Tokyo before it became discount electronics shop to the world, and that means there's still hope. Here's one of the last survivors: an old traditional-style building serving a classical *tonkatsu teishoku*—deep-fried breaded pork cutlet, sliced cabbage, pickles, rice, *miso shiru* soup. Remember: you don't *have* to soak the cabbage in that sickly brown sauce, or even eat it at all. Invaluable for a lunchtime break on long nerdy shopping days.

一般論として、お腹を空かすにはあまり良くない場所だと思われているが、忘れてならないのは、秋葉原も今のような巨大な電気製品の安売り屋街になる前は、古き良き東京の一部であったことだ。この店は、そんな昔の名残りのようなビルの中にあって、古典的な　とんかつ定食を出している。コンピューターのショッピングで費やす長い一日のランチには欠かせない店だ。

MARUMO

5-5-11 Akasaka,
Minato-ku
Tel: 5570-9438
Open: 11:30am-3pm &
5:30-10:30pm (last order)

Italian
¥¥
★★
Map 1

マルーモ

Marumo could pass for a smaller, somewhat down-market **Granata**. Despite the similar, slightly bogus feeling to the decor (maybe this goes with the Akasaka territory?), the cooks show every sign of competence, especially with the fish. Recommended: the generous bouillabaisse for two.

Eastern Tokyoites, note the branch at 6-18-17 Higashi Koiwa, Edogawa-ku (5693-6050).

ここは『グラナータ』を小さくして、庶民
的にしたような店で、インテリアも同じ
ように偽物っぽいが、シェフの腕は確か
で、特に魚料理は旨い。量たっぷりの二
人前ブイヤベースがお薦め。東京東部、
東小岩に支店（☎）5693-6050 がある 。

MATSURIBAYASHI GINJOKURA

Notwithstanding the *ginjo* in its name, this is decidedly not one of the uppity nihonshu establishments frequented by TV connoisseurs and Nagatacho bosses. This is just a bit of the good stuff for the masses—fine sakés and saké-flattering food at prices and hours geared to locals who have neither big budgets nor worries about catching trains.

Centerpiece of an evening here will be the specials of the month, eight or so *ginjo* selections and an equal number of *junmaishu*. The staff seem to take real pleasure in matching you up with ones you'll enjoy. If you're in doubt they'll even bring out the bottles for a taste of several. The food is workmanlike: assorted choose-it-yourself *o-toshi*, sashimi, yakitori and *chinmi* ("delicacies") like *mentaiko* and *kusaya*.

The decor pushes the nihonshu motif to the limit, with labels plastering the walls and one whole table inside a giant saké barrel. Various branches including Shibuya (3464-5832) and Shimo-Kitazawa (3419-8419), but without the emphasis on saké.

4-22-15 Taishido,
Setagaya-ku
Tel: 3419-8225
Open: 5pm-midnight

Izakaya
¥¥
★★ 1/2

Map 64

近所にある『赤鬼』が、本格的な通向きの店とすれば、こっちは良い酒と、それに合うつまみを揃えた大衆酒場といったところだろう。壁は酒のラベルで埋め尽くされ、巨大な酒樽の中に置かれているテーブルもある。夜には、今月のお薦めとして8種類ほどの吟醸酒や純米酒を出している。もし自分で銘柄を決められないときは、何種か利き酒をさせてくれるし、従業員もアドバイスしてくれる。料理は、自分で選べるお通し、刺身、焼き鳥から、明太子、くさやなどの珍味がある。渋谷(☎) 3464-5832、下北沢 (☎) 3419-8419 など、いくつかの支店があるが、酒に関してはこの店ほどではない。

祭ばやし吟醸倉

MATSUYA

1-13 Kanda Sudacho,
Chiyoda-ku
Tel: 3251-1556
Open: 11am-8pm;
closed Sun. & hol.

Soba
¥
★★★

Map 13

Our token soba shop isn't quite the city's most famous (that would be **Yabu Soba**, two blocks away at 2-10 Kanda Awajicho, Chiyoda-ku, 3251-0287). It's hardly luxurious—everyone sits elbow-to-elbow at three-quarters scale tables and chairs—and soba fanatics might prefer the noodles elsewhere (like the revered **Masuoto** at 2-25-18 Hirai, Edogawa-ku, 3681-5610). It's simply the quintessential Tokyo sobaya, as it has been for 120 years and, with any luck, will be long after the rest of this book is history.

知名度では近くにある都内で最も有名な『神田薮そば』(千代田区神田淡路町2-10 (☎) 3251-0287にはかなわないし、味は一部のそば通たちの間で伝説的になっている『増音』(江戸川区平井2-25-18 (☎) 3681-5610)の方に支持者が多いかも知れない。しかし、豪華とはいえない狭い店内はいつも混雑している。創業120年の東京の蕎麦屋の神髄は、運さえ良ければ今後1、2世紀続くだろう。

神田まつや

Lottery jackpot? Sell that screenplay? Here's a sampler of *sky's-the-limit Tokyo dining*. The cheapest will run at least ¥60,000 for two; with a little ingenuity, easily double that. Reservations, need it be said, are *de rigueur*.

Kiyota 6-3-15 Ginza, Chuo-ku (3572-4854): Some of the finest sushi in the world, served in a decor of almost stark elegance. No fish on display and essentially no ordering.

Tsujitome 1-5-8 Moto-Akasaka, Minato-ku (3403-3984): The *kaiseki* meal as tea ceremony. Experience in the "less is more" aesthetic of this type of food is advised.

Fukurinmon Shuka 6-13-16 Ginza, Chuo-ku (3543-1989): Otherworldly Cantonese fare at what is widely regarded as Tokyo's finest Chinese restaurant.

Aragawa 3-3-9 Shinbashi, Minato-ku (3591-8765): "Steakhouse" isn't quite the term for a place where the steaks *start* at ¥40,000. Then drop some real money on a '61 Petrus.

Maxim's de Paris 5-3-1 Ginza, Chuo-ku (3562-6291): An exact scale model of the Paris original. Kitsch, yes, but also magnificent in its own museum-piece way, and we mean every aspect of food, service and bill.

MEKONG GAWA

2-16-4 Kami-Osaki,
Shinagawa-ku
Tel: 3442-6736
Open: Noon-1:30pm & 5-11pm
(last order); closed Sun. & hol.

Cambodian
¥¥
★★

 **Map 14**

メコン川

A long-time standby for good if somewhat Chinesey Cambodian fare, and certainly convenient enough—it's practically on the Meguro Station platform. Dinner courses from ¥3500, but most regulars pick and choose. Top pick: spicy beef salad.

目黒駅のプラットホームにあるといってもよさそうな場所にあるこの店は、長年、中華風カンボジア料理で親しまれている。

MELA

2-25-17 Dogenzaka,
Shibuya-ku
Tel: 3770-0120
Open: 11:30am-2:30pm &
5-11:30pm; Sat., Sun. &
hol., 11:30am-11:30pm

Indian
¥¥
★ 1/2
⬛⬛ **Map 19**

メラ

Despite anecdotal accounts of good meals here, we've more than once found Mela to fall short of Tokyo's elevated Indian food standards. Still, it deserves the support of all fresh air lovers: to our knowledge it's the only restaurant of its type to just say "no" to smoking. Refreshingly un-Indian decor too.

美味い料理に巡り会えるという逸話にもかかわらず、ここは普通のレベルになりつつある。新鮮な空気を愛する人達の為に、東京のレストランでは珍しく全席禁煙。

MESON EL VASCO

1-25-6 Hamamatsucho,
Minato-ku
Tel: 3436-5720
Open: 5-11pm;
closed Sun. & hol.

Spanish
¥¥
★★ 1/2
⬛⬛⬛⬛ **Map 65**

メソン・エル・バスコ

A Spanish chef acquaintance holds that Meson el Vasco does the best Spanish food in the city. It's a tough call, but no one ever seems to regret the trip to this spirited little oasis in the nocturnal no-man's-land of Hamamatsucho. Consistently good tapas, fish (try the stuffed calamari) and paella; fine small list of Spanish wines (recommended: any of the Riojas or Navarras); refreshingly good-humored service by an all-Spanish staff.

スペイン人のシェフたちの間で、いま東京でいちばん注目のスペイン料理店と評判の店。日没後は無人地帯になる浜松町の小さなオアシスといったところ。わざわざ出かけて行っても後悔しないだろう。いつも変わらず美味しいタパス、魚介類（特にイカの詰め物がお薦め）、パエリアと、種類は多くないが充実したスペイン産のワインリスト（お薦めはリオハかナヴァラ）は、なかなかのものだ。従業員全てがスペイン人で、ユーモアたっぷりのサービスが新鮮だ。

MIHOSAI

1-10-1 Shiba Daimon,
Minato-ku
Tel: 3433-1095
Open: 11:30am-2:30pm &
5:30-9pm; Sat. until 10pm;
closed Sun.

Sichuan
¥
★★
Map 66

味芳斉

Now that most of Daimon's famed Chinese restaurants have tarted themselves up for the 21st century, we find ourselves coming back to Mihosai largely for the vintage atmosphere of the place: dark wood walls, worn white plastic tabletops, authentic yellowish fluorescent lighting. Frankly, the food rates only a notch better than at most neighborhood *chuka* places but it's plentiful and not much more expensive. Their ¥770 lunches are eaten, very quickly, by countless local office workers.

For fancier food and surroundings, walk one block over to the main Daimon street and try either the high-rise **New Asia** (3432-8001) or the tasteful **Lanfar** (3435-9266).

大門にある有名中華料理店のほとんどがきらびやかな宮殿風の建物に変わってしまった今、濃い色調の木目の壁、使い古したプラスチック張りのテーブルや何のへんてつもない蛍光灯といった懐かしい雰囲気を求めて通ってしまうのがこの店だ。現代風にしたり、他のレストランと張り合うつもりはまったくないようで、日本風の四川料理の味は昔からずっと変わっていない。安くて量も多く、つまり変わる必要などまったくない本格派なのである。それでももう少し花が欲しいという人は、大門通りに向かって少し歩いたところにある高層ビルの『新亜飯店』(☎) 3432-8001 か、もしくは品の良い『ランファン』(☎) 3435-9266 を試してみると良いだろう。

*Loyal, impassioned, fragrant—garlic lovers are the opera fans of the food world. Ebisu's **Ninnikuya** (3446-5887) made the herb fashionable in Japan in the mid-'80s and is still playing to a packed house nightly. These days we prefer **Ninniku Mura** and **Ninnikuya Goemon** (Seishido Bldg., 5F, 7-14-10 Roppongi, 3475-6173).*

MIKASA CONTINENTAL HIROO

We used to think of Hiroo's Mikasa as a backup in case **Enoteca** was ever full. It's just downstairs, its decor is at least as elegant and its outdoor seating almost as attractive. And we knew from **Buono Buono** that the Mikasa Kaikan people know their trade. Our only concern was the "Continental" in its name—no word covers a greater multitude of restaurant sins.

In fact Mikasa turns out to be well worth visiting on its own merits. The menu, far from being second-hand French, offers dishes as diverse as crab meat and horseradish salad and Peking-style duck crepes. The wine list gets pricey fast, but it's not without a few sound bottles in the ¥3000 range, and decanters of basic red and white for half that. Most enjoyable of all, oddly enough, is the courtly, old-money atmosphere of the place. Usually in Japan, this is a recipe for boredom, if not discomfort. Here, maybe owing to Mikasa's newness or the Hiroo setting, it feels relaxed, even graceful.

5-14-15 Minami Azabu,
Minato-ku
Tel: 3448-8924
Open: 11:30am-10pm;
Sun. & hol. from noon

Continental
¥¥¥
★★★

CC 🗾 🎅 **Map 8**

この店を実のところスペア程度にしか考えていなかったが、目当ての『エノテカ』がたまたま満員だったので、下にあるこのレストランに入ってみて改めて見直した。内装は上の店に負けない程エレガントで、屋外のスペースも同様に魅力的だった。三笠会館が経営するレストランは優れた店であることはすでに『ヴォノヴォノ』で証明済みではあったが、ここも十分に訪れる価値がある。しかし、ちょっとひっかかるのは店の名にコンチネンタルという言葉をつけていることで、これはあまりに曖昧で印象がよくない。料理は美味しく、メニューはカニとホースラディッシュのサラダから北京ダックのクレープまでと幅広い。また、ワインは高価なものが多いが、3000円前後で間違いないボトルが2、3種ある他、赤と白はデカンタで注文できる。豪華さを狙った日本のレストランはとかく気取って堅苦しくなりがちだが、この店のよいところは広尾というロケーションも手伝ってか、肩肘を張らずに上品で優雅な本物の風格を感じさせる点だ。

三笠
コンチネンタル
広尾

MOKICHI

35 Yokoderamachi,
Shinjuku-ku
Tel: 3267-5307
Open: 4:30-11:30pm;
closed Sun. & hol.

Izakaya
¥¥
★★★
cc 大 Map 9

The action at Mokichi centers around two big communal tables, both generally packed with salarymen by six or so. Wooden placards line the walls, offering the complete range of izakaya food and then some. A blackboard lists dozens more, mostly the day's fish. A long banner describes the various sakés (our pick: the house *junmai ginjo*). Another explains the ingredients they use, many of which are shipped down almost daily from Yamagata, the master's home.

The best bet is to go for the day's fish specials, whether humble sashimi like their excellent *iwashi* (sardines), anything grilled or fried, or seasonal exotica like *hotaru ika*, soft, finger-size squid whose name ("firefly") comes from their little navigation lights. Don't be shy about asking what your *Yamagata-ben*-speaking neighbors are eating. Mokichi is a restaurant that rewards the daring.

For fresh air lovers there's a big round table outside, surrounded by beer crates, motorcycles, and a trash can or two. There's also a branch in Nishi Kubo, Musashino-shi (0422-54-7864).

いつもサラリーマンたちに占領されている2つの大きな相席テーブルがこの店の中心になっている。居酒屋料理のほとんどすべての献立がずらりと壁に並び、黒板には魚料理を中心とした日替わりメニューが書かれている。また長い布のメニューには酒の数々(特製玄米吟醸酒がお薦め)の説明があり、山形から毎日のように輸送されている食材についても触れている。特にお薦めなのは日替わりの魚料理、大根ギョーザ、いもご汁などの地方料理だ。ちょっと見慣れない料理も物おじせずに試してみるといい。ただ、肉じゃがのようなスタンダードな料理は逆にいまひとつだ。屋外のテーブルもあるので、ゴミ箱が気にならなければ、外の空気を吸いながらの一杯もいいだろう。武蔵野市西久保店 (☎) 0422-54-7864 がある。

もきち

MOMINOKI HOUSE

2-18-5 Jingu-mae,
Shibuya-ku
Tel: 3405-9144
Open: 11am-11pm;
closed Sun.

Japanese
¥¥

★ 1/2

 Map 11

モミノキ ハウス

A couple of trips here have failed to convince us that the no doubt good intentions of the chef are finding real fulfillment in the food he creates. In a word, it has been pretty patchy. But everyone keeps saying how much they enjoy it, and there's no denying the comfortable multi-level interior, the lovely pottery and the good music. Lunch draws a loyal crowd, too.

東京のヘルシーフード・レストランの中では最もよく知られ、気になる店のひとつである。その魅力は味よりも居心地の良い雰囲気にあり、おしゃれなインテリア、美しい陶器類、センスの良い音楽のすべてが揃っている。これは東京のレストランでは基本だが、自然食の店では希少価値といえる。ランチは割安だが、夜は比較的値段が高くなるようだ。

MONSOON CAFÉ

2-10-1 Nishi Azabu,
Minato-ku
Tel: 5467-5222
Open: 11:30-5am

Southeast Asian
¥¥

★ 1/2

Map 17

モンスーン カフェ

Smallish menu of not especially authentic Southeast Asian snack foods: satay, noodles, spicy Thai and Cambodian salads, Vietnamese raw spring rolls, fried greens. Portions and prices are modest. Monsoon's best feature is its sidewalk patio, looking out onto the green hillside below Aoyama Cemetery. Its biggest drawback: service at times so peculiar you begin to suspect brain damage.

この手の店にありがちな料理よりも内装やムード作りに力が入った店。数少ないメニューには特徴はないが、それなりに美味しいサテ、麺類、スパイシーなタイ・カンボジア風サラダ、ベトナム風生春巻などがある。ボリュームや価格は文句ないだろう。青山墓地の緑が望めるオープンテラスはこの店のハイライトになっている。

MOTI DARBAR

Moti remains just about everyone's favorite Indian restaurant chain, and the standard by which we judge the rest. Darbar is among the newest and best of their branches, with two specialties of particular note: *baigan barta* (made of grilled eggplant and onions) and the buttery, cashew-rich chicken *darbari*. Note the extended hours—it's a great place for a late-night meal.

Another especially recommendable branch is the smallish shop over Akasaka Station by TBS (3584-6640). This one began life as Moti's vegetarian restaurant, and while the menu was soon expanded to include meat (Tokyo just might be Asia's most carnivorous city), the food and the intimacy of the place still set it apart from the others. Pending a facelift, the rather flyblown old Roppongi branch (3479-1939) is worth avoiding.

Roppongi Plaza Bldg., 3F,
3-12-6 Roppongi,
Minato-ku
Tel: 5410-6871
Open: 11am-midnight;
Sun. & hol., noon-11pm

Indian
¥ 1/2
★★★ 1/2

CC 🖊 **Map 18**

モティ ダールバリ店

多くの人に愛されているインド料理チェーンの最新の店。料理はどれも美味しいが、特に baigan barta (炒めたナスと玉ねぎの料理) か、カシューナッツがたっぷり入ってこってりしたチキンの darbari がお薦めだ。遅くまで開いているので夜食にはピッタリ。もう一軒のお薦めは赤坂駅の上にある店 (☎) 3584-6640。始めはベジタリアン部門としてオープンしたが、今では肉料理も出していて、親しみやすい雰囲気は他の店より群を抜いている。六本木店 (☎) 3479-1939 は改装してから出かけた方がよさそうだ。

MR. GARLIC

Seldom as we get the overpowering urge to jump up and rush out for *yoshoku*, Mr. Garlic is the easy favorite when it happens. It's the authentic *shitamachi* experience—cluttered open kitchen, background noise courtesy FM-Tokyo, service by the owner in his black vest and bow tie—all transplanted into an incongruously stylish Azabu Juban basement.

Pastel Azabu Bldg., B1,
1-8-5 Azabu Juban,
Minato-ku
Tel: 3583-6769
Open: 11:30am-2pm &
5-11pm; closed Sun. & hol.

Yoshoku
¥ 1/2
★★
Map 3

We have yet to find anything particularly garlic-intensive on the menu, but touches of quality appear everywhere, right down to the ginger-scented *o-shinko* pickles and the melt-in-the-mouth tofu in the *miso shiru*.

ミスター・
ガーリック

洋食と呼ばれる日本食が食べたくなった
ら、是非行きたいのが麻布十番のここ。黒
いベストに蝶ネクタイ姿のオーナーとFM
東京が流れるオープンキッチン、ここでは
ちょっとした下町の洋食屋さんの雰囲気が
味わえる。店の名前のわりには、ガーリッ
クを強く効かせた料理は少なく、生姜風味
のおしんこや味噌汁の中の豆腐にまで神経
が行き届いている。

MUAN THAI
NABE

2-1 Kanda Jinbocho,
Chiyoda-ku
Tel: 3239-6939
Open: 11:30am-3pm & 5:30-
11pm; closed Sun. & hol.

Thai suki
¥¥
★★ 1/2

 Map 13

The popular (both in Thailand and Japan) new style of *Thai suki* is actually more like shabu-shabu: you plunge your fish, shrimp, pork, dango, wonton and so on into the boiling broth, swish them around till done, then dip in a sauce and eat. The real competition in Thailand is for the sauces, and this one could hold its own even there. Good as this all is, the human body seems to crave a little starch near the end of a meal, for which Muan Thai Nabe provides some fine conventional Thai rice and noodle dishes.

ムアン・タイ・
なべ

タイでも日本でも人気のあるタイスキは、
魚、海老、豚肉、肉団子、ワンタンなどを
熱湯の中でシャブシャブする料理だが、決
め手はつけダレの味にある。この店のタレ
は本場タイでも群を抜く本物の味だ。他に
一般的なタイ料理もある。

MUGYODON

Akasaka Sangyo Bldg., 2F,
2-17-74 Akasaka,
Minato-ku
Tel: 3586-6478
Open: 5-11:30pm; closed
Sun. & hol.

Korean
¥¥
★★★
Map 1

武橋洞

Immensely popular family-style Korean place, meaning countless varieties of kimchi, oyster and crab dishes, and other things unknown to Japanized *yakiniku* places. Good fun, provided you're prepared for crowds, noise, and smoke both from the cooking and the patrons.

韓国家庭料理の店としてかなり有名な存在
だ。いろいろな種類のキムチ、カキ、カニ
料理、そして日本の焼肉屋では食べられな
いような珍しいメニューを揃えているので
人気がある。店内の煙や騒々しさが気にな
らなければ十分に楽しめる店だ。

---

*Yoshoku has two meanings. It can refer to
"Western" food as opposed to Japanese, as in, "What
do you feel like tonight,* yoshoku *or* washoku?" *It also
is a style of Japanese cooking, adapted from European food
back in Meiji times and surviving today mainly in little
neighborhood places in working-class neighborhoods.
Yoshoku standards include* menchi katsu *(breaded, deep-
fried burger),* omuraisu *(rice-filled omelets),* hayashi raisu
*("hashed" rice), croquettes, hamburger steaks and, in latter
times, pilaf and pan-fried spaghetti. One common theme: a
heavily reduced, generic "brown sauce" of mysterious origin.
Perhaps the ultimate yoshoku experience:* **Tawaraya** *(5-35
Kagurazaka, Shinjuku-ku, 3269-2670), an old haunt of
writers Soseki Natsume and Kafu Nagai.*

MUITO BOM

1-13 Kanda Jinbocho,
Chiyoda-ku
Tel: 3296-0774
Open: 11:30am-3pm &
5:30-11pm; Sat. until 10pm;
closed Sun. & hol.

Brazilian
¥¥
★★

  Map 13

ムイト・ボン

Tidy, tiny and competent. There's a bowl of magnificent Brazilian hot sauce on every table, and if the meat's a little tough it's purely in the interest of authenticity. Recommended: the Muito Bom Course, featuring *pasteis* (a kind of deep-fried *empanada* snack), *churrasco* meats and a bowl of *feijoada*. Part of the **Maenam no Hotori** group, all the restaurants of which—by coincidence or sinister conspiracy—begin with the letter "M."

『メナムのほとり』グループが経営しているこざっぱりしたブラジル料理の店。テーブルに置かれているブラジル式の辛味ソースは絶品。お薦めはパステス（肉の詰め物を揚げた料理）、シュラスコ、豆とポークのシチュー、フェジョアーダがついたディナー入門コースだ。

MYUN

AKB Shinjuku Gyoen Bldg., B1,
1-1-11 Shinjuku, Shinjuku-ku
Tel: 5379-5240
Open: 11am-2pm & 5-11pm

Vietnamese
¥
★★

Map 22

ミュン

Also known as (no sniggering there in the back) **My Dung**. It's part time machine: a rather dank, Asian-baroque Shinjuku basement café straight out of the '60s. And part space transporter: an instant trip to Saigon, with reasonably good cheap food and a largely Vietnamese clientele. There's another, marginally less seedy Myun at 4-2-2 Hongo, Bunkyo-ku (3815-1195).

ちょっと時空を超えた旅が経験できそうな店。時は60年代、場所はサイゴン。アジア風バロックスタイルの新宿地下の元喫茶店のインテリアもそのままに、安くて美味しい料理には、ベトナム系の常連客が多い。支店が文京区本郷4-2-2（☎）3815-1195にある。

NANBANTEI

4-5-6 Roppongi, Minato-ku
Tel: 3402-0606
Open: 5-11pm

Yakitori
¥¥ 1/2
★★ 1/2

⟦CC⟧ ⟦◈⟧ **Map 18**

南蛮亭

At least a couple of our respondents
reckon that Nanbantei has been spoiled by
its own international success (branches in
Ginza, Yoyogi, Kichijoji, Kawasaki, Seoul,
Hong Kong, Singapore, Los Angeles and
Copenhagen), and that better value can be
found elsewhere. On the other hand it
doesn't have to cost an arm and a leg—
courses start at ¥2800—and there's no
denying that this is quality yakitori.
Especially useful for visitors, newcomers
and other non-speakers of Japanese.

国際的に広がった支店の成功によって
少々手抜きになったという声も聞かれる
が、この店の焼き鳥の質の良さはやはり
否定できない。コースは2800円からと値
段もまあまあ手頃だ。銀座、代々木八
幡、吉祥寺、川崎、ソウル、香港、シン
ガポール、ロサンジェルス、コペンハー
ゲンに支店がある。

NANKANTEI

4-20-15 Ogikubo,
Suginami-ku
Tel: 3393-3044
Open: 11:30am-2pm & 5:30-
10pm; Sat. & Sun., 5:30-
10pm; closed Mon.

Korean
¥¥
★★★ 1/2

⟦CC⟧ **Map 67**

南漢亭

Comfortable '70s-chic Ogikubo decor, an
accommodating master and creative
Korean food of the highest caliber and at
the fairest of prices. And don't think the
Tokyo food cognoscenti don't know it:
Nankantei wins raves in every other
restaurant guide. Avoid peak hours.

韓国料理といえば日本では『焼肉』のイ
メージが強かったが、東京ではここ10
年、真の韓国料理を出す店が増えて来て
いるので喜ばしい。焼肉が嫌いな訳では
ないが、ここでは数多くのキムチ、麺
類、揚げ物、鍋物が楽しめる。店内は
ゆったりと落ち着いていて、ややレトロ
調の荻窪らしい雰囲気。マスターは親切
で、上等な料理に手頃な値段と文句なし
で、最高の店のひとつだ。

NANPU

1-11-3 Kabukicho,
Shinjuku-ku
Tel: 3200-1285
Open: 6pm-1am;
closed Sun. & hol.

Okinawan
¥¥ 1/2
★★

CC **Map 22**

南風

An Occupation-vintage (1948) dive where waitresses and customers alike are liable to burst forth into song on the *jabisen*, and the chef specializes in raw goat. It's the sort of scene where colorful characters stumble in off the street, down a flagon of *awamori*, then disappear back into the night. They still have their doubts here about *Yamatonchu*, as Ryukyu islanders call main-island Japanese (not to their faces), and gaijin may feel like Admiral Perry. Watch the bill and steer clear of the goat and you're in for Tokyo's most entertaining Okinawan encounter.

1948年創業の沖縄料理の老舗。お客と
ウェイトレスとが代わる代わるに蛇皮線
を弾いては歌い、山羊の生肉を食しては
泡盛りをあおる、そんな感じの店であ
る。山羊の生肉はクセがあってちょっと
食べにくいが、本場の沖縄の味を体験す
ることができる。2階では歌や踊りなど
の伝統芸能が楽しめる。

NATARAJ

3-19-1 Nishi Waseda,
Shinjuku-ku
Tel: 3202-6987
Open: 11:30am-2:30pm &
5-10pm; Sat., Sun. & hol.,
11:30am-10pm

Indian vegetarian
¥
★★ 1/2

▨ ▨ **Map 24**

ナタラジ

Tiny, clean and perhaps a tad too cute, Nataraj delivers fine homemade vegetarian curries and some of the best masala tea in town. Top recommendation: the rich pseudo-meat Nataraj curry. They have a branch in Ogikubo (3398-5108).

こぢんまりとしていて、清潔で、ちょっと
カワイイ感じのするこの店は、自家製のベ
ジタリアンカレーと東京のレストランのな
かでも格別なマサラティーを出す。一番の
お薦めは肉のようなグルテン（蛋白質）が
たくさん入っていて、味、舌ざわりとも本
物のナタラジカレー。荻窪支店 (☎) 3398-
5108

NATURAL HOUSE

6-14-15 Akasaka,
Minato-ku
Tel: 3589-1077
Open: 11:30am-2pm;
closed Sat., Sun. & hol.

Natural foods
¥
★★

 Map 1

ナチュラル ハウス

Another combined natural food store/ restaurant, the latter in a cafeteria format. Meals are simple—say a curry or stew with rice and pickles—and there are only a couple choices per day. Quality, however, is tops: the nutty, perfectly *al dente* brown rice alone is worth the price of admission.

Natural House operates a bigger store (but no restaurant) on Aoyama-dori by Omotesando Station (3498-2277).

自然食料品店とカフェテリアスタイルのレストランがひとつになった店。カレーかシチューにライス、漬物といったシンプルな料理だけだが、その質は高く、完璧に炊かれた歯ごたえのある玄米は東京一。表参道近くの青山通り沿いには食料品のみの支店（☎）3498-2277がある。

NEW YORK GRILL

Excellent
8/5/97 good & wine.
Excellent
fries

Park Hyatt Tokyo, 52F,
3-7-1-2 Nishi Shinjuku,
Shinjuku-ku
Tel: 5323-3458
Open: 11:30am-2:30pm &
5:30-10:30pm (last order);
Sat. from 10:30am; Sun.,
5:30-10:30pm (last order)

American
¥¥¥
★★ 1/2

Map 23

A Bubble-era monument so grandiose that construction only just finished, Shinjuku Park Tower would be worth a visit even if it wasn't for the sparkling new New York Grill up on top. Come hungry: from the *foccacia* on your table (Tokyo's best, we reckon) to the Italianesque starters and the steaks and seafood, it's all of traditional Gotham size and quality. They also have Japan's biggest cellar of California wines, though this wouldn't be the place to expect bargains on them.

Of special note: the Mon.-Sat. ¥3900 buffet lunches and the expansive Sunday brunch (book early).

今になってやっと出来上がった、バブル時代の記念碑ともいうべき新宿パークタワーの最上階にあるレストラン。その壮大なス

ニューヨーク
グリル

ケールを見るだけでも足を運ぶ価値はある
だろう。東京ではここがベストと思える新
鮮なイタリア式のパン "フォッカチア" か
ら、イタリアンスタイルの前菜ビュッ
フェ、ステーキ、シーフードに至るまで、
質、量共にニューヨークに匹敵する。ま
た、カリフォルニアワインは日本で最大級
のセラーを持っている。月曜から土曜まで
は3900円のビュッフェランチ、日曜には
サンデーブランチがある。早めの予約が必
要だ。

All it takes is a few yen and a cast-iron stomach—have a meal in
retro Tokyo. If the likes of Brasserie de Paris and Pilsen have
whetted your appetite, figuratively speaking, here are some more.

● Murgh 2-19-2 Dogenzaka, Shibuya-ku (3461-8809):
Occupation-era (1951) curry house so old and decrepit that it
has to be seen to be believed. Catch it while it lasts.

● Sanshin Bldg. 1-4-1 Yurakucho, Chiyoda-ku: Built in 1928 and
still exquisitely spic and span, this one deserves national
treasure status. Our pick of the shops: the resplendently '50s
New World Service snack bar on the ground floor (3580-1745).

● Palaceside Bldg. 1-1-1 Hitotsubashi, Chuo-ku: Magnificent
'60s kitsch throughout, but for a good time, go to the basement
and have a drink at the Pub Suntorian. It's a Victorian nightmare
come to life.

● Akanoren 1-4-8 Nishi Gotanda, Shinagawa-ku (3491-8118): A
different kind of retro—an izakaya hangout for Imperial Army
vets. War mementos throughout, and the upstairs back room is a
museum of the attack on Pearl Harbor. Please behave yourself
here.

● The Orchid Room Hotel Okura, 2-10-4 Toranomon, Minato-ku
(3582-0111): More Occupation nostalgia, right down to the
uniforms on the waitresses. Recommended for breakfast only,
when it's a favorite coffee stop for international power brokers
like Henry Kissinger and Walt Mondale.

NINNIKU MURA

Look for Ninniku Mura just off Killer-dori behind a door inexplicably labeled "Sand Leek." The place looks to have been many things in its time and appears none too permanent even in its present incarnation. The decor is random—photos of Mick Jagger and Albert Einstein, an upside-down world map from Australia—and the music tends toward loudish funk. Seating is along a counter in front of the kitchen or, with luck, at the single table (it fits eight and can be reserved).

Recommended: deep-fried garlic, spinach and mushrooms in garlic butter, red chili and garlic pasta, steak with garlic chips, tofu salad (yes, it's got garlic in it), garlic rice laced with sesame seeds and topped with an egg. Best of all are eggplant and chicken fried in miso and a shrimp/prawn/squid/octopus and chili oil concoction that will blow the roof off of your mouth. To drink they have a few cautious wines (you'd be cautious, too, around this food) and some very good beers. Note their new branch: Ninniku Mura Hiroo 23 (3449-2943).

2-3-30 Jingu-mae,
Shibuya-ku
Tel: 3404-3463
Open: 6-11pm;
closed Sun. & hol.

Mukokuseki
¥ 1/2
★★ 1/2

 **Map 11**

青山のキラー通りをちょっと入ったところに不可解な『Sand Leek』という言葉が書かれたドアを見つけたら、それがこの店。店内の壁にはミック・ジャガーやアルバート・アインシュタインの写真が貼られ、オーストラリアを上にした逆さまの世界地図が貼られている。音楽はファンク系が中心で、たいていキッチン前のカウンターに座らせられる。テーブルがひとつあり、8人以上なら予約もできる。お薦め料理はニンニクまるごと揚げ、ホウレン草のにんにくバター、ガーリックと赤唐辛子とスパゲッティ、スタミナ焼き、豆腐サラダ、ガーリックライスなど多数。また、ナスと鶏肉の辛ミソ風味、口から火の出るほど辛いエビ、イカ、タコをチリ油で煮込んだスープは一度お試しを。ワインも置いてはあるが、これらの料理には絶対ビールだ。広尾支店『にんにくむら23』（港区南麻布5-14-14（☎）3449-2943）もある。

にんにくむら

Kaiseki: "Japanese haute cuisine." Transcendental as it can be, it's not universally loved. Some find it too precious. Others complain that it's more of an art show than a meal. Après-*kaiseki* stops at McDonald's are not unknown. The course names are worth knowing, since they're often borrowed by other Japanese cuisines. In their approximate order:

- *Shusai* or *zensai*: appetizer
- *Suimono* or *wanmori*: soup
- *Tsukuri*: a "creation" of sashimi
- *Hassun*: savories to accompany the saké
- *Yakimono*: a "grilled food"
- *Takiawase*: cooked vegetables
- *Nimono*: a "stewed food"
- *Agemono*: a "deep-fried food"
- *Sunomono*: a "sour (pickled) food"
- *Gohan* or *shokuji*: rice or noodles
- *Konomono*: pickles
- *Kudamono*: fruit
- *Kanmi*: sweet

ONLY MALAYSIA

3-17-3 Shibuya,
Shibuya-ku
Tel: 3486-0701
Open: 11am-11pm

Malaysian
¥ 1/2
★★ 1/2

 Map 20

オンリー・
マレーシア

Japan's first but no longer "only" Malaysian restaurant has shaken off the blahs and opened this branch on the other side of Shibuya Station. Good rather than great Malaysian food, but that's still a treat. Things are looking up at their original shop too, near the 109 Bldg. at 26-5 Udagawa-cho, Shibuya-ku (3496-1177). Vegetarians take note: there's plenty of good meatless food here.

日本で最初の、でも唯一ではないこのマレーシア料理店は開店当時に比べて一段と味に磨きがかかり、今では渋谷駅の反対側に支店を構えるまでになった。タイレストランはたくさんあるのに、マレーシアレストランの数がまだ少ない東京で、この店の最高級とまではいかないまでも、まずまずの料理は貴重だ。
109ビルの近くに支店（渋谷区宇田川町26-5（☎）3496-1177）がある。

OZ CAFÉ

1-8-13 Nishi Azabu,
Minato-ku
Tel: 3470-7734
Open: 11:30am-2pm &
5:30pm-midnight; Fri. & Sat.
until 4am; closed Sun.

Australian
¥¥
★★

📷 ◪ ✦ **Map 17**

オージーカフェ

An altogether more wholesome scene than Tokyo's best-known Aussie place, **Down Under** (2-2-6 Ebisu Minami, Shibuya-ku 3715-3171), though in the cultural context that's not necessarily praise. They've found a quiet corner here in the residential back streets near Nishi Azabu and built themselves an only partially Japanized version of a Sydney café. Almost-Australian portions of lamb kebabs, Tasmanian salmon, pastas and so forth. No Cooper's Sparkling Ale (when will we ever see this in Japan?), but they do have a few of the more familiar/less interesting Oz brews. Best of all is a breezy outdoor patio that's open almost till the summer sun comes up.

健康的なオーストラリア料理店。確かにオーストラリア人はラフな感じを好むようだが、ここは東京で最も知られたオージープレイス『ダウンアンダー』（渋谷区恵比寿南2-2-6（☎）3715-3171）よりも全体にお洒落であか抜けている。西麻布に近い静かな住宅街の一角にあり、シドニースタイルのカフェを日本風にアレンジしている。巨大でほとんどオーストラリアサイズのラムケバブ、タスマニア産サーモン、パスタなどが食べられる。ビールはお気に入りのクーパーズスパークリングエールは置いてないが、平均的なオーストラリア産が楽しめる。夏の日差しが強くなるまでは風通しの良い中庭がお薦めである。

PAIN PANICO

Not nearly as alarming as its name. In fact it's the gentlest of little Italian places, hidden away up a winding little street from Ebisu to nowhere. The decor owes more to the Japanese coffeeshop esthetic than to the grand European restaurant tradition. On every table is a container of forks and knives . . . and chopsticks. Pain Panico doesn't have a pretension in the world, and in this city that's a promising start.

4-23-12 Ebisu,
Shibuya-ku
Tel: 3444-5687
Open: 6-10:30pm (last
order); hol., 5-9:30pm;
closed Sun. & 3rd Mon.

Italian
¥¥
★★ 1/2

 **Map 5**

The menu comes and it's pretty modest too. A dozen or so appetizers, a few kinds of pasta, two or three fish dishes and maybe some meat or chicken. A small, almost shy assortment of serviceable Italian wines, all priced between ¥2500 and ¥3000.

No one would expect this kind of food to stun, and it doesn't. It's fresh, simple, ingenuous. It has its lapses, but they come across as sincere and simply amateurish rather than careless or unconcerned. And for dessert there's a caramel ice cream that's to die for.

恵比寿の外れにある曲がりくねった小道にひっそりたたずむ静かなイタリア料理店。レストランというよりも、コーヒーショップに近い雰囲気のこの店は、どのテーブルにもフォーク、ナイフ、箸が入った入れ物が置いてある。メニューは12種ほどの前菜、数種のパスタ、2、3の魚料理や、数種の肉、鶏肉料理など。数少なく、控えめな選択のイタリアワインは2500円から3000円まででなかなかイケる。ここの料理には特別な驚きはないが、新鮮でシンプルでちょっと素人っぽい嘘のない味だ。キャラメルアイスクリームは絶品である。

パンパニコ

Nonya food gets our personal vote as the world's most intriguing "small" cuisine. A cross-pollination between Malay and southern Chinese cooking, it's now found in native form only in Singapore and Penang.
*Look for hints of it in Tokyo at **Only Malaysia**, **Mareichan**, **Shinsekai** and the mediocre but strategically located Shinbashi branch of **Indonesia Raya** (3572-7499).*

PALETTE

1-16-8 Ebisu Nishi,
Shibuya-ku
Tel: 5489-0770
Open: 11:30am-4pm &
6-10:30pm

Sri Lankan
¥¥
★★★

 Map 5

パレット

Food in the purest tradition of Serendip. For a start, there's a marvelous range of breads: crisp thin *papadam* for an appetizer; *roti* stuffed with egg or meat, or in its plain, buttery form; familiar types of *nan* as well as a coconut version. Then curries galore: a couple kinds of chicken, mutton, pork, fish, prawn, dhal, and two different vegetarian creations every day. Our favorites are the latter and the green chicken, either of which is guaranteed to wake up your tastebuds after too much *sag* and *biryani* at our many Mogul-style eateries.

We applaud any restaurant that avoids the Indian theme park decor, but this one is so bright and generic that it could almost pass for a small company's executive dining room.

明るすぎて暖かみに欠ける店内の内装は、腕の良いスリランカ人シェフの料理によって気にならなくさせてくれる。豊かなバリエーションのパンは申し分なく、コクのあるココナッツカレーにビールと紅茶、そしてデザートはすべて美味しい。東京の数あるレストランの中でも最高の店のひとつだ。

PANIC CAFÉ

There's a very good restaurant indeed waiting to emerge from the tiny Panic Café. It's just the right distance from the nightly circus called Roppongi. It's cozy, yet with a sense of energy and style. The music swings and the clientele doesn't giggle or shriek. Begin with the salads, say a swordfish/avocado. Next some teppan fries, maybe scallop and asparagus or chicken and garlic sprouts. For a main course it's hard to improve on the charbroiled steak or chicken. There's lots else, too, from pastas to Japanese side dishes like *agedashidofu* (deep-fried tofu). The simpler things they've already got right; the more ambitious ones may take a while. Either way, this is one to watch.

KY Bldg., B1,
3-16-14 Roppongi,
Minato-ku
Tel: 3583-4129
Open: 6-11pm; closed Sun.

Teppanyaki
¥¥
★★ 1/2

 **Map 18**

パニック・カフェ

将来がとても楽しみなレストランである。賑やかすぎる六本木の繁華街からは適当な距離を置いているし、こぢんまりとしているもののそこにはセンスとエネルギーが感じられる。お洒落な音楽が流れる中、客層はアダルト、インターナショナル、そして個性派揃いだ。メニューはめかじきとアボカドのサラダから始めてみよう。次は鉄板焼の前菜。帆立貝とアスパラ、もしくはチキンとニンニクの芽がいいだろう。メインディッシュとしては炭火焼きのステーキかチキンをお薦め。その他、パスタから揚げ出し豆腐まで豊富なバリエーションを揃えている。すでに合格点の店ではあるが、よりパーフェクトになるにはもう少し時間がかかるかもしれない。とにかく見守っていたいレストランだ。

PAO

You mean you've never wanted to sit around a smoking campfire in an animal-hide yurt in the middle of 21st-century urban Japan? Hit-or-miss, slightly bizarre foods, but the *karai* (spicy Afghani stew) is highly recommendable. And people ask us why we live in this city. . . .

2-25-6 Higashi Nakano,
Nakano-ku
Tel: 3371-3750
Open: 6pm-midnight;
closed Tue.

Middle Asian
¥¥
★ 1/2

 Map 68

パ包オ

店の真ん中にテントやキャンプファイヤーの場所を設け、屋根にはその煙を出す大きな穴をあけたユニークな店。こんな奇想天外な店があるからこそ東京という街は永遠に魅力的なのだろう。しかし、確かに冬は少々寒い思いをさせられるし、雨が降ったらどうするのかはいまだに不思議でならない。料理も一風変わっていて、お薦めなのはケバブと『カライ』という名の本当に辛いアフガニスタンシチュー。予め前日に予約が必要だが、胡麻ソースで食べる中華鍋もなかなかの味だ。

A nabe *is simply a stewpot, and gives its name to anything that goes into it. It's mainly a winter dish, and never better than when accompanied by saké. The endless varieties include* yose nabe *(various combinations of meat and vegetables),* motsu nabe *(with liver, heart and other innards),* anko *("angler fish")* nabe, Ishikari nabe *(with salmon) and* chige nabe *(spicy Korean style). King of them all is the hearty, sumo-style* chanko nabe. *Face off with a legendary chanko at* **Ichinotani** *(2-10-2 Soto-Kanda, Chiyoda-ku, 3251-8500).*

PAS À PAS

5 Funamachi,
Shinjuku-ku
Tel: 3357-7888
Open: Noon-1:30pm &
6-9pm; closed Sun.

French
¥¥
★★★

Map 69

The case could be made that no French restaurant has had more impact on the Tokyo eating scene this past decade than the industrious little Pas à Pas. The idea has been to charge a single low price (¥1500 at lunch, ¥2500 at dinner), offer a daily menu that lets diners choose a starter, main course and dessert, then simply cook it the way a good French bistro would. Voilà—a revolution. Suddenly an awful lot of our existing French places began to look top-heavy and grossly over-priced.

Make no mistake, it's not haute cuisine, and the crowds and the short hours assure that it will never be much of a romance venue. But for anyone in search of the food France really eats, as opposed to the standard Japanese fantasy of it, this is the place to start.

過去10年、これほど大きなインパクトを与えたフランス料理店があっただろうか。ランチ1500円、ディナー2500円という安い単一価格の日替わりメニューからはオードブル、メインディッシュ、デザートが選べて、見事なフレンチビストロの味が楽しめる。ここに来ると、いわ

ゆるフレンチレストランがいかに高いかと
しみじみ思わされる。もちろんここはヌー
ベルキュイジーヌの店ではないし、混み
合っていて騒がしいのでデートコースには
向かない場所だ。しかし、日本人が抱いて
いる幻想ではない、本当のフランス人が何
を食べているかを見いだすためには、まず
こんな真面目な店から足を運ぶべきだ。

パザパ

PASAR

Passers-by won't miss this one. By day
there's the shocking salmon pink exterior;
by night, the warm postmodern colors
glowing inside. Softly lit, spacious enough
to afford some elbow room and not too
much cigarette exhaust in your face, Pasar
comes off as somehow both elegant and
casual.

Prices are thankfully on the casual
side, with hardly anything on the menu for
more than ¥1000. They've recently shifted
from mukokuseki cooking to Tokyoesque
Italian, but the salads are still the place to
begin, say with something seasonal like
asparagus tips and sweet raw scallops.
Also reliable are the ultra-thin-crust
pizzas—try the shrimp and mozzarella
version.

3-18-7 Takaban,
Meguro-ku
Tel: 3713-0800
Open: 6pm-midnight;
Sun. & hol. until 11pm

Italian
¥¥
★★

 **Map 70**

昼間はショッキングピンクの外装、夜に
なると中から漏れる明かりが目を引い
て、この店に気づかず通り過ぎる人はい
ないだろう。淡い照明に包まれた店内は
ゆったりとした広さがあり、エレガント
とカジュアルの両者の雰囲気を合わせ
持っている。値段は有り難いことにカ
ジュアル寄りで、1000円を超えるもの は
見当たらない。最近、無国籍料理から東
京風イタリアンレストランに移行した
が、アスパラガスや帆立の刺身などの季
節のサラダからスタートすると良いだろ
う。お薦めはエビとモツァレラの極薄
ピッツァ。

パサール

PAS MAL

2-13-3 Mejiro-dai,
Bunkyo-ku
Tel: 3945-9908
Open: 11:30am-1:30pm (last order) & 6-9pm (last order); closed Sun.

French
¥¥
★★★

 **Map 71**

If **Pas à Pas** has proven that a sound French meal can be as casual and affordable as, say, a few rounds of yakitori and a beer, Pas Mal takes the proof even further. For openers it's even cheaper: ¥1000 for lunch, ¥2300 for dinner. In fact, to our knowledge, they haven't changed their prices since the day they opened, back at the dawn of Heisei.

What Pas Mal has raised is the quality of its cooking, now fully on a par with the best of our budget French places. The difference is that they still seem less harried here, less consciously "ethnic," more amateur in the best sense. Other pluses: a decor of near-perfect simplicity, a comprehensive range of bistro standards, non-included but excellent cheap desserts (the *tarte tatin* is a triumph), and espresso that could serve as a model for every restaurant in this city.

『パザパ』はフランス料理が、数本の焼き鳥とビール並の値段で食べられることを証明して見せてくれた店だとすると、ここはもっと手軽にフランス料理を楽しめることを確信させてくれた店だ。ランチは1000円、ディナーは2300円で、これは平成元年のオープン以来変わっていない。変わったことといえば、味が他の安くて美味しいフランス料理店に肩を並べたことだ。でも混雑してはいないし、妙なエスニック調にもなっていないから、今も良い意味でのアマチュア精神を貫いているといえるだろう。シンプルに徹し

パ・マル・レストラン

た内装、ビストロ料理のスタンダードが揃ったメニュー、安くて美味しいデザート（タルトタタンは最高）、東京中のレストランが見習うべき味のエスプレッソなど、誉め言葉は尽きない。

PASTIS

A big bright room overlooking the Aoyama-dori/Kotto-dori intersection, featuring food cooked to the specifications of Chef Yanagidate of the nearby **Le Poireau** (3797-6362), a leader in the battle for real French food in bigger servings at lower prices. Like any decent European café, they'll give you most anything you want whenever you want it, from a cup of real coffee to an ¥800 lunch plate to a five-course meal. Recommended: any of their meals-in-a-pot: *bouillabaisse*, *pôt-au-feu* or *potée*.

5-50-5 Jingu-mae,
Shibuya-ku
Tel: 3499-2565
Open: 11:30am-11pm

French
¥¥
★★ 1/2

Map 2

店は広くて明るく、青山通りと骨董通りの交差点を上から見下ろせる場所にある。近くにある姉妹店『ル・ポワロー』（☎）3797-6362 のシェフによって選ばれた料理は美味しくボリュームがあり、値段も手頃で数あるフランス料理のなかでも随一。ヨーロッパにあるカフェのようにコーヒー一杯から、800円のランチ、本格的な5品のコース料理まで、いつでも好きな時に利用できる。ブイヤベース、ポトフ、煮込み料理のポテがお薦め。

パスティス

本物の築地を探索していて、『江戸銀』は旅行者向けの行楽地だと思っているなら、魚のプロたちが気に入っている寿司屋に行くべきだろう。有名なところとしては、築地市場の隣にある『大和寿司』（☎）3542-1111と『龍寿司』（☎）3541-9517がある。これらの店は夜明けから正午までの営業だが、夜に行くのであれば『浜茂寿司』（☎）3541-9206 がある。

PATA PATA

Pata Pata sends mixed signals, but we like to think that its heart is in the right place. Run by the **Suzume no Oyado** chain, it bills itself as "healthy Italian": organically grown vegetables, free-range chickens, sea salt, etc. Most places committed to protecting their customers from chemical harm would at least set aside a no-smoking section; here there's a cigarette machine. The decor is spacious and casual, but the industrial ductwork design doesn't quite jell. And the food, wholesome as it might be, lags a good ten years behind the state of the art for cheap Tokyo Italian. The chef could use a trip to Europe. Heck, he could use a walk over to **Il Primo**.

So why go at all? Because, as at Suzume, they get first-class fish here, and they know how to cook it. In the evenings they make up their own pasta, and it's good too. To drink there's additive-free, 100 percent fruit juices. Plus it's a bargain by any standard—even the ¥1300 lunch just keeps on coming, course after course. Like it or not, it's big chains like Suzume no Oyado that will shape the way Japan eats, and here at least are the glimmerings of a healthy new approach to Western food.

2-44-1 Koenji Minami,
Suginami-ku
Tel: 5378-0801
Open: 11:30am-1:30pm
& 5-11:30pm (last order)

Italian
¥
★★

 Map 72

自称ヘルシーイタリアンと呼ぶ、『すずめのおやど』チェーンが経営するレストラン。ここの料理については味にバラつきがあって一貫性がないというウワサもあるが、少なくとも心はこもっていると信じたい。というのも、無農薬野菜や放牧されている鶏、天然塩などを使ってお客の健康を守ろうという姿勢があるからだ。しかしその割りには、禁煙席はなく煙草の自動販売機が置いてある。また、スペースを広く取ったカジュアルな内装だが、配管剥き出しのデザインはいまひとつピンとこない。料理も最新の安いイタリア料理屋に10年遅れをとっているといってもいいだろう。それでもなおこの店に来てしまう理由は、新鮮な魚が食べられるからである。夜になると手打ちパスタが用意され、これもかなりいける。無

添加の100％フルーツジュースもお薦めで
ある。そしてその量と値段に感激してしま
うのは、1300円のランチで、やや大盛り
の皿が次から次へと運ばれてくる。好き嫌
いは別として、日本の外食文化を支えてい
るのはこのような大手チェーン店の進出で
あって、少なくともこの店には大衆西洋料
理への新しいヘルシーなアプローチがあ
り、今後が期待できそうだ。

パタパタ

PAUKE

Japan seems to have an insatiable appetite
for this sort of oom-pah-pah, *gemütlich*-
laden beer cellar scene, and Pauke obliges
hordes of salarymen and OLs nightly. We
prefer it to the owner Rudi's old place, the
venerable **Bei Rudi** (3468-9471). They do
a renowned Eisbein and an adequate range
of sausages, sauerkraut and potatoes.
What brings us back though is the Schlosser
Alt, a classic top-fermented (i.e., ale-type)
coppery-colored brew from Düsseldorf.

Unless you're in need of intimacy (in
which case you've come to the wrong place)
avoid the prison-like booths out near the
door—the fun here is up next to the band.

Nomura Bldg., B1,
4-8 Yonbancho,
Chiyoda-ku
Tel: 3264-7890
Open: 5pm-2am;
closed Sun. & hol.

German
¥¥ 1/2
★★

 Map 10

親しみやすくて活気があるドイツスタイル
のビアレストラン。こうした店はアメリカ
やヨーロッパ（もちろんドイツ系の国を除
いての話だが）よりも日本で人気を保ち続
けているようだ。人々が出会い、交流し、
常に楽しめる場所として必要な店といえる
かもしれない。料理は定番のアイザインか
ら、まずまずのソーセージ、ザウアークラ
ウト、ポテトなど。また、変わったメ
ニューでは鉛色をしたデュッセルドルフの
ビール Schlosser Alt。これはライトと
ダークの中間のビールでドイツ料理にぴっ
たり合う。音楽はワルツからドイツの酒盛
り歌まで何でも演奏してくれる、この手で
は東京一のバンドが入っている。

パウケ

PETIT MARCHÉ

1-25-22 Jiyugaoka,
Meguro-ku
Tel: 3723-7907
Open: 11:30am-2pm &
5:30-9pm (last order);
closed Mon. & 3rd Tue.

French
¥¥¥
★★★

CC **Map 12**

プティマルシェ

PM tends to hold itself to a higher level of decorum than we do, but as the last good French food between us and the River Tama, it's a valuable place to keep in your Franco-file. Fine, rather classical food, and as at most of our French restaurants patronized largely by young women, the desserts operate on a very high level.

丁寧な正統派レストラン。外国人の男性がひとりで入るにはちょっと気が引けてしまうほど。しかし、都心から多摩川までの間に位置する優秀なフランス料理店としては知っておくべき店である。料理はどちらかというとクラシックで、店の大部分が若い女性客で占められている。デザートには工夫があって楽しい。

PHRIK KHII NUU

2-9-5 Asagaya Kita,
Suginami-ku
Tel: 3336-6414
Open: 5-11pm; closed Tue.

Thai
¥¥
★★ 1/2

 **Map 73**

A snug little wooden house of a restaurant content to serve good standard Thai food rather than flashy regional dishes or other exotica. Despite its name (a *phrik khii nuu* is the smallest and hottest of Thai chilies) they tend to go easy on the heat unless instructed otherwise. The place is no longer the secret it once was, which presents a problem: they've converted a fairly oppressive upstairs bedroom into additional seating and will try to put you there if it's full below. It's best to resist.

木造のこぢんまりしたこの店は、派手でエキゾチックなものより、オーソドックスなタイ料理を出すことを心掛けているようだ。店名はタイでも最も辛い唐辛子を意味しているが、特にこちらが指定しなければ、どちらかといえば辛さは控え目。ここも以前のように、知る人ぞ知るという店ではなく、今では混雑していて、階下が満席だと2階の寝室を改装した、気が滅入るような部屋に通されてしまう。

ピッキーヌー

*It always has been worth a trip for Inokashira Park. Now **Kichijoji** finally has a good range of worthwhile food, too. Apart from branches of **Nanbantei**, **Samrat** and **Toriyoshi** (see listings), we're fond of the Okinawan cooking at **Ryuku** (1-29-5 Kichijoji Honcho, 0422-21-6015), and the unadulterated Thai food at **Sukhothai** (2-2-10 Kichijoji Honcho, 0422-20-2600).*

PILSEN

6-8-7 Ginza,
Chuo-ku
Tel: 3571-3443
Open: Noon-10pm;
Sun. & hol. until 9pm

Beer restaurant
¥¥
★

  Map 7

Unequaled beer hall ambiance (the building dates from 1929, Pilsen itself from 1951) and exactly the right beverage: the Czech Pilsner Urquell, *ur*-type for the world's favorite style of beer. A mostly liquid diet works best here—their food appears modeled on the hotel restaurants of Moscow—but respecters of tradition will want to order the "chicken basket."

Not quite as atmospheric, but equally famed and even bigger is Sapporo's **Lion Beer Hall** at 7-9-20 Ginza (3571-2590) with marginally better food.

世界で最もポピュラーなピルズナーラガー・ビールの原型となったチェコ産のPilsner Urquellを飲むには、1929年に建てられたビルの中にある1951年創業のこのビアホールはぴったりの雰囲気だ。ただ、料理はモスクワのホテルのレストランを思い起こしてしまい、とてもお薦めできないが、昔から人気のあるチキンバスケットだけはおつまみになる。雰囲気では劣るが、有名で規模も大きい『サッポロライオンビアホール』（中央区銀座7-9-20（☎）3571-2590）は、料理が多少ここよりましといったところだろう。

ピルゼン

PIZZERIA SABATINI

2-13-5 Kita Aoyama,
Minato-ku
Tel: 3402-2027
Open: 11:30am-2:30pm
& 5:30-11pm

Italian
¥¥ 1/2
★★★

CC ⬛ ✈ **Map 11**

ピッツェリア・
サバティーニ

Word has it that *sabatini* is Italian dialect for "to overcharge, to bilk." We've been sabatinied once or twice ourselves, but not here. Sabatini di Roma's "budget" outlet, located in the basement next to the main restaurant on Aoyama-dori, cuts prices without cutting any visible corners. True, a main course of fish or meat quickly moves into ¥¥¥¥ territory, but that's optional: the focus here is on pastas (above average) and pizzas (maybe the best in town). Optional too are their heavyweight wines—the house red will do quite nicely, thanks. And what a pleasure to have truly professional service in a restaurant of this class. But call ahead or prepare for a long wait in a crowded *genkan*.

東京には「サバティーニ」という名の店が多くて紛らわしく、どこも正気の沙汰とは思えない値段であるというところが共通点だ。しかしここは『サバティーニ・ディ・ローマ』の廉価版ということもあって、例外的に良心的な値段だ。魚や肉料理をメインにした高価なコースや、高級なワインもあるが、中心はピッツァ（東京でナンバーワンといわれている）やパスタだ。サービスは高級店にも負けないが、予約をしないと混雑した入口で長時間待たされることを覚悟しなくてはならない。

It seems Japan always has a cheap all-you-can-eat meat cuisine of the moment. A decade ago it was *yakiniku* Korean barbecue. Today it's *churrasco*: great masses of meat carved off spits directly onto your plate, Brazilian style. Insatiable carnivores might want to start with Barbacoa Grill (4-3-24 Jingu-mae, Shibuya-ku, 3796-0571), a branch of the São Paulo original, and Super Bacana (6-8-5 Ginza, Chuo-ku, 3573-5499), featuring live samba.

POMME DE TERRE

5-31-3 Daita, Setagaya-ku
Tel: 3419-6981
Open: 11:30am-2pm &
5-11pm; closed Mon.

French
¥¥
★★

[cc] 🏯 **Map 21**

ポム・ド・テエル

Along with **Gorger**, the best of the Jackpot ventures. Similar wine and food (fish is best avoided at all Jackpots in favor of meat and especially duck and chicken). Less appealing seating inside—just a long cramped row of tables—so come early (or reserve) and capture a table on the front patio, where the summer fragrance of jasmine mixes with the wafting smoke of the mosquito coil at your feet.

『ゴージェジャックポット』と同じく、ジャックポット系列では一番のレストラン。ワインも食事の味も、値段の安いところも同じだ。この店に限らず、ジャックポットのどのレストランでも魚料理はお薦めしないが、肉料理は美味しく特に鶏肉、鴨料理がお薦め。

PONTE VECCHIO

2-1-1 Shibuya,
Shibuya-ku
Tel: 3400-7765
Open: Noon-3pm & 6-11pm;
Sat., noon-3pm & 5-11pm;
Sun. & hol., 5-11pm

Italian
¥¥¥
★★★ 1/2

[cc] 🔁 **Map 20**

ポンテベッキオ

Seafood specialists with a Japanese sensitivity for their materials. Ask for the ¥5000/person dinner and prepare for an orchestrated progression of dishes. This is real-time dining: between courses they come to your table and you work out the next course together. Superlative date venue; it couldn't be cozier or more intimate, and they have a knack for making you feel like honored guests *and* personal friends.

ここの魚介類料理には和食の繊細な気遣いがなされている。店内の居心地もよく、サービスも完璧。ひとり5000円のディナーコースを注文すると、最高のタイミングで美味しい料理が次々と運ばれてくる。ロマンティックで最高の気分だ。

RAJ MAHAL

Urban Bldg., 4F,
7-13-2 Roppongi,
Minato-ku
Tel: 5411-2525
Open: 11:30am-10:30pm

Indian
¥ 1/2
★★★

  Map 18

ラージ・
マハール

Perhaps it's unfair to think of Raj Mahal, as many of us tend to, as simply a **Moti** competitor. Certainly they offer many of the same curries and tandoori dishes, though not always to the same high standard (notably their *nan*). But the Raj chefs excel at vegetarian curries, particularly the specials on the menu insert. With 99 percent of their customers always ordering the same dozen or so Mogul clichés, no wonder they try a bit harder when challenged. There's a branch near Tokyu Hands in Shibuya (3770-7677).

ついついこの店を『モティ』の競争相手としてしか見ないが、それではここを正しく評価出来ないかも知れない。確かに両者は同じようなカレーやタンドーリ料理を出している。味は必ずしも同レベルとはいかないこともあるが、ベジタリアンカレー、特に日替わりスペシャルはこちらが上回っている。客の99％が決まり切ったインド料理を注文する中で、オリジナルなものを生みだそうとする努力は評価できる。渋谷東急ハンズの近くに支店（☎）3770-7677がある。

REIKYO

2-25-18 Dogenzaka,
Shibuya-ku
Tel: 3461-4220
Open: Noon-2pm & 5pm-12:30am; closed Thur.

Taiwanese
¥¥
★★

Map 19

麗郷

So bustling and Asian that it took us years to realize that the cooking here isn't really as wonderful as everyone seems to assume. Not that it needs to be: Reikyo is a Tokyo classic. Recommended: *chimaki* (leaf-wrapped sticky rice with pork and spices), *chozume* (sweet Taiwanese sausage with garlic) and steamed or fried *asari* clams. Non-smokers, bring aqualung.

あまりにも有名で人気があるために、この店の料理は多くの人が思うほどのものではないことに気付くまで、ずいぶん時間が掛かってしまった。どうしたことか、今では東京の名所になっている。ちまき、腸詰め、蒸したもしくは炒めたアサリがお薦め。

REQUIEM

An unfortunate name to be sure—the owner dotes on Mozart—but Requiem is beyond question the city's finest wine bar. The list bristles with ¥10,000-plus Bordeaux and Burgundies, names to gladden the hearts of the Nihon Wine Academy (just upstairs). Fortunately, Mr. Tamaoki, Requiem's sober young manager and guiding light, will happily find you something good for less than half that.

Among the attractions are dozens of new-wave Italian wines available nowhere else in Japan, a huge French collection, a decent-sized stock of Germans and Californians and even the rogue Southern Hemisphere bottle. Recommended food: stews (oxtail if they have it), cream sauce pastas and cheese plates.

6-24-4 Jingu-mae,
Shibuya-ku
Tel: 5485-1426
Open: 6pm-midnight; Sat.
until 2am; closed Sun. & hol.

Wine
¥¥¥
★★★ 1/2

[CC] **Map 6**

モーツァルトの「レクイエム」を店名にしていて、どうもこれからは葬式を連想して、縁起が良くないが、何といってもここは東京でいちばんのワインバーだ。分厚いワインリストの1万円以上のところにはボルドーやバーガンディーから、店の2階にある「日本ワインアカデミー」の関係者が見たら生唾を飲み込むような銘柄まで書かれている。もちろん、若いが落ちつきのあるマネージャーの玉置氏は、もっと大衆的な値段のものも親切に教えてくれる。日本中でこの店でしか飲めない12種類ほどのイタリアワインから、フランス、ドイツ、カリフォルニア、オーストラリア産まで、数多く揃っている。シチュー各種（もしオックステールに巡り合えれば幸運だ）、クリームのパスタ、チーズの盛り合わせなどがお薦め。

レクイエム

For a closer look at Japan's *health food* scene, pick up the *Natural Restaurant Guide* (Shibata Shoten). It's in Japanese, but with English summaries of about 60 vegetarian, organic and macrobiotic restaurants around Tokyo, and another couple dozen in Kansai.

RERA CHISE

It took until 1994, but now Tokyo has its first Ainu restaurant since pre-Yamato times. Apart from sheer obscurity value, it's well worth a trip for the food: *chiporo imo* (mashed potatoes, *ikura*, and *tsubukai* shellfish); fresh, simply prepared fish like *chep* (Ainu for *shake*, i.e. salmon) and *nishin* (herring); and game in season including boar and venison.

Rera Chise is as much a casual drinking scene as a restaurant, so simply order as you go along. The low prices attract an enthusiastic young crowd (Waseda University is just down the street), and the place is already becoming a magnet for interest in Ainu culture and activism.

YK Bldg., B1,
2-1-19 Nishi Waseda,
Shinjuku-ku
Tel: 3202-7642
Open: 11am-2pm & 5-11pm;
closed Sun. & 3rd Mon.

Ainu
¥
★★

Map 24

レラ・チセ

東京にようやく初めて出来たアイヌ料理の店。珍しいだけでなく、その料理の味は足を運ぶ価値が十分ある。お薦めはチポロ・イモ（マッシュポテトにイクラとツブ貝を混ぜたもの）、新鮮でシンプルに調理されたカヌイ・チェップ（シャケ）やニシンなどの魚類、またイノシシやシカの肉も楽しめる。ここはレストランであると同時にカジュアルな飲み屋でもあり、値段が安いことと、早稲田大学が近いことで若者たちが多く集まり活気がある。そして今や、アイヌ文化や社会問題について語り合う東京の中心的存在になりつつある。

RICE TERRACE

The cream of the current Thai crop. Unbeatable food and an ambiance that somehow combines coziness and sophistication, provided you get a table downstairs—upstairs feels a little plain and claustrophobic.

Recommendations here can only scratch the surface, but consider the *nam phrik kapi*, which is carved vegetables with the fiery, fermented shrimp dip that expatriate Thais miss more than anything else (perhaps because it's so inexplicably

2-7-9 Nishi Azabu,
Minato-ku
Tel: 3498-6271
Open: Noon-2pm & 6-11pm;
closed Sun. & hol.

Thai
¥¥
★★★1/2

 **Map 17**

hard to find outside of Thailand). Rice Terrace reins in the chilies a bit, but the taste is right on target. So, too, the *khaao kluk kapi*, a heaping plate of rice fried in shrimp paste surrounded by morsels of sweet pork, dried shrimp, raw mango, slivers of egg and little purple onions.

The only disappointments to date: the curries can be variable, and the less said of the wines, the better.

タイ料理店の中では最近もっとも気に入っている店で、抜群の料理と洗練されてはいるが親しめる雰囲気を合わせ持っている。ただ2階は1階とは違い狭い息苦しく感じる。タイ本国以外ではなかなかお目にかかることのできない生野菜をエビを発酵させた激辛ソースに付けるナム・プリック・カピも、一度試す価値はある。多少唐辛子を控え目にしているこの味付けは的を得ているようで、エビのペーストを甘い豚肉、マンゴ、卵、玉ねぎでくるみ、揚げたお米に盛ったカオ・クルック・カピに、その特徴が見える。欲をいえば、もう少しカレー種類を増やしてもらいたい。

ライス テラス

*An encouraging example of Asian culinary cross-fertilization: **Thai suki** began with sukiyaki in the Japanese restaurants of Bangkok. The Thais jazzed it up with various other meats and fish, and added a spicy dipping sauce. Now it has been reimported into Japan and enjoys cult popularity at places like Kinshicho's **Thailand** (3625-7215) and **Tokyo Koka** (3280-0008) in Shirokane. Also becoming known as Thai shabu.*

ROBATA

Japan abounds with restaurants that excel at whatever style of cooking they've chosen to recreate. Much rarer is the place that has fashioned cuisine of its own, one that eludes categorization and transcends description. Robata, in its Taisho-era farmhouse setting in the heart of Hibiya, is one.

Consider a typical platter of *o-tsumami no moriawase* ("mixed appetizers"): chunks of tender marinated octopus and onion; beef tongue in *moromi* (saké lees); spinach leaf and cherry tomatoes in a tart white dressing; a stir-fry of green beans, shrimp, ginko nuts and eggs; a curry-spiced paté; a big sheaf of fresh *wakame* tips; a couple plump marinated oysters; spicy sautéed beef with garlic sprouts; melt-in-the-mouth salmon in an orientalized tartar sauce; and at least one or two more things, unidentifiable but luscious. Then it's time to poke around the kitchen and order some serious soups and stews.

There's no sign to speak of, no menu, no reservations and—need it be said—seldom an empty seat.

1-3-8 Yurakucho,
Chiyoda-ku
Tel: 3591-1905
Open: 6-11pm;
closed Sun. & hol.

Izakaya
¥¥
★★★★
Map 7

詩人でもある主人の井上さんは、自らの料理を「おふくろの味」と称している。しかしその料理は芸術の域に達しているといえて、和食とも洋食とも簡単には区別できず、彼自身の興味、実直や正直さを反映したものになっている。前菜の盛り合わせだけでも、柔らかいタコと玉ねぎのマリネ、牛タンのもろみ漬け、ホウレン草とプチトマトのホワイトドレッシング和え、グリーンピース、エビ、銀杏、卵の炒めもの、カレー風味のパテ、生わかめ、カキのマリネ、牛肉のソテーにニンニクの芽の和え物、とろけるようなサーモンの和風タルタルソースかけなどと、とにかく美味しいものが勢揃いしている。メニューは置いていないから、キッチンを見渡して美味しそうなものを探し出すのが楽しい。

炉端

ROGOVSKI

Owada Bldg., 2F,
16-13 Sakuragaokacho,
Shibuya-ku
Tel: 3463-2911
Open: 11:30am-10pm

Russian
¥¥
★★ 1/2

 **Map 19**

ロゴスキー

The **Moti** of our Russian restaurants: big, efficient and deservedly popular. Favorite orders: rich, tangy Ukranian borscht; flavorful, non-greasy piroshki; the ravioli-like Siberian *perimeni* in its buttery broth; and the Chicken Kiev cutlet. To drink they have Russian wines, vodkas and even *kvass*, the summertime cooler brewed from bread.

Despite a move into a new building a few years back, Rogovski has managed to recreate its old overwrought Disneyland czarist decor and music. But then who could imagine it any other way? For Russian food in a more authentic environment, check out the ancient, moldering **Samovar** nearby at 2-22-5 Dogenzaka, Shibuya-ku (3462-0648).

ロシア料理界の『モティ』ともいえる、巨大でパワーがあり、そして人気がある店。リッチな味のウクライナ風ボルシチ、脂っこくなく香り高いピロシキ、こってりしたスープに入っていて水餃子に似ているシベリア風ペリメニ、キエフ風チキンカツレツなどがお薦め。飲み物は、ロシアワイン、ウォッカ、パンから作られヒンヤリした夏向きの飲み物クヴァスがある。数年前に新しいビルに越したが、ディズニーランドとロシア帝政風を折衷したようなこの店独特の内装と音楽は再現されている。横浜に支店（☎）045-321-6666 がある。

ROS MARINO

2-19-1 Miyasaka, Setagaya-ku
Tel: 3706-8580
Open: 11:45am-2pm &
5:30-11pm; closed Mon.

Italian
¥
★★
Map 74

ロス・マリノ

A clean, simple neighborhood place worth at least a detour (it's near Kyodo Station on the Odakyu Line). Reduced to its basics—a couple pastas to share, a few baskets of bread, a ¥2200 bottle of Corvo red—a civilized Southern European meal here will cost as little as anywhere in town.

小田急線経堂駅近くにあって、洗練された南欧料理が気楽に安く食べられ、一度は回り道をしてでも、立ち寄ってみたいと思える店。ふたりで2種類のパスタとパン、2200円の Corvo の赤を一本注文してシェアするのが似合うような素朴な雰囲気だ。

ROSOKANABEJO

1-6-14 Hyakunincho,
Shinjuku-ku
Tel: 3200-3515
Open: Noon-3am

Taiwanese
¥¥
★★ 1/2
Map 22

Well, at least they think their name in Japanese is Rosokanabejo. It's part of the charm here that no one seems quite sure. Run by a young Taiwanese couple with some short-term cooks shuttled up from Taipei, it's a place that serves good food in almost TV sit-com style. Drop by here for a night of that old just-off-the-boat fun.

Recommended for appetizers with your beer: clams with garlic, goose with sweet basil, duck with ginger, pig's feet or beef tendon with coriander leaf, spiced tofu, *chozume* sausage and *aona* ("green vegetables"), quick fried with plenty of garlic. The main dish of choice: Taiwanese-style "shabu-shabu," which is in fact closer to a Singapore-style steamboat of fish balls, fish, shrimp, tofu and heaps of vegetables. Old China hands will insist on drinking *shokoshu* (*shaohsing* in Chinese), a brown rice wine of moderate but deceptive strength.

若い台湾人のカップルが経営している店。台北から短期的に来日した料理人が腕をふるってくれるので、活気ある雰囲気の中で美味しい料理が食べられる。お薦めは、まずビールによく合う前菜か

老曹火鍋城

ら。アサリニンニク、ガチョウのスイート
バジル風味、鴨のショウガ和え、豚足、牛
スジのコリアンダー風味、豆腐、腸詰め、
青菜のニンニク炒めなど。メインとして
は、ここではシャブシャブと呼んでいる特
製台湾鍋。これはつみれ、魚、海老、豆
腐、野菜などを入れたシンガポール鍋に近
いもので美味しい。飲み物はやはり紹興酒
にしたい。

---

*Despite the recent boomlet in Iranian restaurants,
Tokyo still lags behind most other culinary
capitals in **Middle Eastern food**. But here's an
inexpensive newcomer that can match the best of
them: the Israeli-run **Adama** at 3-12-32 Moto-
Azabu, Minato-ku, tel. 5411-2735.*

ROYAL BENGAL

Gyoeido Bldg., 5F,
2-3-2 Nihonbashi Ningyocho,
Chuo-ku
Tel: 3249-6919
Open: 11am-10:30pm
(last order)

Bangladeshi
¥¥
★★

 Map 16

ロイヤル・
ベンガル

Curries much in the style of **Moti** & co., but
the emphasis rather seems to be on kebabs
and other meat dishes, all prepared to *halal*
standards. It's easily the best Indian food in
this corner of town. Royal Bengal has a
branch at 1-16-14 Shibuya (3498-0916).

『モティ』系のカレーを出す店だが、ここ
ではすべてハラル（ムスリムのしきたり）
の基準で作られているケバブを中心とした
肉料理に力を入れている。この界隈では文
句なくナンバーワンのインド料理店といえ
よう。渋谷支店（渋谷区渋谷1-16-14（☎）
3498-0916）もある。

RYUKYU SHUKAN

Ukeshima Bldg., 2F,
5-57-2 Nakano,
Nakano-ku
Tel: 3388-2379
Open: 5pm-midnight

Okinawan
¥¥
★★
Map 15

Down-home Okinawan cooking buried in the alleyways of Nakano. We're addicted to the *goya champuru* (a stir-fry of tofu and the bumpy, bitter *nigauri*), *konbuirichi* (seaweed and pork, and better than it sounds) and *tofuyo* (an ultra-concentrated salted tofu, to be nibbled in the tiniest of bites). To drink, there's *awamori*, Okinawa's native rocket fuel.

Tokyo has more atmospheric Okinawan places (like Shinjuku's **Nanpu**) but none that better captures the easy-going—dare we say it?—un-Japanese flavor of the southern isles.

中野の裏道に、埋もれたように佇む沖縄家庭料理の店。ゴーヤ・チャンプル、昆布イリチ、豆腐ヨウなどを、アルコール度数の選べる泡盛とともに試すと良い。東京にはもっと雰囲気のある沖縄料理店（例えば、新宿の『南風』）もあるが、琉球風の気楽な空気を楽しむならここだろう。

琉球酒館

RYUNOHIGE

31-8 Udagawacho,
Shibuya-ku
Tel: 3461-5347
Open: 11am-11pm (last order)

Taiwanese
¥¥
★★
Map 19

Debate still occasionally arises over which is better, Ryunohige ("The Dragon's Whisker") or the nearby **Reikyo**. Once inside, is there really any difference? We suggest the usuals: the sweet Taiwanese sausage with garlic, some *chimaki*, a couple stir-fries and maybe a big plate of noodles.

近所にある『麗郷』と比較され、どちらが美味しいかと議論されることが多いが、どちらも似たようなものだ。腸詰め、チマキ、炒めもの、麺類などのスタンダードなものを注文すれば良い。

龍の髭

RYUNOKO

Kato Bldg., B1,
1-8-5
Jingu-mae,
Shibuya-ku
Tel: 3402-9419
Open: 11:30am-3pm
& 5-10pm

Sichuan
¥¥
★★★
Map 6

龍の子

A bit of a dive, unless they've finally gotten around to redecoration between press time and when you read this. Let's hope not—its habitués would feel lost.

Recommended: *banbanji* (cold sliced chicken and cucumber in rich sesame sauce), the cold pork in garlic sauce, *suigyoza*, the Sichuan-style spicy fried eggplant or chicken, and the *tantanmen* (noodles with minced meat, chilies and sesame paste).

10年以上も通っている間に、値段は上がり、店内はどんどん汚れていくが、本物の四川料理を食べるならやっぱりここだ。棒々鶏、冷やし豚肉のニンニクソースかけ、水餃子、茄子や鶏肉の揚げ物四川風、担々麺などは相変わらず旨い。

SABADO SABADETE

5-3-2 Shirokane-dai,
Minato-ku
Tel: 3445-9353
Open: 6-11pm;
closed Sun. & hol.

Spanish
¥¥
★★

Map 14

サバドサバデテ

Benito used to make a living making jewelry. Then he started cooking the food of his native Catalonia at parties, and one thing led to another. Best to go light on the *tapas* here—they're better elsewhere—and focus on the good paella and chicken dishes.

オーナーのベニート氏はかつてジュエリーを作っていたが、パーティーなどで故郷のカタロニア料理を作って出したのがきっかけとなって、今ではレストランを始めてしまった。ここではパエリアやチキン料理が何といっても美味しい。

SACÌ PERERÊ

Mitsuoka Yotsuya Bldg., B1,
9 Hon-Shiocho, Shinjuku-ku
Tel: 3226-5888
Open: 6pm-midnight;
closed Sun. & hol.

Brazilian
¥¥¥
★★ 1/2

[cc] **Map 75**

pepper or garlic steak rounds good.

*Samba Band
Meal ¥4000
Caipernesa Cocktail*
サッシペレレ ¥800

Songstress Lisa Ono's dad has been running this bar/restaurant/dance club longer than most of us have been of legal drinking age. Apart from live samba—dancing is practically mandatory here—the big draw is Tokyo's best *feijoada completa,* OK the Brazilian national meal of black beans, pork and all the trimmings. Authenticity demands either Brahma Beer or *cachaça* (sugar cane liquor) with crushed limes, sugar and ice. Prices invariably mount, but there's seldom cause to regret it.

歌手、小野リサの父親が長年経営している店で、ここはバー、レストラン、ダンスクラブを兼ねている。この店になくてはならないライブのサンバダンスは別として、東京一の美味しさと評判なのが黒豆と豚肉などを入れたブラジルの国民的料理フェジョアーダである。また飲み物では Brahma ビールやライムと砂糖、氷を入れたサトウキビのリキュール、バチーダも見逃せない。値段はどれも高めだが、楽しい夜は保証付きだ。

SAIGON

1-7-10 Higashi Ikebukuro,
Toshima-ku
Tel: 3989-0255
Open: 11:30am-10:30pm

Vietnamese
¥¥
★★ 1/2

Map 76

We complain elsewhere about the current lack of quality Vietnamese food in Tokyo, but Ikebukuro's Saigon should satisfy most cravings in the meantime. True, their shrimp and pineapple soup—sour seafood soups are one of Vietnam's finest culinary achievements—disappoints sadly. But the appetizers, like the fried and raw spring rolls, are more than serviceable, and we'll definitely give two thumbs up for the *gyuniku no tsuboyaki*: a pot of spiced beef, to be rolled up piece by piece with lettuce and sauce (great dipping sauces here) in a rice pancake.

東京ではタイ、カンボジア、ビルマの美味しい料理を出す店はかなりあるが、ベトナムとなるとグッと少なく、どうしてもここに足が向いてしまう。エビとパイ

ナップルのスープ（この酸味のある魚介類のスープはベトナム料理が生み出した究極の味である）には、残念ながらがっかりさせられるが、牛春巻や揚げ春巻などの前菜は美味しいし、レタスやソースと一緒に米のパンケーキに包んで食べる牛肉の壷焼きは絶対お薦め。また、10種類以上もの世界のビールも安く楽しめる。

サイゴン

SAKANA-TEI

Casual decor in the concrete bunker genre, four communal counter-style tables, service by friendly *o-basan*—this has to be one of Tokyo's most approachable outlets for top-quality saké. Sakana-tei features about ten featured labels per day, plus a regular list of dozens of small and large bottles. They do take the stuff seriously: you're limited to one beer at most, and only three of the sakés can even be ordered warm. (Realize that asking for a *ginjoshu* to be served warm is like ordering the sommelier to heat up your Montrachet.)

Lots of thoughtful touches with the food, from the *aonori* (fresh raw *nori* seaweed) to the Shizuoka *wasabi* root and sharkskin grater that comes with the sashimi. Recommended: *kakuni* (Chinese-style stewed pork), and crab and scallop *tamago-yaki* (not unlike a Spanish omelet).

Koike Bldg., 4F,
2-23-15 Dogenzaka,
Shibuya-ku
Tel: 3780-1313
Open: 5:30-11pm (last order); closed Sun. & hol.

Izakaya
¥¥
★★★

 **Map 19**

東京に数ある安い居酒屋で、料理も地酒も充実した店は案外少ない。そんな中でここは質も値段も文句ない店と自信をもっているのだ。ここでは最高級の酒が気軽に飲めるのだ。店内はカジュアルなコンクリートの打ち放しで、相席テーブルが４つあるだけで、親切なおばさんが給仕してくれる。日本酒リストは常に用意してあるものの他、毎日変わるその日のお薦めが約10種あるが、飲み方にはルールがあって、ビールはひとり１本、お酒は熱燗を３種類までしか注文できない。新鮮な青のり、静岡産のワサビ、刺し身のツマにはフカの皮をおろしたものまでついてきて、細部にまで配慮が行き届いている。

酒菜亭

SAMRAT

Piaza Omiya Bldg., 3F,
2-25-17 Kitazawa,
Setagaya-ku
Tel: 5454-1871
Open: 11am-10pm

Indian
¥ 1/2
★★ 1/2

Map 21

While the older Shibuya (3496-9410) and Roppongi (3478-5877) branches don't stand up to the heavy local competition, Samrat's familiar tandooris and northern-style curries are a welcome addition to Shimo-Kitazawa. They're also hard to beat these days on price: the lunch set is down to ¥850; dinners from ¥1980. And if we have to be beaten about the head with "Indian" decor, this branch is about as tasteful as it gets—lots of dark wood and low-keyed lighting. Also worth keeping in mind are their locations in Ueno (5688-3226) and Kichijoji (0422-20-8670).

古くからある渋谷店（☎）3496-9410 や六本木店（☎）3478-5877 は地域戦争の中で苦戦しているようだが、ここ下北沢ではタンドーリや北インドカレーが確実にファンを増やしている。最近では値段も安くなり、ランチが850円、ディナーは1980円から楽しめる。内装もダークウッドでシックにまとめ、シンプルな照明でかなり上品な雰囲気を出しており、東京のインド料理店の水準を上回っている。上野店（☎）5688-3226、吉祥寺店（☎）0422-20-8670 も覚えておきたい。

サムラート

SANKT GALLEN

Tokyo's first brewpub, and the place we'll be the day the Authorities decide that they can safely legalize microbreweries without howls of protest from Japan's beer oligarchy. In the meantime come here for their refreshing near-beer (0.7 percent alcohol) and a couple full-power brews from Café Pacifica, their sister shop in San Francisco. For non-liquid nourishment they do a complete range of dim sum in cooperation with owner Mitsuo Iwamoto's **Suihan Village** restaurants (3342-5758 in Shinjuku; 3986-6410 in Ikebukuro).

6-3-10 Roppongi,
Minato-ku
Tel: 3408-0607
Open: 11:30am-3pm
& 5-10:30pm; Sat.,
Sun. & hol., 11:30am-10pm

Brewpub
¥¥
★★
Map 18

サンクト・ガーレン

ビールの醸造パブといった店が、ここ数年世界中に広がっているが、ここは東京で唯一の自家製ビールとそれに良く合う料理を出すいわゆるブラッスリー。日本の法律により、普通のビールは醸造できないが、アルコール分0.7％のぎりぎりの類似ビールは新鮮で爽快な気分にさせてくれる。また、サンフランシスコにある姉妹店『Cafe Pacifica』で醸造された本格的なビールも楽しめる。料理はオーナー、岩本光生氏の経営する『翠亨屯茶両』（新宿店（☎) 3342-5758／池袋店（☎) 3986-6410）の飲茶が食べられる。そろそろいい時期だと思うが、正式のビール醸造が解禁になれば、本物が飲める店になるはずである。

SARONIKOS

It's not in Tokyo proper, but we claim historic precedent: Tokyoites have been making the pilgrimage to Yokohama for Greek food for decades. Saronikos is last of the old breed, with no concession to fashion or even decor. Recommended: Greek salad, garlic eggplant, moussaka and the giant liver steak. If you like their retsina they'll sell you a bottle to take home.

3-40 Akebonocho,
Naka-ku, Yokohama-shi,
Kanagawa-ken
Tel: 045-251-8980
Open: 6pm-1am;
closed 1st & 3rd Mon.

Greek
¥¥
★★ 1/2

 Map 77

場所は東京からはずれるがこの店を選んだ理由は、東京人が戦後間もない時代からギリシャ料理を求めてこの横浜まで遠征していたからだ。内装や雰囲気をかたくななまでに守り続けている最後の老舗である。お薦め料理はギリシャ風サラダ、ナスのニンニク風味、ムサカ、巨大なレバーのステーキなど。松ヤニ風味のギリシャワイン、retsina が気に入れば、ボトルを買って持ち帰るのもOKだ。

サロニコス

SASA NO YUKI

2-15-10 Negishi,
Taito-ku
Tel: 3873-1145
Open: 11am-9pm;
closed Mon.

Tofu
¥¥
★★ 1/2

🆑 📰 📑 **Map 78**

Three centuries old and the word is definitely out—they even have a flashy English-language brochure. It's best to call and reserve a place on the ground floor with a view out over the carp pool (the upstairs rooms are viewless). Priced from ¥1400 to ¥4450, the courses offer some of the best value at Tokyo's tofu restaurants—more for your money than at **Goemon** or **Enjuu**—and apart from the occasional bit of chicken, it's good vegetarian fare.

根岸という粋な下町にあり、伝統的なスタイルと300年の歴史を誇る豆腐料理の老舗。ここは世界的に知られている為、派手な英語のパンフレットまで用意されている。鯉の泳ぐ池が眺められる1階の席は予約した方が確実。（2階からでは景色を楽しむことはできない。）1400円から4450円のコースは、東京の豆腐料理店の中で最も価値がある。たまに鶏肉が少し出て来るのを除けば、ベジタリアンにもぴったりの場所だ。

笹の雪

SASASHIN

2-20-3 Nihonbashi Ningyocho,
Chuo-ku
Tel: 3668-2456
Open: 5-10:30pm;
closed Sun. & hol.

Izakaya
¥¥
★★★ 1/2

Map 16

Sasashin comes preceded by so giant a reputation—the most famed izakaya in Tokyo's most famed neighborhood for izakaya—that it's a bit of a shock to find it so small and utterly plain. But that's only before the clientele streams in. Then you see what Sasashin is all about: the ultimate no-frills *Edokko* food and drink. Crowded, noisy, smoky, red-faced and rowdy every single night.

Recommended: sashimi, grilled fish, *nimono* stews and anything else that looks good on the counter. Japanese language ability will not go amiss here.

日本橋ではあまりにも有名な居酒屋だが、実際の店の狭さと地味さには驚かされてしまう。しかし、いったんこの店が混み始めると、さすが江戸っ子の町の居酒屋だけあり、店内は一気に活気づく。お薦めは、刺し身、焼き魚、煮物の他、カウンターに並べられた大皿料理も見逃せない。

笹新

*Japan eats two kinds of **eel**.* Anago *lives in the sea and appears most often at sushi shops (but not raw).* Unagi *is a fresh-water creature, finer textured and more subtly flavored. Both are at their most succulent in winter, but unagi is most often eaten in summer, when it supposedly combats heat and fatigue. For ultimate unagi, splurge at the ****/¥¥¥¥ **Juubako** at 2-17-61 Akasaka, Minato-ku (3589-1085); for good-enough unagi, find the sign that says* うなぎ *on your local shopping street.*

SASHIMIYA

3-6-19 Kita Aoyama,
Minato-ku
Tel: 3499-3438
Open: 11:30am-1:30pm &
5-11pm; closed Sun. & hol.

Japanese
¥¥

★★ 1/2

[cc] **Map 2**

三四味屋

Fish specialists worth knowing about: they're reliable, inexpensive and just a few seconds away from Omotesando Station. They have plenty of what their name promises, but the house specialty is the grilled salmon and whole deep-fried or grilled *anago* eel. To drink there's beer, wine, shochu and comprehensive cocktails—where else in the world could you team up a Moscow Mule with a *geso-age*? Choice of seating: a sushi-style counter, tables for two or *zashiki* mats.

Sashimiya is booming: other branches can be found in Shinjuku (5379-3438), Roppongi (3589-3438), Ginza (3562-3438), Kanda (3251-3438) and Kojimachi (3261-2507).

必見の魚料理専門店。安くて、美味しく、表参道のすぐそばという便利な場所にあり、その名の通り、新鮮な刺し身料理が食べられるのはもちろんだが、あえていいたいお薦めは焼き鮭と一匹丸ごと揚げるか、焼いたアナゴである。飲み物はビール、ワイン、焼酎、カクテルとひととおりあるが、モスコミュールとゲソ揚げなんていう変わったコンビネーションも試してみたい。座席はカウンターでもテーブルでも座敷でも自由に選べる。

SECCA

Landic Bldg., B1,
4-11-13 Roppongi,
Minato-ku
Tel: 3478-0070
Open: 11:30am-2:30pm
& 5pm-midnight

Thai
¥¥
★★ 1/2

Map 18

セッカ

It would be hard not to like Secca. It's a largish basement ornamented in the sort of eclectic post-modern style Japan does best, thoroughly '80s but ageing gracefully. The food is richly spiced but wholesome, and the Thai folks in the kitchen are *cooks*, not vacationing tuk-tuk drivers.

Recommended: spicy seafood salad, stir-fried crab with roasted chili paste, chicken in pandamus leaves, any of the Thai soups or curries. They have courses from ¥3500, and some of the most interesting lunches in Roppongi for just ¥900 to ¥1000.

大きな地下スペースには日本人好みの和洋折衷のポストモダンスタイルが広がっていて、誰もがここを好きにならずにはいられない店。本場タイの料理人たちが作る料理はさすがに香辛料が効いているが、ヘルシーな味わいである。お薦めは辛いシーフードサラダ、揚げたカニの唐辛子ペースト和え、パンダマスの葉に包んだ鶏肉、タイカレー、タイスープなど。コース料理は3500円から。また、ランチはたったの900円から1000円でたっぷり楽しめる。

---

*With a little luck the dull days of **Japanese beer** may be coming to an end. The Big Four (Kirin, Sapporo, Asahi, Suntory) have the expertise and the facilities to make beers as interesting as any in the world. Instead, they pursue marketing gimmickry and endless repackaging of the same basic lager style. Antediluvian law meanwhile inhibits any grassroots brewing movement. But time—and the international microbrew boom— are on the side of real beer. Stay apprised of the situation at **Sankt Gallen** and **Cerveza**.*

SEIRYUMON WEST

5-25-9 Nakamachi,
Setagaya-ku
Tel: 5707-1990
Open: 11:30am-3pm &
5:30pm-4am; Sat., 11:30-
4am; Sun., 11:30am-
11:30pm

Chinese
¥ 1/2
★ 1/2

🆑 **Map 79**

青龍門ウェスト

The food doesn't measure up to that of **Seiryumon East** in Shibuya (3496-7290)—and even theirs isn't thrilling—but then who would notice here? Cavernous post-apocalyptic decor of mangled catwalks, industrial waste and rows of pachinko machines that occasionally fill with water to *son et lumière* accompaniment. It's Tokyo as the world imagines it.

Upstairs is the stylish and intermittently very good **Roy's** (5706-6555), a kind of **Spago** Goes Hawaiian.

料理は渋谷の『青龍門イースト』にも及ばないが、その内装は一見の価値がある。ひびだらけの花道、工業廃棄物、水の入ったパチンコ台に音と光のショウまでついた世紀末的インテリアは、まさに世界が東京をイメージした通りである。2階にあるスタイリッシュな『ロイズ・レストラン』（☎) 5706-6555 は、ハワイアンスタイルの『スパゴ』といった感じ。

SELAN

2-1-19 Kita Aoyama,
Minato-ku
Tel: 3478-2200
Open: 11:30am-9:30pm;
Sat., Sun. & hol., 9am-9pm

Café
¥ ¥
★ 1/2

🆑 ◈ 🎴 **Map 11**

Impersonal service and generally insipid "Continental" food, but the setting excuses a lot: it's along the gingko-lined promenade to Jingu Gaien park. Inside is bright and airy, and they keep their outdoor terrace open year-round. In the winter, they even fire up space heaters on poles and pass out blankets to put over your knees. You feel like a sanitarium patient in the Alps. On a fine Sunday morning it's the city's prime brunch spot.

愛想のないサービスにつまらない "コンチネンタル" 料理だが、この神宮外苑のイチョウ並木沿いというロケーションの良さは見逃せない。中は明るく広々としていて、屋外のテラスもうれしいことに1年中オープンしている。冬には部分温熱器を取り付け、膝掛けまで貸してくれるので、晴れた日曜の午後にはぴったりのブランチスポットである。

セラン

SHABUZEN

10-20 Kamiyamacho,
Shibuya-ku
Tel: 3485-0800
Open: 5-11:30pm; Sat.,
Sun. & hol., 5-11pm

Shabu-shabu
¥¥
★★★

 **Map 19**

しゃぶ禅

Over a dozen branches, but this big newish one behind NHK is our favorite. Their famed all-you-can-eat shabu-shabu course is ¥3300 for the *gyu* (generic "beef," i.e. imported); ¥4300 for the *wagyu* ("Japanese beef"). Beef lovers will note that the price gap is narrowing, but that patriotic *wagyu* eaters receive a free propeller beanie—no, just kidding. In any case, there isn't much reason to stuff yourself on tough, cheap *yakiniku* or *churrasco tabehodai* elsewhere when Shabuzen provides quality merchandise for just a bit more.

12以上の支店がある中で、お気に入りはNHK裏に新しくできたここ。名物のシャブシャブ食べ放題のコースは輸入牛で3300円、和牛で4300円。特に安い焼肉やシュラスコの食べ放題を除けば、ちょっと余計に払うだけで、ここでは質の高い料理が食べられることを覚えておきたい。

SHANFON

Dai-ni Sealand Bldg., B1,
6-33-14 Okusawa,
Setagaya-ku
Tel: 3703-7757
Open: 11:30am-2pm &
5-midnight; Sat., Sun. & hol.
until 10pm

Chinese
¥¥
★★★

 **Map 12**

Designer Ryuichi Hasegawa had helped build enough restaurants for other people to know what he wanted in his own. Open the door and there's an immediate sense of *tojokan* ("arrival"): a pair of ancient painted Chinese doors, and beyond, a narrowish but high-ceilinged room, dramatically lit. Generic modern China gray has become a design statement, subtly contrasting with the richer earth colors of wood and brick. One whole wall is white shoji paper, backlit with bamboo shadows. From the best seats, along the open mezzanine floor, it feels part 1990s Tokyo, part 1930s Shanghai dancehall.

The menu is a similarly stylish production, with photographs of all 150 or so dishes. They cover a lot of geographical territory, from Shanghai and Taiwanese coastal styles to the spicy heart of Sichuan, and both portions and prices are modest enough that even a small group can try a variety.

デザイナーの長谷川隆一氏は数多くの個性的なレストランを作ってきたが、古代中国風の扉を開けるとまず圧倒されるこの店も、彼の作品のひとつである。素晴らしい照明で照らし出される幅は狭いが天井の高い部屋は、チャイナグレイがレンガの色と柔らかいコントラストをかもし出している。障子紙でできた壁には竹の影が映し出され、吹き抜けの中2階にある特等席に座ると、90年代の東京と30年代の上海のダンスホールを同時に体験しているような錯覚にとらわれるようだ。メニューも150もの皿の写真をちりばめたしゃれた作りで、料理は上海から台湾、四川にまで及ぶ。量も値段もほどほどなので、小人数のグループでいろいろな料理を取って楽しむのがいいだろう。

香風

SHINSEKAI

The complete Malay peninsula foodstall experience, tucked into an ex-soba shop behind Kabukicho and serving mostly expat Asians 24 hours a day. By about 4am, you may begin to see some *very* strange things around here. Singaporean/Malaysian standards include *char kuay teow* (flat fried noodles), chili crab, and chicken in hot coconut curry. Mind-bendingly authentic.

1-16-19 Okubo,
Shinjuku-ku
Tel: 3200-5545
Open: 24 hours a day

Southeast Asian Chinese
¥
★★★
Map 22

歌舞伎町裏の以前はそば屋があった場所にできた24時間営業の店。ここは東京に在住する多くのアジア人向けで、東南アジアの屋台そのものといった店だ。午前4時頃がまさにそのピークで、平たい麺を炒めたチャークウェーティオー、唐辛子風味のカニ、ココナッツカレーで和えたチキンなどが美味しい。スタンダードなシンガポール／マレーシア料理はさすが本物の味である。

新世界

SHIN-YOKOHAMA RAMEN HAKUBUTSUKAN

2-14-21 Shin-Yokohama,
Kohoku-ku, Yokohama-shi,
Kanagawa-ken
Tel: 045-471-0503
Open: 11am-10pm;
closed Tue.

Ramen
¥
★★

Map 80

新横浜ラーメン博物館

Surely the world's only *ramen* theme park. Start on the third floor and review the history and making of Japanese-style Chinese noodles. Then on to the real attraction: the bottom two floors, a movie set re-creation of a typical Tokyo neighborhood circa 1957—that watershed year in which instant ramen was allegedly invented. You have your choice of eight ramen shops, chosen by taste-testers from hundreds nationwide. When that tires, there are various other stores to browse, and even a bar and izakaya.

Entry is ¥300 but ramenophiles can buy a three-month pass for just ¥1000.

世界で唯一のラーメンテーマパークである。まず3階へ行って日本の中華麺の歴史を覗いてみよう。そしていよいよ吹き抜けになっている1、2階へ。ここには日本に初めてラーメンが登場したとされる1957年頃の東京の町が再現されている。東宝美術が映画のセットのように作ったものだが、その雰囲気はなかなかよくでている。ラーメン愛好家たちの舌にかなった8種類のラーメン屋が軒を連ねているが、お薦めは博多ラーメン。ラーメンを満喫した後はバーや居酒屋などに寄ってみるのもいいだろう。入場料は300円だが、1000円の3ヵ月有効パスも用意されている。

SHIZENKAN II

Half health food store, half restaurant, Shizenkan II draws a steady clientele of Shibuya housewives, retirees, students and the more health-oriented local office workers, mainly female. Most choose the ¥950 *butikku* ("boutique") *teishoku*, a daily set that includes a smallish main dish, a scoop of brown rice (free seconds) and up to a dozen little *o-kazu*. It's not without its hints of the school cafeteria, but it's varied and interesting, low on the calories and served all day. Shizenkan II makes a fine place for a quiet solo meal, a

3-9-2 Shibuya,
Shibuya-ku
Tel: 3486-0281
Open: 11am-8pm (last order);
closed Sun. & hol.

Vegetarian
¥
★★

❌🚭 **Map 20**

自然館パートⅡ

spot of tea and a good book—Alan Watts or
Gary Snyder would be in order.

On the other side of Shibuya Station is
Shizenkan I (3476-0591), smaller and
plainer but with similar food and the last
public oxygen dispenser we've seen in
Tokyo.

店の半分は自然食料品店、残りの半分が
レストランになっているここは、渋谷の
主婦やOL、学生、健康志向のサラリーマ
ンたち、大部分が固定客で占められてい
る。ちょっとしたメイン料理に玄米が１
膳（２膳目はただ）と、数種のおかずがつ
いた950円のブティック定食に人気があ
る。ここの味付けは時々学食風ではある
が、バラエティに富んでいて毎日食べら
れるのでありがたい。他にもいろいろな
コースはあるが、ここで出される料理は
550キロカロリーを超えるものはまずな
い。ほとんどがカップヌードル１杯分の
カロリーというわけで、ダイエット中の
人にはうれしい店だ。ひとりで静かに食
事をしたい時やお茶、読書にもぴったり
の場所である。渋谷駅の反対側には同様
の支店パートⅠ（☎）3476-0591 がある。

*Mexican and now Brazilian apart, **Latin American
food** remains pretty slim pickings in Tokyo. The best
of the rest: inexpensive, expat-acclaimed Peruvian
cooking at **Arco Iris** (3-32 Nakasaiwaicho, Saiwai-
ku, Kawasaki, (044-541-4572); Bolivian food and
musical entertainment at the long-established
Cantuta (4-9-11 Roppongi, Minato-ku, 3401-
6520); upscale Chilean cuisine at **Isadora** (1-16-29
Ebisu, Shibuya-ku, 5423-4987).*

SHUNJU

An expansive, subtly lit underground room, an impossibly long thick wooden counter cut from a single 350-year-old Nagano chestnut, a *zashiki* (tatami) area with a big *irori* charcoal fireplace, a garden behind glass—designed and lit by two of the best (Takashi Sugimoto and Harumi Fujimoto respectively): Shunju comes as close to a work of art as any basically empty space ever could.

Shunju doesn't assign itself a genre but the closest would be *kappo*, Japanese high cuisine without the contrivance or self-consciousness of kaiseki. It means appetizers like tiny radishes, baby octopus, *nanohana* greens, lightly pickled *myoga* (a type of ginger sprout) and *namako* (sea slug) served in hollowed *yuzu* citrus. Then heartier fare like oxtail soup, and fish or meat *nimono*. If you're at the irori, they'll put on a stew pot, or maybe a chunk of fish on a spit over the charcoal. It's a cuisine of near-perfect materials presented as near to that state as possible. The refinement is absolute, without a trace of fuss or wasted motion.

While Japanese restaurants at this level normally work on the basis of personal introduction, a call here to Miyashita-san (in Japanese, please) should get you in. Set a price per head and leave the rest to him.

Related to this place but considerably more affordable: the two-part Shunju (izakaya **Haru** and bar **Aki**) at 1-3-22 Mishuku, Setagaya-ku (3795-3952).

Akasaka Iinuma Bldg., B1,
2-16-19 Akasaka, Minato-ku
Tel: 5561-0009
Open: 6-11pm;
closed Sun. & hol.

Japanese
¥¥¥¥
★★★★

Map 1

ほのかな照明で照らされた広い地下スペース、樹齢350年という長野の栗の木を使った信じがたいほど長い木のカウンターに大きな囲炉裏のあるお座敷、そしてガラス越しに見える庭園など、ここはインテリアと照明の世界では最高峰に位置する杉本貴志氏と藤本晴美氏の手による、アート空間と呼ぶにふさわしい店である。料理はジャンルにとらわれず、二十日ダイコンやイイダコ、菜の花、ミョ

ウガ、くりぬいたユズの皮に入れられた
ナマコからオックステールのスープ、魚
料理、肉を使った煮物など、しいていえ
ば割烹料理に近いメニューが並ぶ。囲炉
裏端に座れば、鍋物や串にさして炭火で
焼いた魚なども食べられる。値段は高い
が完璧な材料を完璧に調理してくれるの
で納得。大衆派には居酒屋の『春』とバー
の『秋』の、2部に分かれた支店（世田谷
区三宿1-3-22（☎）3795-3952）もある。

春秋

SIAM

Siam has positioned itself as the value
leader in Tokyo Thai food, mainly through
their ¥1000 all-you-can-eat lunch buffet
every day of the year. It's not up to the
level of a good 250-baht Bangkok hotel
buffet, but considering that ¥1000 *is* 250
baht who's complaining? Typically there's
only one curry, but loads of stir-fries,
noodles, rice dishes, soups and even some
Thai desserts and unlimited coffee.
Dinner, either à la carte or by set course
(boring) comes to about three times as
much, and that's still cheap.

Various branches, most convenient of
which are at 5-8-17 Ginza, Chuo-ku (3572-
4101) and 3-9-4 Akasaka, Minato-ku
(3505-0550). Avoid these at all costs
during Japan's official noon-1pm lunch
break.

1-15-8 Jinnan,
Shibuya-ku
Tel: 3770-0550
Open: 11:30am-3pm &
5:30-10:30pm

Thai
¥ 1/2
★★ 1/2

 Map 19

1000円で食べ放題のランチによって一躍
有名になったタイ料理の店。バンコクに
よくある250バーツのホテルのビュッフェ
には劣るが、250バーツが1000円だと考
えると、これほど得なレストランはなか
なか探せないだろう。カレーは一種類だ
が炒めものは豊富で、麺類、ご飯類、
スープ、デザート、コーヒーなどが楽し
める。

サイアム

SICILIA

5-1-1 Roppongi
Tel: 3405-4653
Open: 5pm-2am;
Sun. & hol., 5-11pm

Italian
¥¥
★★

 Map 18

シシリア

Cheap pizza and chianti in graffiti-encrusted catacombs more or less directly below the main Roppongi intersection. It's been here more than 30 years and looks it—and suddenly, in the last couple of years, it's more popular than ever.

六本木交差点のほぼ真下にある、この落書きだらけの穴ぐらみたいなレストランでは、安いピッツァとキャンティが味わえる。オープンしてすでに30年以上もたっているが、いまだ深夜族には人気のようだ。

SIN

Luna House, Part 4, B1,
3-35-15 Jingu-mae,
Shibuya-ku
Tel: 3470-0400
Open: 11:45am-2:30pm
& 6-10:30pm (last order);
closed Sun.

Italian
¥¥¥
★★ 1/2

CC **Map 11**

シン

They call it "Sexy Italian." We say it's Tokyo most frightening dinner: you sit directly below some exceptionally sharp-looking sheets of steel hanging from the ceiling. (A pity Turia isn't still around for dancing afterwards.) Reliable Italianesque food if you don't let them get too inventive, and there's no shortage of wine. It's designed for dating, and judging by appearances, it's devastatingly effective.

自称"セクシーイタリアン"と呼んでいるようだが、私にいわせれば東京で最も恐ろしいレストランである。なぜなら天井からとても鋭利に見える鉄板が下がっていて、その真下に座らなければならないからだ。しかし、シンプルなイタリア料理を楽しむのであれば、ここは悪くない。ワインも豊富に揃っている。デートスポットとしては充分に効果的な店だ。

Potentially the most far-reaching restaurant trend in Tokyo as this book goes to press: *stylish ultra-cheap dining* at a new wave of big American-style eateries. Bellini's Pizza Kitchen is typical: intriguing food and lively atmosphere at "family restaurant" prices. But latest and greatest has to be Farm Grill (2F Ginza 9, 8-5 Ginza, Chuo-ku, tel. 5568-6156), a chic '90s update on the mass-market steakhouses of the '60s. It's colossal in size and remarkable in quality.

SODOTEN

Yomiuri Kaikan,
B1, 1-11-1 Yurakucho,
Chiyoda-ku
Tel: 3213-0056
Open: 11am-3pm &
5-9:30pm; Sat., Sun. & hol.,
11:30am-8pm

Chinese
¥ 1/2
★★ 1/2

Map 7

小洞天

Call it kinky, but we've got a thing about big old Asian dining halls with waitresses in uniforms. Here they're Chinese, in outfits that make them look like airline stewardesses. Ageless funky Asian decor too, with chandeliers and marbled walls and a carpet of indeterminate age and color.

These niceties appear lost upon the masses of diners who come for the famous *shumai*, which are so big and meaty that four of them plus a bowl of rice and soup make a meal. Come summer, fans of *hiyashi chuka* should under no account miss their ¥1200 *gomoku hiyashi soba*, brimming with crab legs, shrimp and grilled meats.

制服を着たウェイトレスがいる古くて大きなアジア的な食堂に長年憧れ続けてきたが、ここはそうした店の中でも最後のそして最高の店のひとつである。スタッフはほとんどが中国人で、スチュワーデスのような制服を着ている。店の内装は大理石の壁にシャンデリアが揺れ、あいまいな色のカーペットが敷かれ、過去40年位昔ならどの年代にも当てはまるような流行を超えたアジア風である。しかし私の個人的な趣味は別として、ここがいつも混んでいるのはひとえにその料理のせいだろう。大ぶりで具のたっぷり入ったシューマイは特に有名で、ライスとスープをとればもう立派な食事といった満足感である。夏にはカニ足、エビ、チャーシューなどが入った豪華版の五目冷やし中華そば1200円が絶対お薦めだ。

SORRISO

Food and value at least a match for **Carmine**, and no wonder: it was started by Carmine and his little brother. It's also bigger, more bustling and a whole lot easier to find. Easiest order for a first visit is the basic dinner course (¥3800). Make a choice or two where needed, and ask for a Chianti or a Barbera if you like red, a Borro della Sala if you want white.

A typical course begins with mixed antipasto—mozzarella, beef tongue and healthy things like broccoli, cauliflower, mushrooms, eggplant and cabbage—or a salad, say of shrimp and ricola and lots of big shards of parmigiana. Then pasta, which could mean spaghetti with olive oil and garlic or penne in a no-nonsense tomato sauce. Then a main course like lamb stew or a filet of fish with a tangy green sauce. Simplicity and good ingredients are the keys to this kind of food. Dessert is included too: say a choice of inevitable *tiramisu*, fashionable *zuppa inglese*, unfashionable banana soufflé, delicious chocolate mousse or reliable fruit tarte.

3-1-15 Kagurazaka,
Shinjuku-ku
Tel: 3235-4477
Open: Noon-2pm & 6-10pm
(last order); closed Sun.

Italian
¥¥
★★★

Map 9

カルミネ氏とその弟が始めた店で、料理も値段も『カルミネ』に匹敵するが、人気は上回っているようだ。初めての人は料理が自由に選べる3800円のディナーコースに、ワインは赤なら、キャンティかBarbera、白なら Borro della Sala を注文してみよう。典型的なコースは、モツァレラ、牛タン、ブロッコリー、カリフラワー、マッシュルーム、ナス、キャベツなどが入った前菜の盛り合わせ、またはエビとリュコラチーズとパルメザンチーズのサラダで始まり、オリーブオイルとガーリックのスパゲティかシンプルなトマトソースをかけた魚料理が続くが、すべて素材の良さが決め手になっている。また、ティラミス、ズッパイングレーゼ、バナナスフレ、チョコレートムース、フルーツタルトなどのデザートもついてくる。

ソリーソ

SPAGO

5-7-8 Roppongi,
Minato-ku
Tel: 3423-4025
Open: 11:30am-2pm & 6-
10pm (last order); Sat., Sun.
& hol., 6-9:30pm (last order)

American
¥¥¥¥
★★★

 Map 18

スパゴ

Opinion divides sharply. "Tourissimo!" shouts one of our respondents, "for trendy wannabes who don't even realize that this is a shadow of the L.A. namesake." Others love the studied Californian casualness of the place, the still-inventive pizzas, the decadent desserts. Perhaps we can all agree that it's intriguing, new-wave American food priced higher than you'd want to pay on a daily basis. For something closer to a bargain, by local standards anyway, try **Lunchan** or **Tableaux**.

個性的な店に対しては賛否両論、様々な意見があるようだ。中にはこの店をロサンゼルス店のイミテーションに過ぎないという人もいるし、またある人はカリフォルニアのカジュアルな空気を感じさせる工夫を凝らしたピッツァやデザートは官能的だ、とまで評価を下す人も多くいる。もし値段のことを気にかけないなら、誰でもがここの新アメリカ料理に興味をそそられることは確かだろう。気軽にモダンなアメリカ料理を試すなら低価格の『ランチャンバー＆グリル』や『タブロウズ』がある。

SPIRAL CAFÉ

5-6-23 Minami Aoyama,
Minato-ku
Tel: 3498-5791
Open: Sun., 11am-2pm
(brunch)

Café
¥ 1/2
★★

 Map 2

スパイラル・カフェ

Normally just a nice big space for coffee or tea that's expensive even for Tokyo. Come on Sundays, though, and they'll treat you to a decent ¥3000 brunch. Dress the part: you'll be under observation. Afterwards there's usually a worthwhile art exhibition of some sort in the adjoining Spiral—Tokyo's mini-Guggenheim—and the shop upstairs is always worth a browse.

青山にある広々としたカフェとはいえ、東京の基準からいってもコーヒーや紅茶の値段は少し高い。しかし、日曜日には3000円でなかなかのブランチが食べられる。特に印象に残る料理ではないが、ゆったり過ごせるスタイリッシュなスペースとインターナショナルな客層が作り出す雰囲気は充分に楽しめるはずだ。

STOCKHOLM

Sweden Center, B1,
6-11-9 Roppongi,
Minato-ku
Tel: 3403-9046
Open: 11am-11pm;
closed Sun.

Swedish
¥¥¥
★★ 1/2

 Map 18

The bigger and the hungrier you are, the more you're going to like Stockholm. Bigger, because you'll fit: everything here, notably the chairs, is built to Viking scale. Hungrier because of the day-long smorgasbord of 50 to 60 different dishes, generally of fine quality and not at all unreasonable at ¥4300 for lunch or ¥5800 for dinner. Seriously, the only problem with this place is that we always feel compelled to eat till we're incapacitated.

Any book that mentions the smorgasbord feels bound to repeat the time-honored way of eating it. Once more for the record: pickled dishes, smaller fish and other savories first; then bigger fish, cold meats, cheese, and sausages; then hot dishes; and finally desserts. The slower the pace, the more enjoyable the meal. Allow at least a couple hours.

ストックホルム

何もかもがラージサイズのここは、在日外国人の人気を集めている。店内のテーブルや椅子の大きさに始まり、料理の種類と量には圧倒される。終日50～60種類の料理が食べられるスモーガスボードが昼は4300円、夜は5800円と申し分ない。長期間日本に暮らしているといつの間にか小食になってしまい、こういうことに感動しなくなるのだが、もしあなたが大食漢か空腹、または誰かを食事に招待するのなら、ここはお薦めの店だ。

SUJATHA

Among the best of our new crop of Sri Lankan restaurants. While it isn't among the cheapest, you'll get what you pay for here. The showpiece is a magnificently incendiary oxtail curry (they claim they stew it for two days for tenderness and flavor). Also recommended: the potent Sujatha curry and the unusual *gyumino* curry (order in advance).

Now that Ceylonese food is entering the Japanese mainstream—often by being billed as "mild," which it isn't—it's a pleasure to find a restaurant that pulls no punches.

Colins 14 Bldg., 2F,
4-21-18 Chuo,
Nakano-ku
Tel: 3380-3960
Open: Noon-1pm &
6-11:30pm; closed Wed.

Sri Lankan
¥¥
★★★

CC ◈ ✕   **Map 81**

スジャータ

Diners new to this kind of food and shy of
spices might prefer to start at **Sigiriya**, by
Meguro Station at 2-16-1 Kami-Osaki
(3446-2555).

スリランカ料理の代表的な店。東京のイ
ンド料理店の9割までが出しているインド
北部の料理に飽きてしまった人にはピッ
タリだ。スリランカ料理は味がマイルド
と思われがちだが、実際にはかなり辛
く、値段は安い場合が多い。口に火がつ
くようなオックステールカレーは、風味
と柔らかさを出すために40時間も煮込ん
だもので、さすが味に深みがある。特製
カレーや、予約が必要だが珍しい牛ミノ
カレーもお薦めだ。

SUSHISEI

3-11-14 Akasaka,
Minato-ku
Tel: 3582-9503
Open: 11:30am-2pm &
5-10:30pm; Sat., 4:30-10pm

Sushi
¥¥
★★★

CC   **Map 1**

寿司清

Between the hyperactive chefs in front of
you and the customers waiting three deep
behind you, Sushisei is no place for a long,
leisured evening. On the other hand the
value for money is sensational, and there's
a rowdy *shitamachi* energy to the place
that's near irresistible. Various other
reliable branches too, including Ginza (3571-
2772) and even New York.

日本に居住している我々外国人が、この国
を離れて最も懐かしく思うのは何といって
も寿司だろう。幸運にもこの店はニュー
ヨークに支店があるが、ここ赤坂店では目
まぐるしく寿司を握る職人と列を作って待
つ客とで大盛況だ。ゆったりできる場所で
はないが、この値段で、こんな上質の寿司
を食べさせてくれる店はなかなかない。店
内にみなぎる荒々しいほどの活気も魅力の
ひとつとなっている。銀座店（☎）3571-
2772 他、多くの支店がある。

*Rice wine is the raison d'être of the **Nihonshu Center** (5-9-1 Ginza, Chuo-ku, 3575-0656) and as part of their promotional effort they'll give you a glass of quality saké for just ¥300. Then another, and another—five brands are available for tasting each day. Various special food and saké events every week or so too. Open: 10:30am-6pm; closed Thur. & hol.*

SUZUME NO OYADO

A self-styled "Natural and healthy casual gourmetic bar," and they look pretty sincere: no MSG, no-pesticide and low-pesticide vegetables and their own additive-free soy sauce and miso. More to the point, the food is cheap, plentiful, and better than the decor or the clientele might indicate. The big photo menu also makes it easy to order. If you're in Kawasaki, it's close to the station and a whole lot preferable to most of the alternatives. Almost a dozen branches on this side of the Tama, too.

Recommended: *nigari yakko*, *tarabagani* (king crab) salad and the daily fish specials.

Recruit Kawasaki
Higashiguchi Bldg., B1,
3-1 Ekimae Honcho,
Kawasaki-ku, Kawasaki-shi,
Kanagawa-ken
Tel: 044-211-9500
Open: 5pm-1am

Izakaya
¥
★★ 1/2
Map 82

"自然で健康的、気楽なグルメの酒場"と店内に多少変な英語で謳っているように、この店ではすべての料理にいっさい化学調味料を使わず、無・低農薬栽培の野菜や無添加の自家製醤油と味噌を用いている。加えて値段は安価でボリュームがあり、安っぽい居酒屋風内装にもかかわらず、味も驚くほど良い。メニューは注文しやすい写真入りだし、都内や多摩地区に10軒以上ある支店のどれもが駅から1、2分の距離にあって便利だ。ニガリヤッコ、たらば蟹サラダ、日替わりの魚料理がお薦め。

すずめのおやど

TABEMONO MURA

When it comes to decor, Japan's natural food restaurants seldom stand on ceremony. Few, though, seem so blithely unconcerned with their looks as Tabemono Mura. Brace yourself: it's like wandering into the kitchen of a Japanese summer camp. Everyone sits around a big dining room table. You serve your own tea. People tend to take their own trays back to the counter when they're done. And heaven help you if you haven't eaten all your rice.

You're just one of the family here, and the cooking reflects it: apart from maybe **Tsubakiya**, it's the most ingenuously homemade food of its type we've found in Tokyo. There's only one thing to order—the ¥750-¥800 *teishoku* meal set—but you're given a choice of main dishes, say *mabo-dofu* (spicy Chinese tofu), grilled fish or croquettes. For a couple hundred yen more they'll add on a bowl of the daily *nimono* stew. Both the volume and variety of the dishes is a good notch above average, and while they do use some fish and poultry, vegetarians will have no problems.

3-36-4 Shimo-Renjaku,
Mitaka-shi,
Tokyo-to
Tel: 0422-49-4789
Open: 11:30am-2:30pm
& 5:30-9:30pm (last order);
closed Sun. & hol.

Japanese
¥
★★ 1/2

 **Map 83**

地味さの究極ともいえる自然食レストラン。店内はまるでサマーキャンプの台所といった感じだ。大きなテーブルにみんなで座り、お茶は各自で入れる。食べ終わるとお盆をカウンターに返しに行く人も多く、ここにいると家族の一員になったような気さえしてくる。料理も『椿屋』を除けば、おそらくここが東京で一番家庭的な自然食を出す店ではないだろうか。メニューは750円から800円の定食しかないが、その中のメインの料理を例えば、麻婆豆腐か焼き魚、またはコロッケというように選択できる。あと数百円追加すれば日替りの煮物もつけてくれる。質も量も平均以上のこの店はベジタリアンにとっても親しめる場所だ。

たべもの村

An uncanny number of Tokyo's **natural/vegetarian restaurants** *have taken root along the Chuo Line. In addition to* **Guruppe, Korinbo** *and* **Pata Pata** *they include the convenient but institutional* **Green House** *(2-13-26 Nakano, Nakano-ku, 3380-8022); "organic izakaya"* **Gaburi** *(3-58-3 Koenji Minami, Suginami-ku, 3314-6060);* **Sumire-ya Bun'an** *(4-27-14 Ogikubo, Suginami-ku, 3393-0688), a long-time gathering place for natural food enthusiasts; purely vegetarian, Seventh Day Adventist-run* **Elim**, *also in Ogikubo at 3-7-14 Amanuma (3220-0550); and the highly regarded* **Demeter** *way out at 2-14-5 Honmachi, Kokubunji-shi (0423-23-9924).*

TABLEAUX

Eclectic without being silly, elegant with a sense of fun, Tableaux extends itself over the culinary landscape from quesadillas, pastas and salads to fish sautéed with *gobo* and fennel, rosemary-scented duck in a honey glaze and Maine lobster with grapefruit and tomato. You'll either love or hate the Ottoman Empire bordello decor. Be sure to ask the *maître d'* for his own recommendations: the menu makes everything sound wondrous, but it isn't always.

Sunroser Daikanyama Bldg., B1,
11-6 Sarugakucho,
Shibuya-ku
Tel: 5489-2201
Open: 11:30am-10:30pm;
Fri. & Sat. until 11pm

American
¥¥¥
★★★

  Map 4

『スパゴ』や『ランチャンバー＆グリル』の線をいく、ニューアメリカンキュイジーヌに焦点を当てた店。『ラボエム／ゼスト』チェーンのデラックス版である。内装は19世紀と21世紀が入り交じったような不思議な舞踏会場風だ。料理はパスタ、サラダ、ゴボウとフェンネルを添えた魚のソテー、ハチミツを塗って焼いたローズマ

リー風味の鴨、グレープフルーツとトマトを添えたメイン州産のロブスターと幅広い。メートルディー（支配人）に彼自身のお薦めを聞くのも忘れずに。メニューでは素晴らしく見える一品が必ずしも美味しいとは限らないのだから。

タブロウズ

TAILLEVENT ROBUCHON

Post-modern Japan still has its problems with the thin line between high class and high kitsch. Fans of the latter are going to love this one: a slavish, full-scale reproduction of a Louis XVth-style chateau on the site of the former Sapporo beer factory (burp!). And for those who feel that a tie-up between two of France's grandest restaurants is meaningless overkill cynically aimed at a public more obsessed with brand names than devoted to fine food . . . aw, lighten up.

Lunch courses from ¥7000; dinner from ¥18,000. Think of it as a theater ticket with a drop-dead meal attached.

Yebisu Garden Place,
1-13-1 Mita,
Meguro-ku
Tel: 5424-1338
Open: Noon-2:30pm
(last order) & 6-9:30pm
 (last order); closed Sun.

French
¥¥¥¥
★★★★

Map 5

ポストモダンの日本であっても、依然としてハイクラスとハイ・キッチュを明確に区別するのは難しいようだ。個人的には後者が好きだが、例えば、サッポロビールと2軒の高名なフランス料理店が提携してサッポロビールの工場跡地に、ルイ15世スタイルの城を忠実に再現したレストランをオープンさせたのは素晴らしい。もちろん、ここまでしたからといって必ずここが最高のレストランになるとは限らないが、忘れられない思い出を作ってくれることは確かだ。ランチのコースは7000円、ディナーは18000円から。

タイユバン・ロブション

TAINAN TAAMI

Unsurpassed price/performance ratio and boisterous Chinese street stall atmosphere. For Taiwanese food lovers short on money and claustrophobia—everyone is wedged in around low round tables—there's hardly reason to go anywhere else. TT serves the Southeast Asian way: small plates, small prices. The photo menu shows over 50 dishes, most around ¥500. Better yet is just to look around and see what other people are eating. Always reliable are the steamed clams, bean sprouts with sauce, *chozume* (sausage), *chimaki* (leaf-wrapped rice), *aona* (stir-fried green vegetables) and noodles. Main shop in Shibuya (3464-7544); the many branches include Ginza (3571-3624), Ikebukuro (3988-1158), Roppongi (3408-2111), Shinjuku (3232-8839) and Suidobashi (3263-4530).

2-1-13 Nishi Kanda,
Chiyoda-ku
Tel: 3263-4530
Open: 11am-2pm & 5-11pm;
Sat. & Sun., 11am-11pm

Taiwanese
¥¥
★★★
Map 13

財布の中身が寂しい時にも安心して行ける台湾料理店。背の低い丸いテーブルを囲んで食べるここの台湾料理は、値段も皿もスモールサイズでいかにも東南アジア風。写真のついたメニューには500円前後の料理がざっと50種以上も揃っている。オーダーに迷ったら、周囲を見回して通らしき人が食べている料理を参考にするのも手。お薦めは、蒸したアサリ、ソースで和えたモヤシ、腸詰、チマキ、青菜など。手頃な値段で人気を保つこの店は屋台風の活気に満ちている。渋谷本店（☎）3464-7544の他、銀座店（☎）3571-3624、池袋店（☎）3988-1158、六本木店（☎）3408-2111、新宿店（☎）3232-8839、水道橋店（☎）3263-4530がある。

台南担仔麺

THE TAJ

Among the oldest and most Establishment of our Indian restaurants (the other is **Ashoka**), The Taj still has its share of loyalists. The key is to ignore the rather faded decor and concentrate on the range of regional foods: *samosas* and *pani poori*,

3-2-7 Akasaka, Minato-ku
Tel: 3586-6606
Open: 11:30am-2:30pm &
5:30-10pm; Sat., Sun. & hol.
until 9:30pm

Indian
¥¥¥
★★★

📷🔲 **Map 1**

tandoori-baked fish and especially the
southern-style vegetarian curries and
masala dosa.

『アショカ』と並ぶ東京のインド料理の老
舗であり、依然として忠実なファンがつい
ている。古臭い内装には目を向けず、イン
ド全域を網羅したという豊かな風土料理に
注目しよう。お薦めはサモサ、パニプー
リ、ボンベイ風野菜カレー、タンドーリで
焼いた魚、南部の野菜カレー、マサラドサ
（詰め物をした米のパンケーキ）、ニューデ
リー式のデザートなど。

ザ・タージ

TAMAKYU

2-30-4 Dogenzaka,
Shibuya-ku
Tel: 3461-4803
Open: 4-10:30pm;
closed Sun. & hol.

Izakaya
¥¥
★★

Map 19

Shibuya's true monument to loyalty and
perseverance isn't that statue of the
confused dog by the station. It's this stub-
born old izakaya, for years underdog in a
battle against behemoth Tokyu Corporation.
Tamakyu refused to budge, and Tokyu
finally had no choice but to build its shiny,
great 109 complex *around* this genial
eyesore. Also spared was the last old tree
along the street, and what a lovely tree it is.
Despite being pointedly ignored by most
Japanese-language guidebooks (and not
because there's anything wrong with the
food or drink), Tamakyu has thrived on
public goodwill ever since.

ここが立ち退きを拒否したため、東急はこ
の愛すべき邪魔物を囲むような形で109ビ
ルを建てるほかなかったという話はあまり
にも有名だが、私にとって渋谷の象徴はあ
る意味で忠犬ハチ公よりもこの頑固な居酒
屋といえる。立ち退きを巡って長年争いを
続けているこの店のお陰で、路傍の老木も
救われたが、この木がまた何ともいえなく
美しいのだ。この正直な居酒屋は、一般の
人の好意によって今も大繁盛している。

玉久

It's interesting, if not an unmixed blessing, to see the splash the *omori* ("big portion") phenomenon is making in '90s Japan. Restaurants are learning that for a small marginal cost they can put gigantic dishes of food on the table. Diners are realizing that for years they've been paying too much for too little. It's a boon for groups and the impoverished and hungry, less appealing if there's just a few of you and you prefer variety to volume. Most are Italian, French or Chinese, and tend to cluster around larger stations like Shibuya, Shinjuku and Ikebukuro. Look for 大盛り or "Big Plate" (sic) in English.

TANTO

1-26-2 Shoto,
Shibuya-ku
Tel: 3466-3292
Open: 11:50am-2:30pm &
5:30-10:20pm; Sat. & hol.,
5:30-10:20pm; closed Sun.

Italian
¥ 1/2
★★ 1/2

 **Map 19**

タント

A big, bright mustard-colored house, filled with earnest young couples at tables a little too close together. Tanto calls itself an *omori shokudo* ("large-portion dining hall") and it's advisable to take them at their word—servings are huge. Despite that, quality is first-rate, from the big mixed Tanto salad to the thick, pie-sliced country-style omelet with fresh tomato sauce. The various pizzas come closer to the real rustic Italian item than at a lot of places with bigger prices and smaller portions.

明るいマスタード色の建物にあるこの店は、テーブルどうしの間隔がくっついていることもあって、若いカップルたちの熱気で一杯だ。最近の傾向になっている"大盛食堂"で、時としてふたりでは食べ切れないほどの量が出てくる。タント風サラダ、フレッシュトマトソースのかかった田舎風オムレツ、田舎風ピザがお薦めだ。

TAVERNA AZZURRA

3-38-12 Jingu-mae,
Shibuya-ku
Tel: 3497-1586
Open: 6-11pm; closed Thur.

Time is catching up with Azzura. It's still a delightful basement hideaway, filled with an interesting mix of people and refreshingly real-life waiters. They still have their cross-cultural fun in the kitchen: lotus root in the ratatouille, *gobo* garnish with the saltimboca, touches of *shiso* when least expected. But what felt like state-of-the-art Tokyo Italian food ten years ago no longer really stands out in the crowded field today. Nor have they cured themselves of the bad old habit of packing in so many tables that

Italian
¥¥ 1/2
★★ 1/2

 **Map 11**

タヴェルナ・
アズーラ

you feel likeyou'resittinglikethis. We'll keep going back, but in the hope that they'll shift up a gear and stay in the running.

地下にあって隠れ家のような雰囲気もあり、種々雑多な客で賑わっている。和食の素材を生かしたイタリア料理、例えばレンコン入りラタトゥイユ、サルティンボカ（ローマ風牛肉料理）のゴボウ添え、シソのユニークな使い方などなかなか楽しい料理が多いが、東京のイタリア料理の世界ではここ10年の間にこれも特に珍しいものではなくなってしまった。

TENMI

1-10-6 Jinnan,
Shibuya-ku
Tel: 3496-9703
Open: 11:30am-2pm &
5-9pm; Sat., 11:30am-7pm;
Sun. & hol., 11:30am-6pm;
closed 2nd & 3rd Wed.

Macrobiotic Japanese
¥
★★★

 **Map 19**

Arguably the oldest (1961) and most illustrious (John Lennon ate here) of our city's natural food restaurants. That gives them every right to rest on their laurels but, in fact, they're still one of the best, serving macrobiotic food in a purely Japanese mode. Even the basic *bento* shows unusual care—even flair—and for just ¥1000. Also recommended: *agedashidofu* and *genmai mochi*. Apart from an occasional hint of fish on the menu, it's all vegetarian. The decor too is a genteel cut above the health-food norm, and at night they offer brown rice saké (*genmaishu*), a kind of anti-*ginjoshu*.

Our one gripe: a constant sense that the staff is doing you a favor simply by serving you.

1961年創業の東京で最古、そしてかつてはあのジョン・レノンも訪れたことがあるほど有名な自然食レストラン。一度有名になると駄目になる店が多い中で、ここは依然として最上の長寿のための純和食を出し続けている。例えば最も基本的な1000円の弁当にも並々ならぬ気遣いが見られ、揚げ出し豆腐、玄米餅などがお薦め。またベジタリアン用の料理ばかりではなく魚料理もあり、夜は玄米酒も呑める。インテリアやサービスは普通の自然食レストランよりはましだ。

天味

TOFUYA

3-5-2 Akasaka,
Minato-ku
Tel: 3582-1028
Open: 11am-1:30pm
& 5-10pm; closed Sat.,
Sun. & hol.

Japanese
¥¥
★★ 1/2
Map 1

豆腐屋

If this book seems to be accumulating a lot of tofu restaurants, it's less for any unnatural passion for the stuff than for the honesty and humility of the people who serve it. The clean, green Tofuya—a perfect name—in fact offers a whole range of classically simple Japanese cooking, from sashimi to *yakizakana* (grilled fish) to winter stews and soups. It's an ideal place should you find yourself in Akasaka, surrounded by Japanese restaurants but with no idea of which one to try. For initiates of *yuba*, *ganmodoki* and other secrets of the tofu world, it's well worth a trip of its own.

このガイドブックに少々豆腐屋が多くなってしまったのは、豆腐が好きだからというよりも、そこで働く人々の実直な態度や謙虚さに魅かれたからである。この店もしかり、清潔で緑が多く使われていて、メニューには湯葉やガンモドキ料理はもちろん、刺し身、焼き魚、煮物といったシンプルな日本の伝統食が幅広く揃っている。和食料理屋が軒を連ねる赤坂で、どの店に行こうか迷った時には最適の場所である。

もしあなたが飲食業に従事しているか、飲んだり食べたりすることが好きというなら、『日本ワインアカデミー』（渋谷区神宮前6-24-49（☎）5466-9847）に行き、ワインについて学ぶと良い。そこで身につけた知識を、階下にある素敵なワインバー『レクイエム』で生かすことができる。

TOHKALIN

Hotel Okura, 6F,
2-10-4 Toranomon,
Minato-ku
Tel: 3582-0111
Open: 11:30am-4pm
& 5:30-9:30pm

The créme de la créme of Tokyo's many grand Chinese dining emporia. In spite of the red carpet luxury and the stunning dinner prices, the hotel location makes it easy to walk into for, say, a ***1/2/¥ bowl of noodles and a beer. They also do good-value lunches followed by an excellent if premium-priced *yam cha* service from 1-4pm (Sun. & hol. from 11:30am). An

Cantonese
¥¥¥¥
★★★★

📷 ◈ ✄ **Map 1**

桃花林

additional bonus: diners at Tohkalin have access to the Okura's entire wine cellar.

東京にいくつかある有名な中華レストランの中でもとりわけ豪華。贅沢な赤いカーペットが敷かれ、値段も高いが、ホテル・オークラの中という便利さと、麺類とビールだけでも入れる気楽さがあって嬉しい。午後1時から4時（日祝日、午前11時30分から）までの飲茶は値段は高いが絶品。またホテルと共通のワインリストは天下一品。

TOHRYU

2-4-5 Azabu Juban,
Minato-ku
Tel: 3451-0514
Open: 11:30am-10pm; Fri. &
Sat., 11:30am-10:30pm;
closed Tue.

Chinese noodles
¥¥
★★★

📷 ◈ **Map 3**

Nothing has changed much since the '60s: faded gilt walls, waiters in bow ties, a rose in a peeling silver cruet on each table. There's fine *ippin ryori* ("à la carte") but the attraction is noodles: super-rich *shisenmen* (with Sichuan-style sesame paste and chilies), *torisoba* (with chicken), *shin-torisoba* (with "tree fungus" and vegetables) and superb *yakisoba* fried either hard or soft to order. All these run around ¥1500, about twice the Tokyo average and worth it. Big spenders can indulge in either of the two soba dishes that have made Tohryu known as "the world's most expensive noodle shop" (which we doubt, but it has a nice ring to it): the ¥7000 *awabi* (abalone) or *fukahire* (sharkfin).

Branches in Kojimachi (3264-6628) and the basement of the World Trade Center in Hamamatsucho (3435-5364).

色あせた金色の壁、蝶ネクタイのウェイター、テーブル上のバラの花と銀色の薬味入れというスタイルは1960年代から何も変わっていない。一品料理も良いが、贅沢な味の四川麺、鳥そば、そして硬、軟の焼きそばは最高だ。お金に余裕があれば「世界一高価なそば屋」としてここを有名にした7000円のアワビとフカヒレそばを試すのも良い。麹町（☎）3264-6628と浜松町の世界貿易センター地下（☎）3435-5364に支店がある。

登龍飯店

TOKUJU

3-11-8 Shinbashi,
Minato-ku
Tel: 3434-2822
Open: 11:30am-3am; Sat.,
noon-11:30pm; Sun. & hol.
until 10:30pm

Yakiniku (Korean barbecue)
¥¥¥ 1/2
★★★

[cc] 🔷 **Map 84**

Tokyo's top name in premium *yakiniku*, and
further evidence of an old irony: the more
you pay for non-Japanese cuisine in Japan,
the less authentic it's likely to be. For the
assertive marinades and surprising side
dishes of *real* Korean barbecue, go to a
dive like **Kotchan** or **Hallelujah Bussan**.
For exquisite meat and Japanese refinement, come here. It's the epitome of an
old-line, Ginza/Shinbashi restaurant:
choice of counter, tables and private
rooms; "high-class" '60s-ish decor, gracious service, lots of men in suits. Sample
it on the cheap at lunch: a good *yakiniku
don* (grilled beef on rice) for ¥950; for ¥1400,
a choice of big, grill-it-yourself lunches.

有名焼肉店のひとつ。韓国料理として
は、『こっちゃん』や『ハレルヤ物産』のよ
うに安くて新しい店ほど本格的ではない
が、肉の質とサービスではここが群を抜
いている。ランチは特にお薦めで、焼肉丼
が950円、大盛ロースかカルビランチは
1400円で食べられる。遅くまで開いてい
るので、映画や観劇の帰りに最適。ちなみ
にここは、シャブシャブの『八山』六本木
店 (☎) 3403-8333 や渋谷12ヵ月ビルの中
にあるステーキや肉料理のレストランも
経営している。

徳寿

TOKYO DAIHANTEN

5-17-13 Shinjuku,
Shinjuku-ku
Tel: 3202-0121
Open: 11am-10pm

Unless you're a high-rolling Taiwanese
wedding party, Japan's biggest Chinese
restaurant is mostly missable—except for
the giant *yam cha* hall on the 3rd floor.
Leisurely Sunday dim sum brunch here is a
Tokyo tradition. Advisory: sit along the
main route of the food carts. Hide yourself
away in a back corner and you risk going
hungry for hours.

Yam cha
¥¥
★★ 1/2
Map 22

東京大飯店

台湾スタイルの派手な結婚披露宴でもなければ、日本最大の中華レストランでの小人数の食事は楽しくないかも知れない。ただ、3 階の巨大な飲茶ホールでする日曜日のブランチには多くのファンがいる。この時はフードワゴンの通る道に隣接したテーブルに座ることを薦める。そうしないと長い間食べ物にありつけないことになるから ...。

TOKYO JOE'S

*Exc food &
atmosphere.
— quite expensive
~ ¥11,000 / hd.*

2-13-5 Nagatacho,
Chiyoda-ku
Tel: 3508-0325
Open: 11:30am-3pm &
5-11pm; Sat., Sun. & hol.,
11:30am-11pm

American
¥¥ 1/2
★★★

Map 1

Sweet and meaty as stone crabs are, is it really worth paying their airfare from the Florida Keys? We say "yes," if only because this cavernous crab emporium can offer better value for money than most any place serving local seafood. The staff, though trained to military precision, are perfectly friendly if you talk to them.

Recommended: ¥2800 crab lunch (there's crab in four of the five courses) and the ¥7000 Florida dinner. Both finish with a big piece of cheesecake-rich Key Lime Pie. Home base in Miami (worth a visit for tradition, but we actually prefer the food here); branch in Osaka (06-344-0124).

31/1/98

東京ジョーズ

フロリダのストーンクラブはわざわざ高いお金を払ってでも、アメリカから空輸する価値があるほどカニ肉がたっぷり入っていて美味しい。この洞窟みたいな広い店では、そんなとっておきのシーフードが他のどんな店よりも納得のいく値段で食べられる。スタッフは教育が行き届いていて一見堅く見えるが、話してみると意外にフレンドリーだ。5 コースのうち 4 つまでがカニ料理の2800円のカニランチと7000円のフロリダディナーがお薦め。どちらもビッグサイズのチーズケーキのようなライムパイがついてくる。マイアミが本店、大阪に支店 (☎) 06-344-0124 がある。

TOKYO KAISEN MARKET

2-36-1 Kabukicho,
Shinjuku-ku
Tel: 5273-8301
Open: 5pm-midnight; Sat.,
Sun. & hol., noon-midnight

Seafood
¥¥
★★★

Map 22

Cross a New York fish market with a Hong Kong seafood emporium, toss in some Bangkok spice and a little L.A. chic and you could conceivably come up with something like Tokyo Kaisen Market. But even then would it occur to you to plonk it down dead center in Kabukicho, Tokyo's raunch mecca?

The white-tiled ground floor really is a market. Fish, crab, clams, shrimp, lobster, abalone—take your purchase home or direct it to their kitchen. For ¥800 or so, a team of mostly Southeast Asian chefs will steam, boil, bake, broil, or fry it to order and serve it to you upstairs. Or just work from the extensive menu of Japanese, Chinese and Thai-style seafood, stir-fries and noodles. Don't neglect the house specials, printed in the traditional red.

Upstairs is a rambling, multi-level collection of rooms, complete with high-tech sushi/oyster bar. Exposed beams and lots of glass create an airy, half-indoor-half-outdoor feeling, the whole thing suspended over the urban jungle outside. It's Tokyo at its *Blade Runner* best.

ニューヨークのフィッシュマーケットと香港のシーフードレストラン、それにバンコクのスパイスとL.A.のスマートさをミックスしたのがこの店だ。床一面に白いタイルを敷き詰めた1階は魚市場で、新鮮な魚、カニ、ハマグリ、エビ、ロブスター、アワビなどを買って持ち帰ってもいいし、2階で食べることもできる。およそ800円で東南アジアのシェフたちが注文により蒸したり、茹でたり、焼いたり、あぶったり、揚げたりと腕を振ってくれる。また、豊富なメニューの中から和食、中華、タイ風シーフード、炒めものや麺類などを選んでもよい。赤い字で示してあるこの店のスペシャルメニューはぜひ注文して欲しい。この2階は雑然としていて寿司とオイスターバーがあり、梁がむき出しになった壁はガラスで覆われ、室内にいながら外の雰囲気が味わえる。歌舞伎町ジャングルが眼下に見下ろせるここは、まるで「ブレードランナー」さながらの世界だ。

東京海鮮市場

TOKYO PARIS SHOKUDO

3-7-3 Iidabashi, Chiyoda-ku
Tel: 3222-5400
Open: 11:30am-2pm
& 6-9:30pm; closed Mon.

French
¥¥
★★ 1/2
Map 9

Uh-oh . . . Toulouse-Lautrec posters papering every square centimeter of the walls and teeny tables so close together you could throw a sock hop on them. Someone should also break it to these people that real little Parisian restaurants these days don't play loud chanson on their stereos. Pearl Jam, maybe; Juliette Gréco crooning "*Les feuilles mortes*," no.

Yes, they try a bit too hard here, and not least in the kitchen. It's the kind of place where everything is diced a little finer than it needs to be and where the bread is bestowed one piece at a time. But then it's great dicing and excellent bread. For that matter, all the food is fully satisfactory in its simple way, and the house red is among the best we've found at this class of place. At the price—¥1200 for a generous lunch, ¥2800 for an even bigger dinner—it's a steal.

ロートレックのポスターが壁一面に張られ、小さなテーブルが所狭しと置かれ、ステレオからはシャンソンが大音量で流れているこの店は、小粋なパリのレストランを気取っているつもりかもしれないが本当のパリのスタイルではない。料理はなかなか美味しく満足できる。そしてハウスワインの赤はこのレベルの店ではピカイチといえそうだ。1200円のランチとボリューム満点の2800円のディナーは超お得。ただ、インテリアと音楽だけはもうちょっと何とかして欲しい。

東京パリ食堂

TOMOCA

1-7-27 Yotsuya,
Shinjuku-ku
Tel: 3353-7945
Open: 6-10pm;
closed Sun. & hol.

Sri Lankan
¥¥
★★ 1/2

 Map 85

Only one choice to make here—fish, shrimp, chicken, mutton, beef or liver—and one price, a flat ¥4200. The food simply arrives: papadam chips, lentil stew, jackfruit curry, a sambal or two, cucumber salad, eggplants with cloves and whatever meat or fish you've picked, done up in a rich curry. For ballast, rice flour pancakes and rice. To drink, Sri Lanka's own Lion Lager or Royal Pilsner.

Fugitives from the '60s will feel at home amid the batik bedspreads and potted palms and droning subcontinental music. It's the sort of place where you keep smelling incense, then notice they don't have any.

4200円のコースのみのメニューは、油で揚げたおつまみパパダムチップ、豆のシチュー、ジャックフルーツカレー、ライスにかけて食べる辛いサンボール、キュウリのサラダ、ナスのクローブ風味、そして魚、エビ、チキン、マトン、ビーフ、レバーのなかからひとつ選ぶカレーの7品に米粉のパンケーキとライス、紅茶がつく。ビールはスリランカのライオンラガービールかロイヤルピルスナー。バティックのベッドカバーや鉢植え、エキゾチックな音楽は60年代の雰囲気をかもしだしていて、まるでお香まで漂ってくるようだ。

トモカ

TONKI

1-1-2 Shimo-Meguro,
Meguro-ku
Tel: 3491-9928
Open: 4-10:45pm;
closed Tue. & 3rd Mon.

Tonkatsu
¥
★★ 1/2

Tokyo *tonkatsu* (pork cutlet) mecca for generations. Success certainly hasn't spoiled their famed *hire* ("filet") or *rosu* ("roast") *teishoku*—still among the best of their type, and starting at just ¥1550—but come early or prepare to wait in line and eat in polite haste. Branches include Jiyugaoka (3718-5006), Koenji (3339-7548) and Komagome (3949-7387).

Good, but perhaps not quite as good (though even cheaper), is Tonki's renowned competitor **Maisen**, at 4-8-5 Jingu-mae, Shibuya-ku (3470-0071).

 **Map 14**

この店は永年にわたって東京のとんかつの
メッカだ。混んでいることが多いので待つ
ことを覚悟しなくてはならないが、1550
円のヒレカツ、ロースカツ定食は相変らず
美味しい。自由が丘（☎）3718-5006、高
円寺（☎）3339-7548、駒込（☎）3949-
7387 に支店がある。味は少し落ちるが安
い青山の『まい泉』（渋谷区神宮前4-8-5
（☎）3470-0071）も悪くはない。

とんき

TONY ROMA'S

"Grease and formica," comments one of
our corespondents, obviously not a fan of
Tony's meaty grilled ribs and the big loaves
of French-fried onion rings. Maybe it helps
to be American. Other locations in Akasaka
(3585-4478), Aoyama (3479-5214) and
Roppongi (3408-2748). But our heart be-
longs to the branch by Katase Enoshima
Station at the end of the Odakyu Line
(0466-22-7337), where you can sit outside
by Sagami Bay under big, flaming torches
straight out of the native dance scene in
Mothra.

1 Sanbancho,
Chiyoda-ku
Tel: 3222-3440
Open: Noon-3pm & 5-11pm

American
¥
★★

 **Map 10**

「油っぽくて合成樹脂の匂いがする」という
知り合いもいるが、そういう人たちは、こ
の店のいかにもアメリカ人好みの、肉の
たっぷりついたスペアリブと巨大なオニオ
ンリングのフライが好きではないのだろ
う。赤坂（☎）3585-4478、青山（☎）
3479-5214、六本木（☎）3408-2748に支
店があるが、小田急江ノ島線の終点、片瀬
江ノ島店（☎）0466-22-7337では海辺の大
きな松明の下に座って食事をしていると、
映画「モスラ」に登場する原住民のダンス
シーンを思い出してしまう...。

トニーローマ

TOP DOG

1-25-12 Jiyugaoka,
Meguro-ku
Tel: 3724-5351
Open: 11:30am-11:30pm

¥
★ 1/2
▨ ✕ **Map 12**
トップドッグ

Good omelets and dogs amidst a friendly
young crowd, but the best reason to drop by
here has always been the outdoor porch,
now, alas, a little too closed in by awnings
and shrubbery. Perhaps we could send
over a gardener?

ホットドッグはもちろんだが、オムレツ
も美味しい。しかし何といっても、つい
ここに寄ってしまいたくなるいちばんの
理由は、最近多少狭くはなったが、生垣
に囲まれたポーチがあるからだ。

Yakitori endeavors to use every part of the bird. The farther
down the following list you eat, the greater your claim to
epicureanism:

● *Torinegi:* Beginner's yakitori—hunks of white meat with skin
alternating with scallions
● *Tsukune:* Balls or slabs of minced chicken meat, onions, and
herbs
● *Sasami:* Skinless white breast meat
● *Tori no shisomaki:*Sasami wrapped in *shiso* leaf, often with a
touch of sour *umeboshi* plum paste
● *Tebasaki:* Wings
● *Rebaa* (or *kimo*)*:* Liver
● *Motsu:* Giblets; the prize is reckoned to be *sunagimo*
(gizzard); also popular is *hatsu* (heart)
● *Kashira:* Head
● *Kawa:* Skin
● *Nankotsu:* The ultimate challenge: crunchy white cartilage

For truly deluxe yakitori—yes, that's a contradiction in terms—
make for Hitori Shizuka (41-27 Udagawacho, Shibuya-ku, 3463-
4935) or Monsen (2-13-8 Azabu Juban, Minato-ku, 3452-2327).
Both offer splendid atmosphere (dark and rustic at Hitori
Shizuka, polished and chic at Monsen), lavish ingredients,
expert cooking and the uniquely Japanese thrill of having no idea
how much it's going to cost until they slip you the bill.

TOPKAPI

3-6-26 Kita Aoyama,
Minato-ku
Tel: 3498-3510
Open: 5-11pm; closed Sun.

Turkish
¥¥
★★★

 Map 2

トプカピ

Tokyo's tiniest Turkish restaurant serves just one big square table, but they're always willing to try to shoehorn in another person or two. You can't help but meet your neighbors: you're practically in their laps. Superlative versions of all the standards: vegetable dips, spicy stews, kebabs and fresh-baked flat bread.

東京で最も小さなトルコ料理のレストラン。店内には大きな角形のテーブルがひとつだけあって、混んで来るとどんどん詰め込まれてしまうので、まるで隣の人の膝の上に座っているような気にさせられる。トルコ料理のスタンダード、野菜のディップ、辛いシチュー、ケバブ、フラットなパンが味わえる。

TOPS

3-20-8 Shinjuku,
Shinjuku-ku
Tel: 3354-6525
Open: 5-11pm;
Sun. & hol., 5-10:30pm

Kushiyaki
¥¥
★★ 1/2

 Map 22

串焼処トップス

Kushiyaki (expanded, upmarket yakitori) that's still within financial reach. It's always packed these days, and often just too smoky, but that's the price of being good and just a block away from Shinjuku Station. Men needn't be shy about ordering the "Lady's Course": for ¥3500 it offers the best price/performance ratio here.

"串焼き" というとしばしば「値段の高い焼き鳥」というように思われてしまうが、この店は手頃な値段で心配ない。最近ではいつも行列ができていて店内は混み合い、騒々しく、煙でモヤっている。でもこれは良心的な値段と新宿駅のすぐそばという理由からだろう。男性もぜひ3500円の "レディース・コース" を恥ずかしがらずに注文したらよい。コストパフォーマンスはこれが最高だ。

TORIFUJI

Wine with yakitori? Well, why not? It's barbecue, after all, and owner Harii-san is a no-nonsense enophile who knows a thing or two about matching European drink to Japanese food. Showcased each month are a half dozen bottles, mostly French whites in the ¥3500 to ¥4500 range. Or go potluck, and ask for a carafe of red or white. It'll be about a third of a bottle of whatever he has open at the moment. Intriguing stuff too: we've glimpsed names like Listrac and Coteaux des Baux.

Most regulars settle on one of the four courses (¥2600 to ¥3600). Even the basic model offers two different *o-toshi*, a salad and eight kinds of yakitori. We favor the ¥3150 version, which finishes with an assortment of cheeses. The sole flaw with this system is that the food has to be cooked in a separate room—fine wine doesn't appreciate smoke—and arrives all at once on a big platter. And, frankly, yakitori loses its charm after a few minutes of congealing on your plate. Perfectionists will want to order stick by stick.

6-7-19 Ginza,
Chuo-ku
Tel: 3571-4391
Open: 5:30-11pm;
closed Sun. & hol.

Yakitori and wine
¥¥
★★ 1/2

 Map 7

焼き鳥にワインなんて合わないと思うかもしれないが、実は焼き鳥もバーベキューの一種であり、ワインはバーベキューにぴったりなのだから不思議ではない。この店のオーナーの針井氏はそんな和食と洋酒をマッチさせる達人。毎月変わる店のワインは6種類あって、ほとんどが3500円から4500円程度のフランス産の白。常連のほとんどは、2600円から3600円の4つあるコースの中から選んでいるが、最もベーシックなものでも2種のお通しにサラダ、そして8種の焼き鳥がついてくる。お気に入りは3150円のコースで、最後にチーズの盛り合わせが出てくる。ただ唯一の欠点はワインが火に弱いため、料理は別の部屋で調理され、大皿に盛られて一度に運ばれてきてしまう点で、焼き鳥はその生気をみるみるうちに失ってしまう。完璧主義者は一本ずつオーダーするのが得策かもしれない。

トリフジ

TORIGIN

As much as we like the food and the atmosphere in Ningyocho, there's a clannish feel to many places that can make an unintroduced, first-time visitor feel more tolerated than welcomed. And that's if he's Japanese. Gaijin may feel as if they have just beamed down from the Starship *Enterprise*.

Torigin is different. It's warm and friendly, even to strangers. To their astonishment they even found their way once into an English-language tourist guide, so by now they're used to non-Japanese too. Yet it's classically *shita-machi*—the miniature scale, the family-style service, the simple, decent food.

Specialty of the house is *kamameshi* (literally "food in a pot"), a mixture of rice and bits of whatever meat or vegetables the cook can scrounge up. It's a dish so modest that you might as well try it in its most modest form, *takenoko* (bamboo shoot) *kamameshi*. There's also yakitori and other snacks, as well as a dozen or so fine sakés, including your author's much beloved Suigei ("The Drunken Whale").

Note that Torigin and its retro chicken trademark are a franchise. There are many about town, and they vary widely in style and quality.

2-24-6 Nihonbashi
Ningyocho, Chuo-ku
Tel: 3667-0084
Open: 5-11pm; closed Sun.

Izakaya
¥¥
★★ 1/2
Map 16

なぜか初めての人には入りにくいという店があり、特に人形町辺りではそういった店が多いようだが、ここは違う。フレンドリーでオープンだから自然に足が向いてしまう。外国人旅行者向けのガイドブックにも紹介されたことがあるので、店のほうでも今では外国人慣れしている。しかし、ここは純然たる下町そのもので、こぢんまりした店内や家庭的なサービス、シンプルで美味しい料理が信条だ。特に釜飯、中でもタケノコ釜飯はなかなかの味。また、焼き鳥や小料理もいいが、美酒「酔鯨」を始めとする酒の種類も豊富だ。この店のレトロな鶏のトレードマークはフランチャイズでたくさんの支店があるが、店のスタイルと味はそれぞれ違いここがベストだ。

鳥ぎん

TORIYOSHI

4-28-21 Jingu-mae,
Shibuya-ku
Tel: 3470-3901
Open: 11:30am-2pm
& 5-11pm; Fri. & Sat.
until midnight

Japanese
¥¥
★★
Map 6

Specializes in *tebasaki* (chicken wings) but they do a complete range of home-style Japanese food, with an emphasis on chicken. Mainly we like coming here for the space—it's far bigger inside than the Harajuku backstreet entry would ever suggest—and the chic contemporary Japanese design. Lunch is a terrific value.

Toriyoshi's original shop is in Kichijoji (0422-46-7652), and there are various others around town. Fans of this place should also check out **Kiku**, a couple streets over at 4-26-27 Jingu-mae, Shibuya-ku (3408-4919), offering inexpensive Japanese fare in equally stylish surroundings in a more traditional vein.

手羽先の専門店だが、鶏を中心とした幅広い日本の家庭料理を扱っている。原宿の裏通りとは思えないほどゆったりした広いスペースに、現代的なしゃれた和風デザインのインテリアで、気分のいい店になっている。お得なランチがお薦め。本店は吉祥寺（0422-46-7652）にあるが、その他自由が丘支店（）3718-1678、二子玉川支店（）3709-4149、立川支店（）0425-29-2960、横浜支店（）045-242-9822 などがある。この店が気に入ったら、もう少し伝統的な店構えではあるが、やはりイマ風の和食屋『きく』（渋谷区神宮前4-26-27（）3408-4919）もすぐ近くにあるので、のぞいてみるのをお薦め。

TOYA

Koike Bldg., 2F,
2-6 Kanda Ogawamachi,
Chiyoda-ku
Tel: 3233-0018
Open: 5-11:15pm;
closed Sat., Sun. & hol.

A quality operation. The tidy, compact Toya serves up possibly the best food we've found at any *jizake* (regional saké) specialist. Meat, fish or vegetables, these people are obviously willing to pay top dollar for their materials. You do too, of course, and they don't make it easy to economize—seldom have we been told so assertively what to eat and what to drink. But you sense that it's less out of a profit motive than a sincere desire to give you the best they have. The sakés, by beaker or bottle, are in a class of their own.

Izakaya
¥¥¥
★★★★

🆑 **Map 13**

と屋

質にこだわる地酒専門店。こぢんまりと
したこの店では、肉、魚、野菜、すべて
の材料費を惜しまずに、いい素材で最高
の料理を出している。食べる方も財布の
中身を惜しむようではここには不向き
だ。儲けることが第一ではなく、より良
い品質のものを提供したいというポリ
シーが感じられる。もちろん地酒も極上
の逸品を出してくれる。

TRADER VIC'S

Mouth-watering Polynesian cuisine in an
exotic South Seas ambiance of balmy
breezes redolent of frangipani and—no,
hold it, rewind. Vic himself was the first to
put Polynesian food in its place ("the worst
stuff you'll ever eat"), and the fantasy he
created instead remains less interesting for
its imaginary cooking than the wonderfully
tacky Bali Hai decor.

　　But the enduring reason to come here
is the ¥6000 champagne brunch under the
tribal masks and tiki torches every Sunday
and holiday. It's real French bubbly in
unlimited quantities, and the buffet isn't
half bad either: big salads, grilled seafood,
barbecued spare ribs and so on, all the way
through to dessert and endless coffee.

Hotel New Otani, 4F,
4-1 Kioicho, Chiyoda-ku
Tel: 3265-4707
Open: Sun. & hol.,
11:30am-2:30pm (brunch)

Brunch

¥¥ 1/2
★★ 1/2

🆑 🔲 📅 **Map 1**

トレイダー ・
ヴィックス

海外における『トレイダー・ヴィックス』
の評判はどちらかというと時代遅れで、
キッチュなものであり、億万長者のドナル
ド・トランプでさえ、そのプラザホテル買
収の際、当時中に入っていたこの店を安っ
ぽいと呼び、閉店させようとしたという。
しかし、東京支店はいまだに人気を保って
おり、日本のビジネスマンたちはインター
ナショナルな料理を出す店と考えているよ
うだ。南太平洋風の内装も何だか遊園地み
たいで白々しいが、日曜祭日にやっている
6000円のシャンパンブランチはお薦めし
たい。フランス産のシャンパンが飲み放題
で、スープ、サラダ、シーフード、バーベ
キュースペアリブ、デザート、コーヒーが
つくビュッフェはなかなかである。

TRATTORIA THEO

1-26-6 Umegaoka,
Setagaya-ku
Tel: 3426-8867
Open: Noon-10pm;
closed Mon.

Italian
¥¥
★★★

 Map 86

Overpriced wines apart, Theo is the little neighborhood Italian place you wish you had in your own neighborhood: relaxed and affordable, with food that ranges from merely pleasant to flat-out terrific. It's related to the excellent **Ponte Vecchio**, and it shows. We like the ultra-thin crust pizzas, and you won't go far wrong with any of the pastas or fish dishes.

トラットリア・テオ

高すぎるワインは別として、ゆったり落ち着いた雰囲気と美味しいイタリア料理は、こんな店が近所にあったら最高と思うほどだ。あの『ポンテベッキオ』の姉妹店というのもうなずける。生地が超薄いピザがお薦め。

TSUBAKIYA

1-33-4 Senju,
Adachi-ku
Tel: 3870-8761
Open: 11:30am-2pm;
closed Sat., Sun. & hol.

Japanese
¥
★★★

 Map 87

Down a winding, narrow alley and up an outdoor staircase, it's a bright, tiny, high-ceilinged loft of a place. Inside are crammed a few miniature tables and chairs, a small library of food- and health-related books and a ghetto blaster quietly playing Billie Holliday or Bill Evans. Each day, they prepare a single *teishoku*—main dish of fish on Monday, *agemono* (deep-fried food) on Tuesday and Friday, *nimono* (stew) on Wednesday and tofu on Thursday—and charge ¥800 (¥980 with a good cup of coffee). Nothing fancy, nothing exotic. Just a classically simple Japanese meal made of unimpeachable materials (a whiteboard describes the provenance of the day's ingredients), put together with the kind of personal care that no proper restaurant would ever be able to afford. It's like having a mom in Kita Senju.

曲がりくねった細い路地を通って2階へ上がると、そこには明るくて小さい、天井の高いロフトのような店がある。小さなテーブルと椅子がぎちぎちに置かれ、料理と健康に関する本がたくさんあり、ミニコンポからはビリー・ホリデイとビル・エバンスが流れている。毎日800円の定食が1種類のみで、月曜日は魚、火曜日と金曜日は揚げ物、水曜日は煮物で木曜日は豆腐というのが決まりメニュー。980円で美味しいコーヒーをつけてくれる。特別豪華でもエキゾチックでもないが、その日の料理の食材をホワイトボードに書いて説明したり、細かい部分に気を配ったりと、大規模な営利本位のレストランでは到底できないことをこの店ではやってくれる。申し分のない材料で典型的な家庭料理を提供している。まるで北千住に自分の母親がいるみたいだ。

椿屋

While the Wedgwood Tea Room probably comes closest to serving a proper English *tea*, Tokyo offers various other serious tea experiences of note:

● Chugoku Sakan, 1-35-2 Nishi Ikebukuro, Toshima-ku (3985-5183): A *yam cha* joint with a twist: buy a tin of the tea of your choice and they'll keep it for you for future visits.

● Lai Lai, 2-15-13 Tsukiji, Chuo-ku (3541-2595): One of Tokyo's surprisingly few traditional Chinese teahouses, featuring oolong and jasmine teas and Chinese sweets.

● Lipton Tea House, 3-5-3 Ginza, Chuo-ku (3564-3921): A standard selection of English teas and homemade scones.

● Mariage Frères, In The Room, 2F, 1-12-13 Jinnan, Shibuya-ku (3477-1854): A mind-boggling 400 varieties of Indian, Ceylonese and Chinese tea, to take home or to sip in their genteel no-smoking tea room.

● Tsukimasa, 5-28-16 Daizawa, Setagaya-ku (3410-5943): Traditional Japanese teas and cakes in an unexpected locale: a back street just beyond Shimo-Kitazawa's youth promenade.

● A snob's guide to saké classifications

Category	Permitted ingredients	Ratio of added alcohol	Typical style	Recommendation
Junmaishu ("pure rice saké")	Rice, *koji* rice, water	0%	Rich, full-bodied	Many devotees settle for nothing less
Honjozo ("true brew")	Rice, *koji* rice, water, alcohol	25% or less	Slightly softer, often more fragrant	Good for drinking warm
Futsushu ("ordinary saké")	Rice, *koji* rice, water, alcohol, sugar	About 50%	Generic "saké" flavor	If you must, find one without sugar
Sanzoshu ("triple-extended saké")	Almost anything	About 67%	Wartime hardship	Serve to unwanted guests

● Saké label terminology revealed

Daiginjoshu ("grand ginjoshu")	Rice must be polished to 50% or less of original weight	A match for *ginjoshu*, but seldom much better
Ginjoshu (roughly, "saké celebrated in song")	Rice must be polished to 60% or less of original weight	Note that these can be either *junmaishu* or *honjozo*
Genshu ("*ur*-saké")	Undiluted to saké's standard 16% alcohol level	Raw 40-proof power for strong foods, running lawnmowers, etc.
Namazake ("draft saké")	Unpasteurized (other sakés normally get zapped twice)	Headstrong young brew for drinkers of similar persuasion
Nigorizake ("cloudy saké")	Unfiltered and turbid	Range from light and fizzy to thick and sublime
Shiboritate ("freshly pressed")	Shipped before the usual six-month ageing	Saké nouveau: sprightly and often on the wild side
Yamahai	An older style: no lactic acid added before fermentation	Uncommon, complex, distinctive—worth the search

TSUNAHACHI
TSUNOHAZUAN

3-28-4 Shinjuku,
Shinjuku-ku
Tel: 3358-2788
Open: 11:30am-3pm &
5:10-9:30pm (last order)

Tempura
¥¥

★★★ 1/2

Map 22

exc. value

Some masterfully polite people greet you on the ground floor of this elegant monolith and an attendant in kimono takes you up in the elevator. You're seated at a black marble counter in a room of simple, radiant beauty. Across the counter is a tank of bubbling cool water and a pan of bubbling hot oil. Under the guidance of the single chef, the sea creatures in the former make a short but memorable transit to the latter, then, a moment later, to your plate. They taste as if they have lived for this moment alone, and so they have. Afterwards, you're asked if you're ready for *o-shokuji*: rice, pickles, and *akadashi* soup. At the end comes coffee in a bone china cup.

Even allowing that Tsunahachi made its name on gourmet-grade tempura at realistic prices, the bill for this lunchtime *tempura teishoku*— ¥2500—seems extraordinarily reasonable for such high culinary theater. It is more expensive in the evenings, but still only a fraction as much as anywhere else of comparable quality.

Tsunahachi operates various branches around town (the old original shop is just around the corner), all less elevated in style and even lower in cost.

つな八
つのはず庵

つな八チェーンは手頃な値段でグルメを満足させる天ぷらを出すということで一躍有名になったが、ここは別格。エレガントな黒い大理石のビルに構えたこの店では、レベルが全く違う天ぷらが食べられる。ランチの天ぷら定食は生けすから出した活魚をその場で揚げて出してくれる。これで2500円なら大満足だ。

*The only significant step up in **tempura**
from **Tsunohachi Tsunohazuan** is to the very
top—traditionally considered to be the ****/¥¥¥¥
Ten-ichi (6-6-5 Ginza, Chuo-ku 3571-1949).*

UKAI
TORIYAMA

3426 Minami Asakawacho,
Hachioji-shi,
Tokyo-to
Tel: 0426-61-0739
Open: 11am-8pm;
Sun. & hol., 11am-7pm

Kushiyaki
¥¥
★★

🎴 🔷 🎌 ⮕ **Map 88**

Fantastic Setting
Better to go
  a la carte.
Set > ¥8000, ¥3200 for
        kids
うかい鳥山

This one has been passed around the
Tokyo Journal community since the early
days, and remains one of the great culinary
getaways. Take a Chuo Line or Keio Line
express from Shinjuku, get off at Takao
Station—it's the end of the line—and catch
a bus or cab to Ukai Toriyama. The staff
will lead you to a little open hut by a stream
on the hillside, and take your order for food,
beer, and saké. The food is *kushiyaki*:
skewers of chicken, beef, vegetables, and
other things, which you grill over your own
irori, the traditional charcoal hearth. When
you need more, ring them up and they'll
bring it. It's a world of its own, simple and
timeless, and there is always a sadness
when the time comes to leave.

かねてから『トーキョージャーナル』のス
タッフご用達の串焼きの店。新宿から中
央線か京王線に乗り、高尾駅で下車。バ
スかタクシーでようやく辿り着くと、店
のスタッフが丘のふもとの小さなせせら
ぎ沿いにある小屋に案内してくれる。そ
こで料理と飲み物を注文し、自分専用の
囲炉裏で串焼きを焼いてアツアツを食べ
る。肉や野菜の追加もできる。都会の喧
噪を離れたのどかな場所で時を忘れて食
事を楽しんだ後、ここを離れる時にはい
つもちょっとセンチメンタルになってし
まう。

Belgium brews more, and more interesting, styles of beer than
any other country. In the space of the past few years Tokyo has
become the best city outside of Europe to sample them, provided
1) you look at the bottle *before* it's opened and check the
expiration date, and 2) money is no object. Among the most
distinctive: fruity *gueuze* of any brand, refreshing "sour" beers
(Rodenbach Grand Cru), old-fashioned wheat beers (Hoegaarden
White), heady Trappist ales (Chimay, Orval) and the strong,
seductive, one-of-a-kind Duvel. Best places to hoist them: Bois
Celeste, Brussels, Cerveza, Kaiseitei East.

UN QUINTO

7-12-23 Roppongi,
Minato-ku
Tel: 3408-1795
Open: Noon-2pm & 6-11pm;
Sat., Sun. & hol., 6-11pm

Italian
¥¥
★★ 1/2

[cc] [symbol]　**Map 18**

ウン・クイント

Home base in Fussa (0425-52-6052) features outdoor tables only for the hardy: diners sit practically in the slow lane of National Route 16. Though it's more peaceful here in midtown, Un Quinto still manages to recreate the Yokota Air Base experience: rustic, shack-like decor, unsubtle Italian food heavy on the garlic and an international staff who aren't exactly gunning for Excellence in Waiting awards. A useful antidote to the rest of Roppongi. Recommended: soft-shell crabs.

横田基地の近く、福生に本店 (☎) 0425-52-6052 があり、そこでは大きなトラックが走る国道16号線脇にテーブルを出して食事を出している。ここ六本木の支店は打って変わって静かだが、どこか本店に似た雰囲気があり、ガーリックがいっぱいの料理はラフでエネルギッシュだ。さまざまな国籍のウェイターたちの仕事ぶりも決して型にはまっていない。六本木駅から3、4分のところなのに、ここはいわゆる六本木とは別世界である。

VALENÇAY

6-5-6 Jingu-mae, Shibuya-ku
Tel: 5466-2601
Open: 11:30am-10:30pm;
closed 3rd Sun.

Cheese
¥
★★

[cc] [symbol]　**Map 6**

ヴァランセー

Tokyo's flashiest cheese shop showcases its products in its attached restaurant. A little antiseptic, but unbeatable value for money: meals are essentially a loss-leader. Pastas with multiple cheese sauces, quiches, etc.

東京で最も派手なチーズ屋さん。ここのチーズは隣接したレストランで食べられる。少々防腐剤臭いのが気になるが、値段は手頃。ここではチーズで作ったソースのパスタやキッシュも味わえる。

*Ningyocho, and more generally the area between Nihonbashi and Kanda, offers the greatest concentration of good traditional Japanese eating places in Tokyo. Most cater to a regular clientele; few appear in guides of any sort. Prices tend to be either extremely cheap or very pricey indeed, but value for money is uniformly high. Two to try at opposite ends of the spectrum: bargain-basement yoshoku at **Raifukutei** (3666-3895) and an izakaya that truly rates ****/ ¥¥¥¥: **Kikuya** (3664-9032).*

VEGETABLE MAGIC II

1-3-12 Nakane,
Meguro-ku
Tel: 3725-1188
Open: 11:30am-1:30pm &
5:30-11pm; Sat. & Sun.,
5:30-11pm

Mediterranean
¥¥
★★

 **Map 25**

ベジタブル
マジック

Pumped up on petrochemicals, doped with pesticides, gassed or waxed or colorized, the modern Japanese vegetable is nothing if not beautiful. But the bionic gleam that seduces shoppers doesn't interest organic greengrocer Kazuo Yoshiki. His priorities are flavor and wholesomeness. So he buys his produce from farmers who grow it the way their grandparents did. Then he gives it to a team of French and Japanese cooks in a big open kitchen right in the middle of the restaurant and lets them whip up whatever comes to mind: salads and soups of the day, pôt-au-feu, cassoulet, paella, couscous, moussaka, you name it. It's good healthy eating, although—the name notwithstanding—there's not a lot here for vegetarians.

オーナーの吉木氏は見た目はきれいだが、化学肥料と殺虫剤がたっぷり使われた現代の野菜を嫌い、直接農家から有機野菜を買っているこだわり派。店の真ん中にある広いオープンキッチンで、フランス人と日本人のスタッフがその新鮮な野菜をふんだんに使って料理している。その日のサラダとスープ、ポトフ、豆とポークを煮込んだカスーレ、パエリア、クスクス、ムサカと種類は豊富。店の名前に反してベジタリアン向きのメニューが少ないが、素材を生かした料理は美味しい。

VENENCIA

2-15-6 Kami-Meguro,
Meguro-ku
Tel: 3760-7310
Open: 6:30pm-1:30am;
closed Sun. & hol.

Spanish
¥¥
★★★

 Map 4

ベネンシア

An old Spain hand and certified *experto en brandy y vinos de Jerez*, proprietor Takeshiro Naito can guide you through dozens of his favorite sherries (¥700 to ¥800/glass), including limited bottlings never seen in stores. Superior cured ham, giant Spanish olives, Spanish omelets and other tapas-type snacks too.

スペインのブランデーとシェリーに関してはエキスパートのオーナー、内藤氏は他ではめったに飲めないような、限定版や珍しいシェリーを一杯700円から800円で提供してくれる。生ハム、大粒のスペイン産オリーブ、スペインオムレツ、そして小皿料理などどれもスパニッシュ・テイスト満点だ。

VICTORIA STATION

4-9-2 Roppongi, Minato-ku
Tel: 3479-4601
Open: 11am-midnight;
Sun. & hol., 11am-11pm

American
¥¥
★★

 Map 18

ヴィクトリア ステーション

Authentically synthetic "American" decor and reputable roast beef at mass-market prices. Salad lovers dismayed by Japan's lack of understanding of the genre can take matters into their own hands here: VS's all-you-can-eat salad bar is the real thing. Lots of branches; notably Ogikubo (3399-1129), Shibuya (3463-5288) and Waseda (3205-0844).

列車の中をイメージしたちょっと古くさい内装とローストビーフ、そして値段の安いことでは定評があるが、本当に注目して欲しいのは種類が豊富なサラダバー。これこそ日本ではなかなかないアメリカらしいサービスだ。荻窪店（☎）3399-1129、渋谷店（☎）3463-5288、早稲田店（☎）3205-0844 がある。

VINO HIRATA

Endo Bldg., 2F,
2-13-10 Azabu Juban,
Minato-ku
Tel: 3456-4744
Open: 6pm-2am;
closed Sun. & hol.

Wine
¥¥
★★★

CC ◆ **Map 3**

ヴィーノ・ヒラタ

Founder of **La Patata** (3403-9664), **I Piselli** (3442-9771) and **Cucina Hirata** (3457-0094), Chef Hirata had all but priced himself beyond the means of many of his fans until he opened this simple upstairs wine bar. While the list even here is skewed toward big-ticket wines, there are bargains to be found, and they'll give you a fine antipasto misto plate at no great cost.

シェフの平田氏は『ラ パタータ』、『イ・ピゼリ』（☎）3442-9771 や『クッチーナ・ヒラタ』（☎）3457-0094 の創業者であり、今回シンプルなこのワインバーをオープンさせた。他店に比べて手頃な値段で料理やワインを楽しめるこの店に、数多い平田ファンたちは大満足だろう。ワインリストのほとんどは高価で名の知れたものばかりだが、中には求めやすいボトルもみつけられる。料理にはメインコースはないが、美味しい前菜の盛り合わせが食べられる。

VOLGA

3-5-14 Shiba Koen, Minato-ku
Tel: 3433-1766
Open: 11am-2:30pm &
5-10pm; Sat., Sun. & hol.,
noon-3pm & 5-9pm

Russian
¥¥
★

CC ◆ **Map 89**

ボルガ

Our respondents' comments ranged from "Even Dostoevsky's novels aren't *this* dreary" to "Made me feel like a dead czar" and "A nest of spies!" It's not every city where you can dine in what appears to be a Russian Orthodox crypt. Volga would make the perfect Halloween date. Recommended: more vodka.

ハロウィーンの日のデートには最適な店かもしれない。なにしろロシア正教の教会の地下室みたいな場所で、食事ができるチャンスなんてめったにないのだから。料理は特筆するほどではないが、ちょっと変わっていて不気味な感じのするこの店には、一度足を運んでみる価値がありそうだ。

WAIGAYA

1-5-10 Kami-Meguro,
Meguro-ku
Tel: 3713-2611
Open: 5pm-midnight

Mukokuseki
¥¥
★★

 Map 4

わいが屋

Imagine a place that cooks the food of an imaginary land, and a staff that speaks its language. Dishes like *pata-pata* ("flap-flap") gyoza, *gutsu-gutsu* (mystery stew) and pumpkin gratin. Cooks and waitresses with names like household pets ("Go-chan," "Dora-chan," etc.), and big name tags, as if they want you to call them that too. Flourishes and theatrical bows as dishes are passed and bottles uncorked. It's a pajama party. It's a cartoon. No, it's the parallel world of Waigaya. Once you get past the Mouseketeer style, you see this place for what it is: an *izakaya* for a new generation. After us, the deluge.

架空の土地の食べ物と、その土地の言葉をしゃべる人たちがいる場所を想像してみて欲しい。パタパタギョーザ、グツグツなどという名の料理に、例えば「ありがとうございます」の代わりに「ありやす」などというスタッフ。料理を運んで来たときやワインの栓を抜くときのおおげさなアクションは、まるでマンガかパジャマパーティーのよう。しかし、一度この雰囲気に慣れてしまえば、この一風変わった世界が 新世代の居酒屋だということがわかるだろう。

WARUNG I

2-29-18 Dogenzaka,
Shibuya-ku
Tel: 3464-9795
Open: 5:30pm-midnight

Indonesian
¥¥
★ 1/2

 Map 19

ワラング・アイ

Things have straightened up a little since the early days when the staff seemed to be smoking something stronger than *kretek*. Still a convivial late-night scene, and idiosyncratic but not bad versions of satay, *gado-gado*, fried rice and noodles, etc.

かつては、何か悪いものでも吸っているような不思議な雰囲気を漂わせていた従業員の質も多少はましになったようだ。かなり個性的だが、サテー、ガドガド、焼き飯、麺類の味は悪くない。

WEDGWOOD TEA ROOM

11-6 Sarugakucho,
Shibuya-ku
Tel: 5458-8024
Open: 11am-8pm

Tea (the meal)
¥
★★ 1/2

 Map 4

There are days, as Oscar Wilde knew so well, when the presence or absence of cucumber sandwiches becomes a matter of some urgency. Days, in short, when there is a need for the art of tea as practiced by that other island nation. This is the place to come then: a civilized sanctuary of Earl Gray and Darjeeling and Queen Mary, of scones and clotted cream, dainty cakes and sandwiches, Wedgwood pots and cups and cozies, even tea maidens in white aprons. It's ¥2000 all in, and just speak up when you want them to refill your pot with hot water.

ウェッジウッド ティールーム

英国流茶道を体験できる場所として人気がある。種類豊富なお茶はもちろん、サンドイッチ、ケーキ、固めに練ったクリームを添えたスコーンが、ウェッジウッドのポットやカップでサービスされる。ティーポットの保温カバーや白いエプロンをしたウェイトレスもお洒落で居心地が良い。2000円でひととおり楽しめ、お茶のポットにはお湯の継ぎ足しもしてくれる。

YATANA

1-11-31 Hyakunincho,
Shinjuku-ku
Tel: 3361-1349
Open: 11:30am-11pm

Burmese
¥¥
★★

 Map 22

Relocated (just down the street from their original place), expanded and better than ever. Yatana is home away from home for the surprising number of young Burmese studying and working in Tokyo. It's also the only exception we'll make to eating in a place with a karaoke machine. In fact here you may even want to sing. Recommended tune: "Won't Be Long" (The Bubblegum Brothers).

珍しいビルマ料理のレストラン。タイやインド料理より少し粗削りといった感じの家庭料理が中心になっている。独特な田舎風カレー、野菜のフライ、歯ごたえがあり香辛料の効いた麺類、小鳥の串焼きなどが食べられる。新しくて広くなった店は入りやすく、意外と数の多い在日ビルマ人たちに故郷の味を満喫させてい

る。また、カラオケが置いてある店で、食事が耐えられるのはここぐらいだろう。この店の他、東京にあるビルマレストランはニュースポット、天王州アイルの豪華な『パレ・ドゥ・ローテュス』(☎) 5460-5453 と『ビルマの竪琴』(☎) 5723-2464 である。

ヤタナ

YETI

Minimalist, to put it politely: the entire decor could have been hauled here in a backpack from Katmandu. There's a similar attractive innocence to the food, notably the *momo*, *pokouda* and Nepalese curries (try the pumpkin). They're less successful when they try to be Indian—forget the *sag* curries. And why, oh why, even here, the mound of shredded cabbage, sliced cucumber, and pink-tinted Kewpie "mayonnaise" that Japan takes to be Indian "salad"? But we like the prices, the portions, and even the Nepalese music, which is considerably more soothing than the usual Indian droning.

2-14-8 Takadanobaba,
Shinjuku-ku
Tel: 3208-1766
Open: 11:30am-11pm

Nepalese/Indian
¥
★★

 Map 24

よくいえばミニマリストとも呼べるこの店の内装は、カトマンズから手荷物にして運ばれてきたような感じで、料理も素朴さが魅力になっている。モモ(ネパール風ギョーザ)、ポクーダ(ネパール風天ぷら)、カレー類(カボチャのカレーが美味)がお薦め。しかし、いわゆるインド料理はいまいちで、特にサグカレーはお薦めできない。また、なぜか日本人がインド風サラダだと勘違いしているキャベツの千切りにキュウリの輪切り、ピンク色のマヨネーズも付いてくる。値段は手頃で、量も多く、食べやすい料理が揃っている。店内に流れるネパール音楽も心地よい。

イエティ

YURAKUCHO YAKITORI ALLEY

2-1 Yurakucho,
Chiyoda-ku
Open: Roughly sunset to midnight; opens earlier on weekends

Yakitori
¥
★ 1/2
Map 7

Tokyo's quintessential post-war, under-the-tracks, open-air eating/drinking scene and, well, it's seen better days. The remaining shops make little attempt at quality, not that the usual clientele would notice it anyway. For good rowdy Occupation-era fun, it's still unmissable and irreplaceable.

有楽町高架下の飲み屋街

第二次大戦後の東京では沢山あった屋外やガード下の飲食店街の中ではもっとも親しまれているところだ。ここをおいて、米軍占領時代の楽しみを今に伝えている場所はないだろう。

ZEST CANTINA

Another arm of the **La Bohème/Tableaux** empire. The Zest chain styles itself as a purveyor of "Southern California" cooking, which is a pretty good clue that authenticity isn't going to be a priority. That said, for Americanized Mexicana-like burritos and fajitas, these places are cheap and convenient. Other Zests can be found in Harajuku (3499-0293), Iikura (5570-6555), Nishi Azabu (3400-3985), Roppongi (3478-0222) and Yokohama (045-662-0941). All are open until 5am.

3-29-4 Ikejiri, Setagaya-ku
Tel: 5486-0321
Open: 11:30-5am

American
¥
★ 1/2
Map 90

ゼスト カンティナ

『ラボエム』、『タブローズ』の傘下のひとつ、ゼストチェーンによれば、"南カリフォルニア料理" を出す店ということだが、それでいかにここが本物志向の店でないかがわかってしまう。なぜなら"南カリフォルニア料理"なんていうはっきりとしたものがないからである。しかし、アメリカナイズされたブリトーやファヒータなどを食べるなら、こうした店は安くて便利

だ。原宿店（☎）3499-0293、飯倉店（☎）
5570-6555、西麻布店（☎）3400-3985、
六本木店（☎）3478-0222、横浜店（☎）
045-662-0941 があり、どの店も午前5時
まで営業している。

ZIA

Shibutoh Cinétower Bldg., B1,
2-6-17 Dogenzaka,
Shibuya-ku
Tel: 5489-6655
Open: 11:30am-11pm

American
¥¥
★★ 1/2

　Map 19

Nouveau Southwestern U.S. cuisine in the
(brand new) tradition of its progenitor,
Santa Fe's Coyote Cafe. Native American
ingredients—chilies, corn, squash, tomatoes—form the base, but in com-bination
with anything from anywhere. The menu, in
fact, ranges so widely over so unfamiliar a
territory that you're probably best off to put
yourself in the hands of the chef. Name a
price per head and he'll assemble a course.

The biggest revelation here for the
skeptic is the sheer variety of flavors: it's
not all cilantro and mesquite. A touch of
Mexico here, a little Provence there, a hint
of Chinese stir-fry. Portions are small, but
there's a fresh, honest taste to things that
moves the Japanese menu to call it "health
food for the unstoic." Add a colorful,
slightly bizarre decor and not-so-Old West
music of the Dan Hicks and his Hot Licks
school and you've got a worthy adult refuge
in the heart of the Shibuya teen jungle.

サンタフェにあるサウスウエスト料理の元
祖『コヨーテ・カフェ』の伝統を取り入
れ、新しいスタイルも加えた新アメリカ料
理店。チリ、トウモロコシ、カボチャ、ト
マトなどのアメリカ原産の素材をベースに
し、それに様々な土地の様々な材料を加え
ている。メニューは多岐にわたり、名前か
らはどんなものか分からないので、ひとり
当たりの予算と好みをいって、あとはシェ
フに任せるのが良い。メキシコ料理、プロ
バンス料理から中華料理の炒めものまで、
種々のエッセンスが料理の中にうかがえ
る。量は少ないが、素材は新鮮で真面目な
味付けだ。カラフルで奇抜なインテリア、
バックに流れる通好みのカントリーミュー
ジックもカルトっぽくて面白い。

ジア

ZUIEN BEKKAN

2-7-4 Shinjuku,
Shinjuku-ku
Tel: 3351-3511
Open: 11am-10pm

Chinese
¥¥
★★ 1/2
Map 22

随園別館

If we're not quite as enamored of this old-time favorite as most guidebooks, it's only because there are so many other interesting alternatives these days that didn't exist when ZB first opened its doors. It's drab and dingy, the service tends to be brusque and the menu hardly ever changes. In other words, it's uncompromisingly Chinese and—quite a feat for Tokyo—remains so after decades of popularity. Still a relative bargain, too. Recommended: Peking duck.

この店は開店当時、どのレストランガイドにも登場し、大評判だった。でももうここに魅力を感じなくなってしまったのは、最近になって興味をそそる店が次々と出現したからなのだろう。店内は薄汚れ、サービスも悪いし、メニューも昔と変わらない。だがそれにもかかわらず、この東京でそこそこの人気を保っていられるのは、頑固一徹、変わらない味と手頃な値段のお陰だろう。北京ダックはお薦めだ。

『東京大飯店』を除けば、東京には飲茶をカートに乗せ、大勢の客であふれる広い店内を回るという正統派の店は少ない。そんなことから、ほとんどの店では客はメニューの中から料理を選び調理して貰っている。結果として、冷凍や作り置きの料理を食べさせられることが多い。これを承知なら、麻布十番店 (☎) 3505-9688をはじめとして、各所に支店のある『Cox-Top』や、新宿 (☎) 3342-5758 と池袋 (☎) 3986-6410 にある『翠亨屯茶両』、最近味が落ちたが六本木で人気の『点心之家』(☎) 3478-8608がある。また、満州式の飲茶で、皮の厚い餃子を食べるなら、新宿の『老辺餃子館』(☎) 3348-5810 がお薦め。

MAP
LISTINGS

マップ・リスト

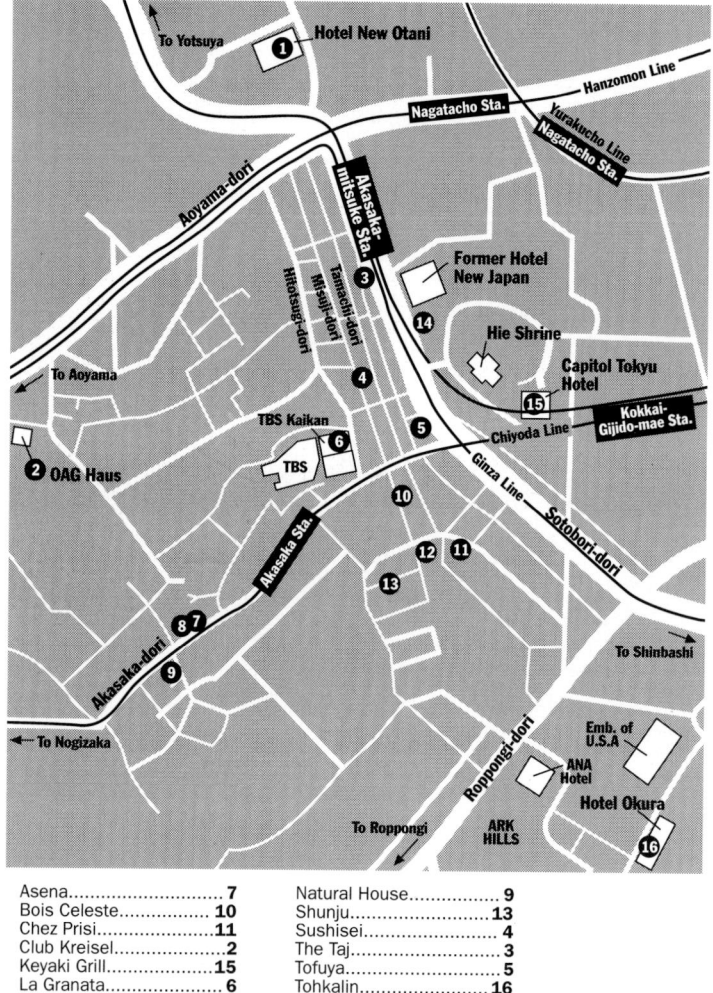

2 AOYAMA　青山

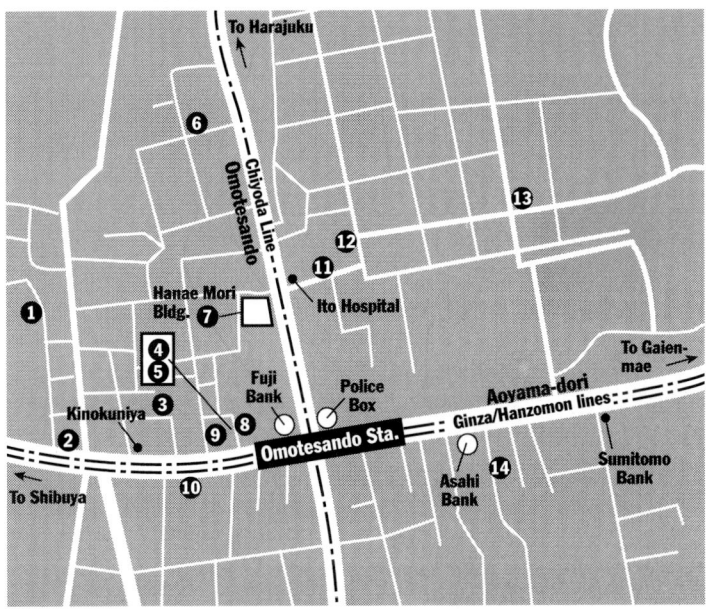

3 AZABU JUBAN 麻布十番

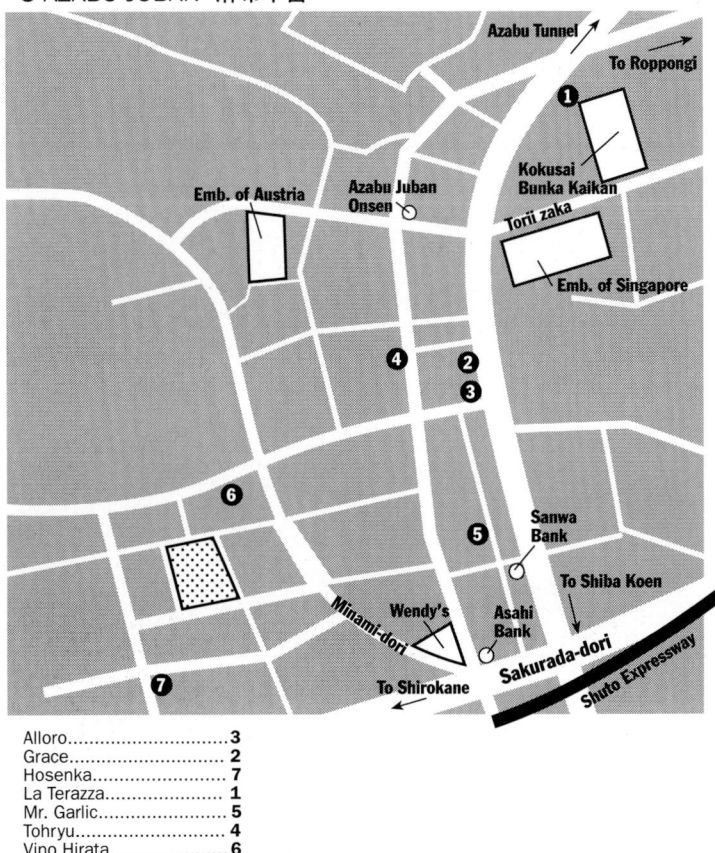

4 DAIKANYAMA/NAKA-MEGURO　代官山／中目黒

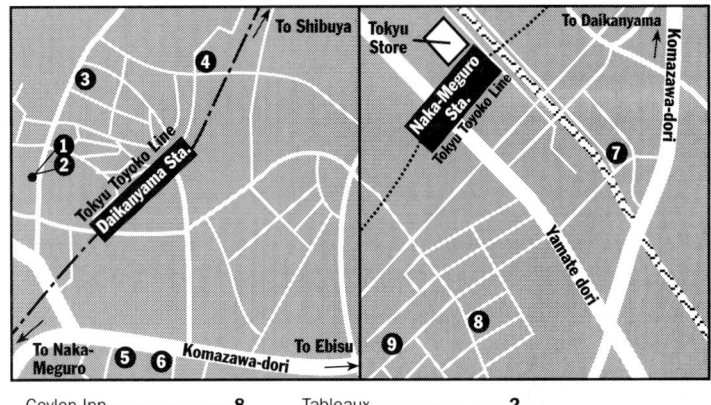

5 EBISU　恵比寿

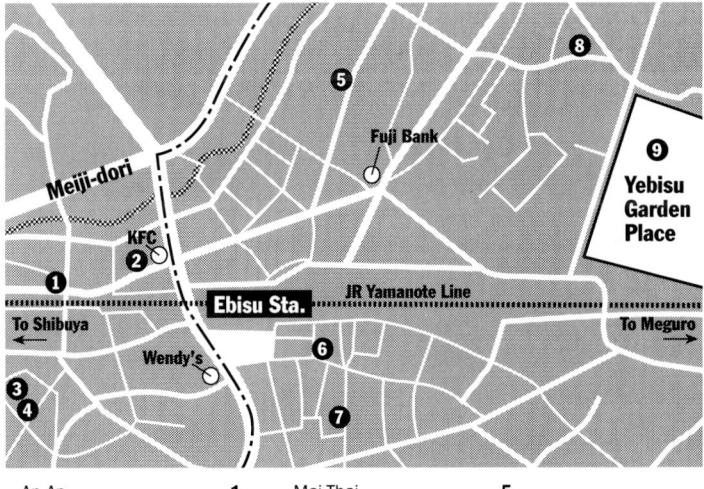

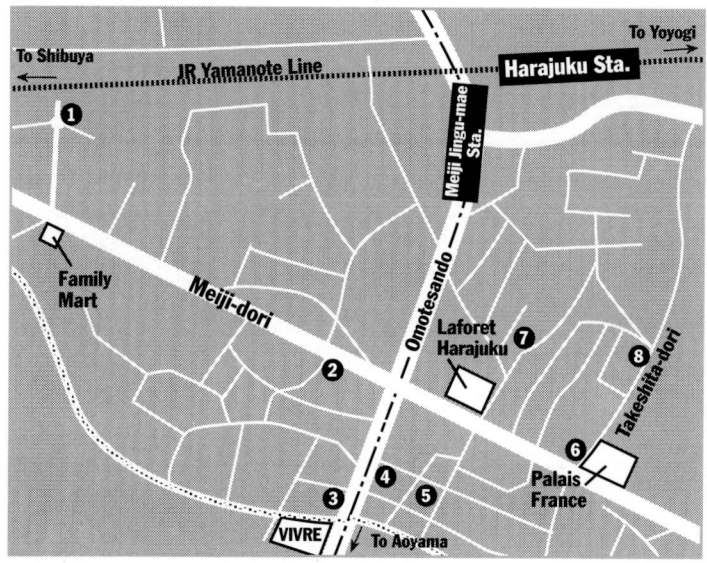

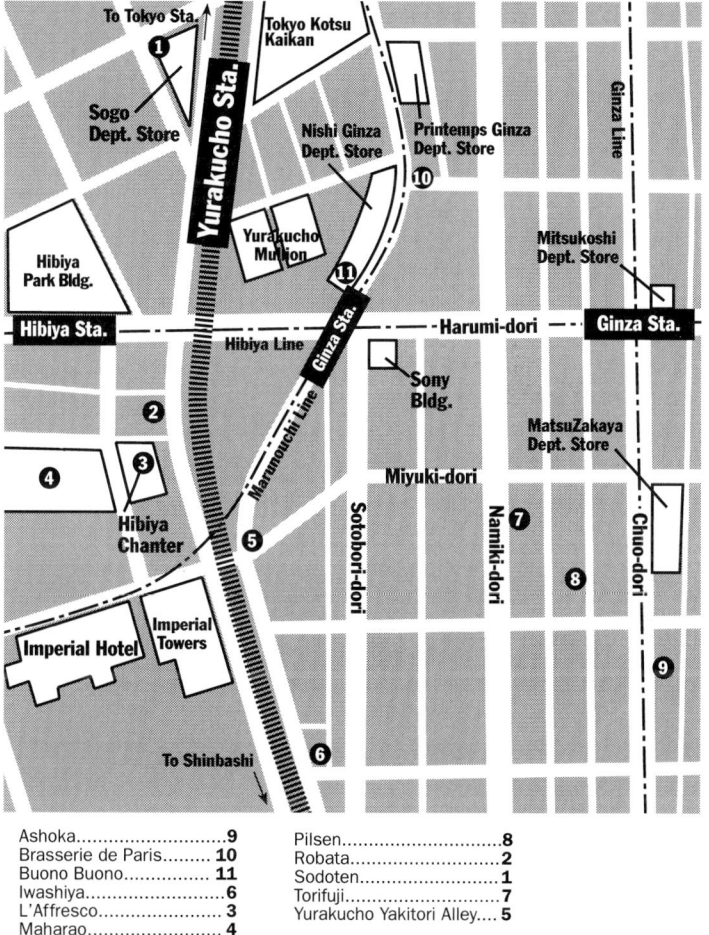

8 HIROO 広尾

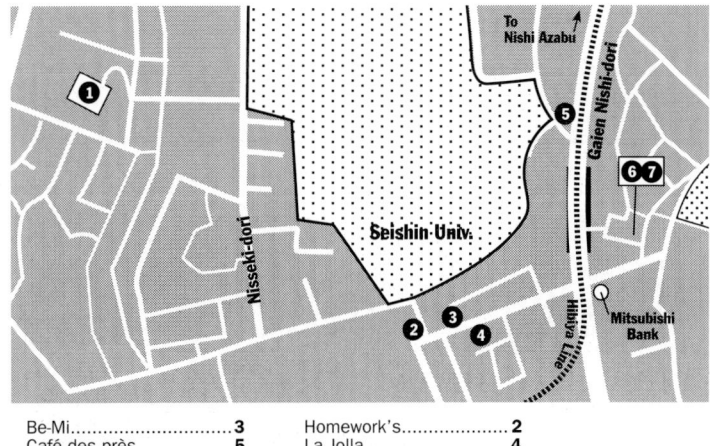

9 IIDABASHI 飯田橋

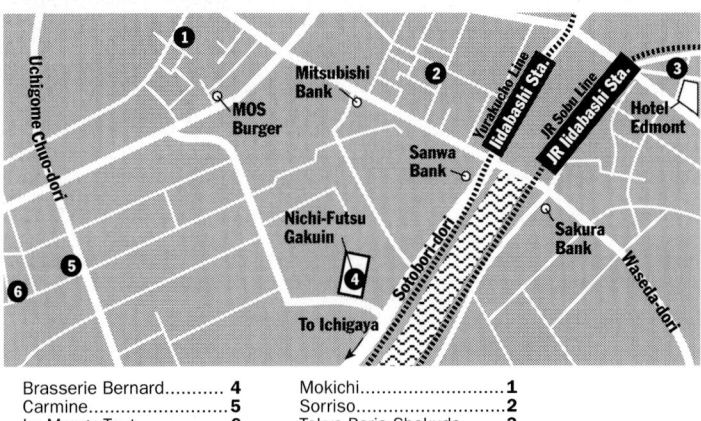

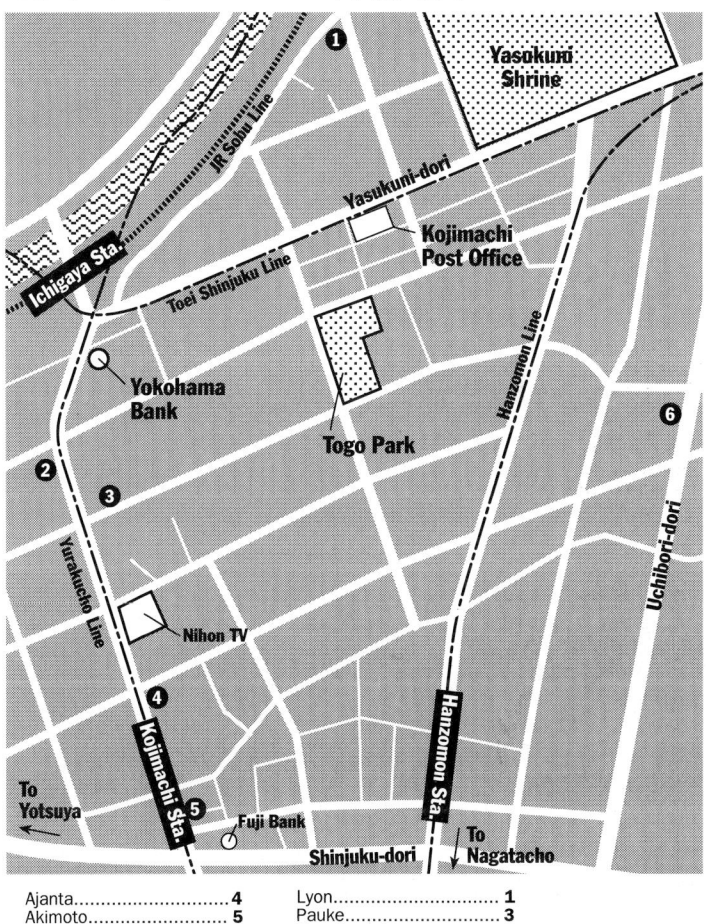

11 JINGU GAIEN 神宮外苑

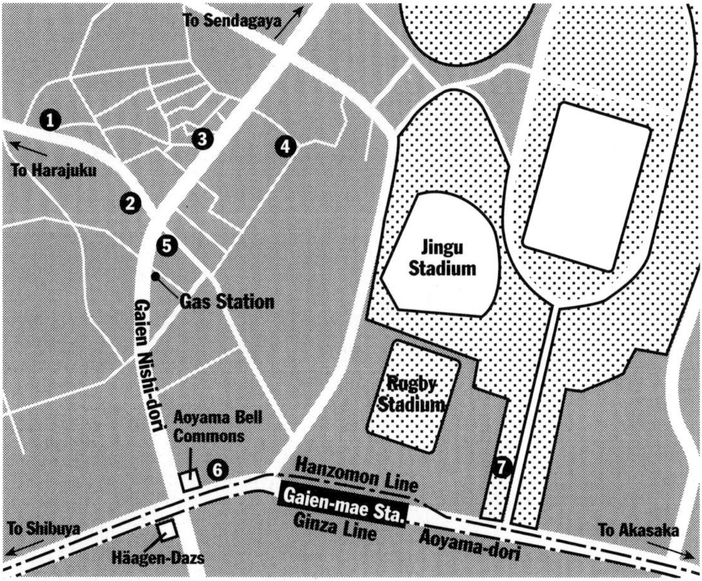

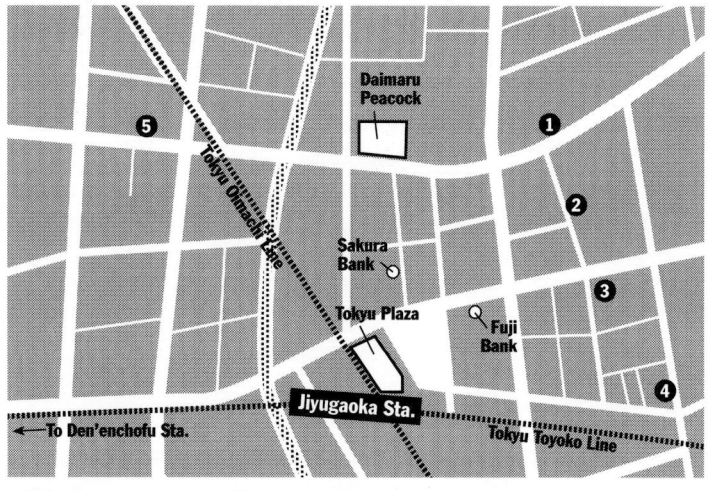

La Patata........................ 3	Selan............................... 7
Mominoki House............. 1	Sin.................................. 2
Ninniku Mura.................. 4	Taverna Azzurra.............. 5
Pizzeria Sabatini.............. 6	

12 JIYUGAOKA 自由が丘

Chianti............................ 2	Shanfon........................... 5
Gold Leaf........................ 1	Top Dog........................... 3
Petit Marché................... 4	

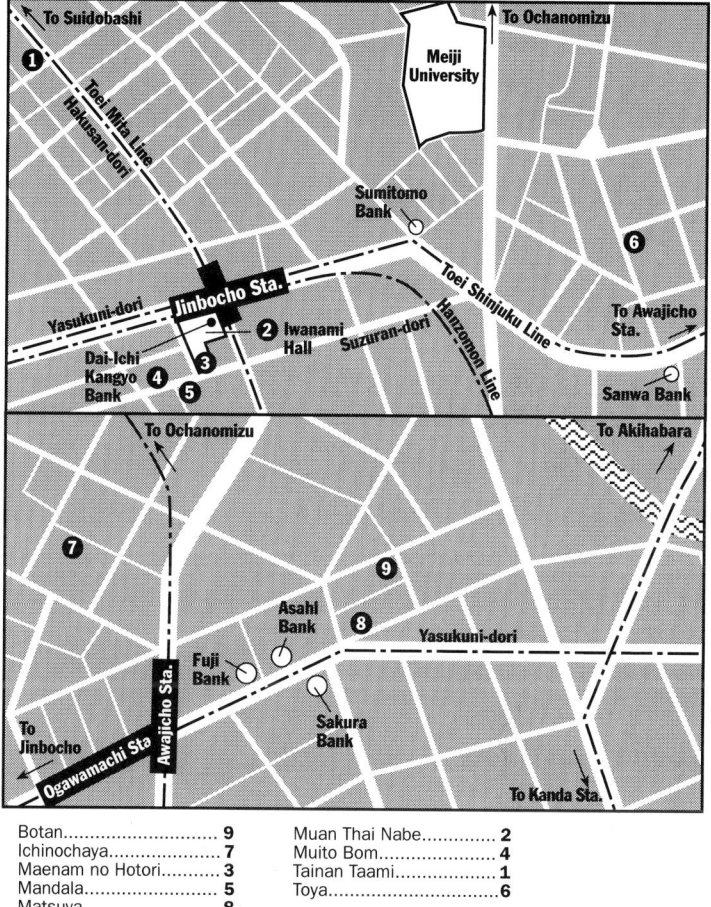

14 MEGURO/GOTANDA 目黒／五反田

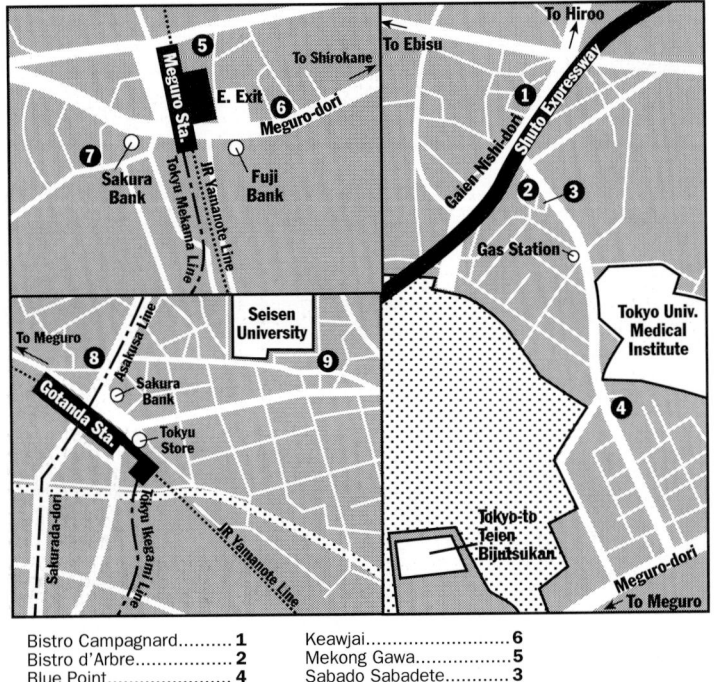

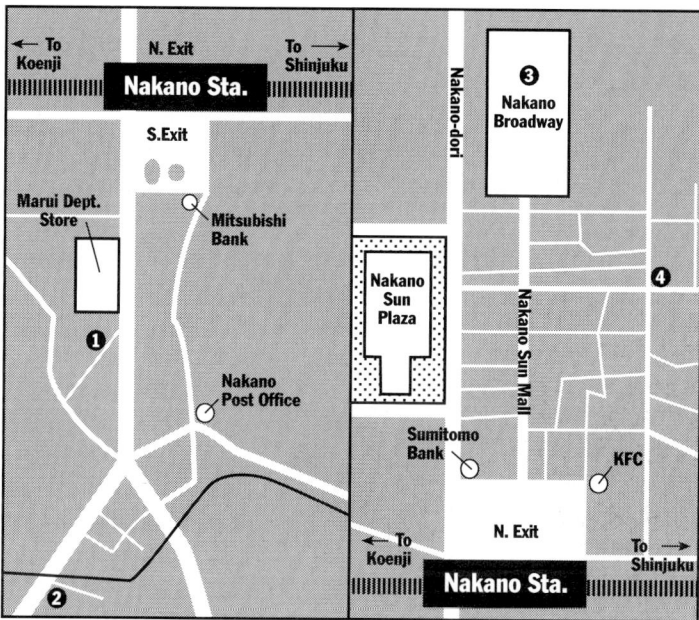

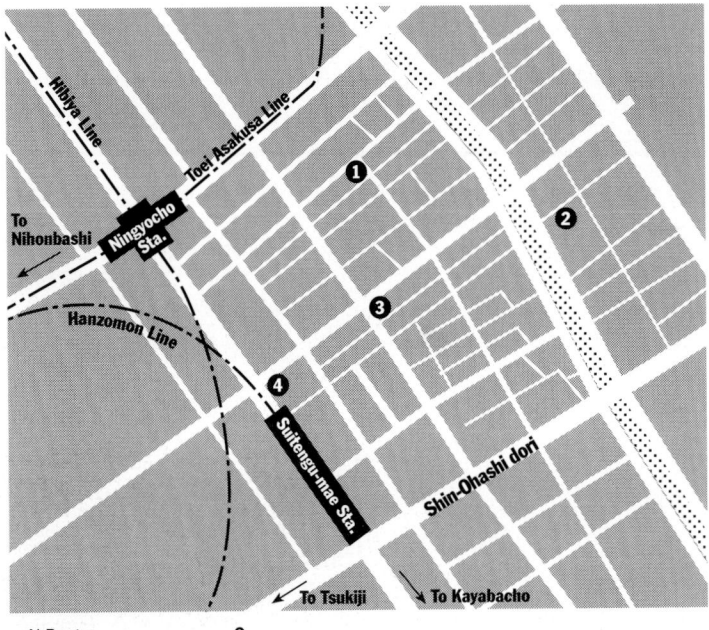

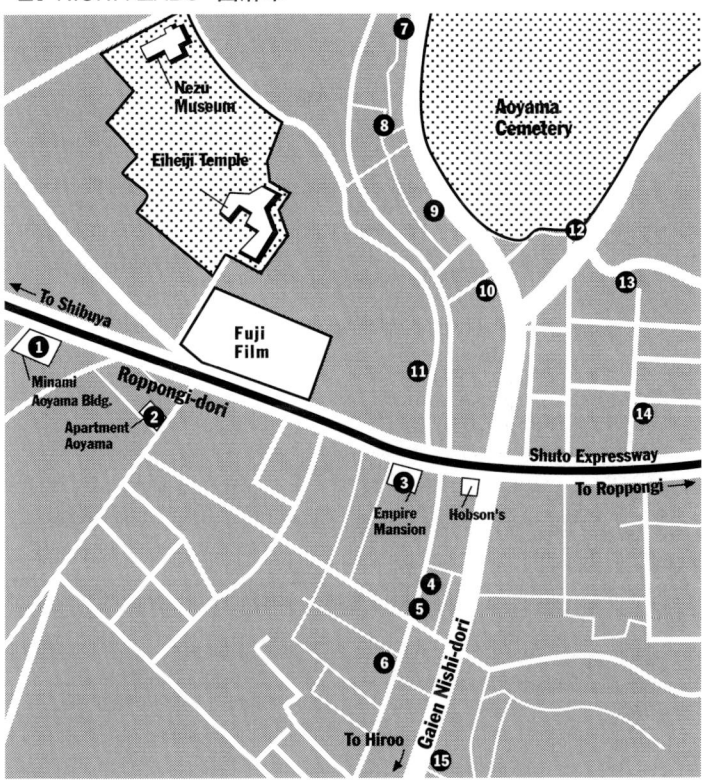

18 ROPPONGI 六本木

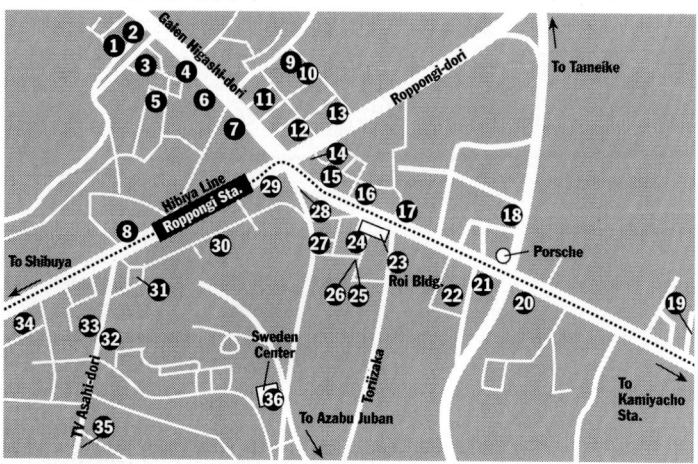

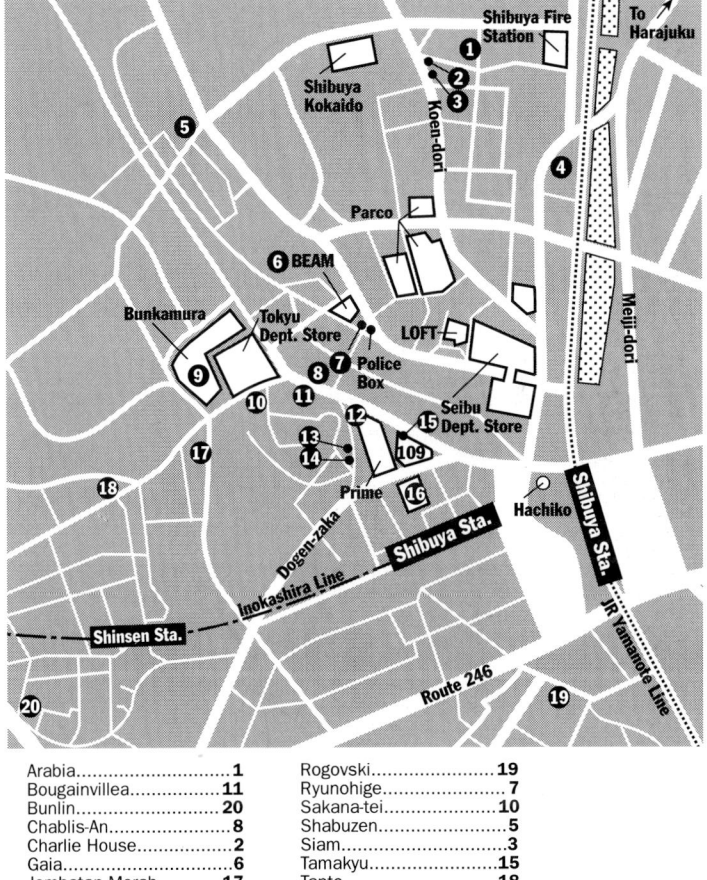

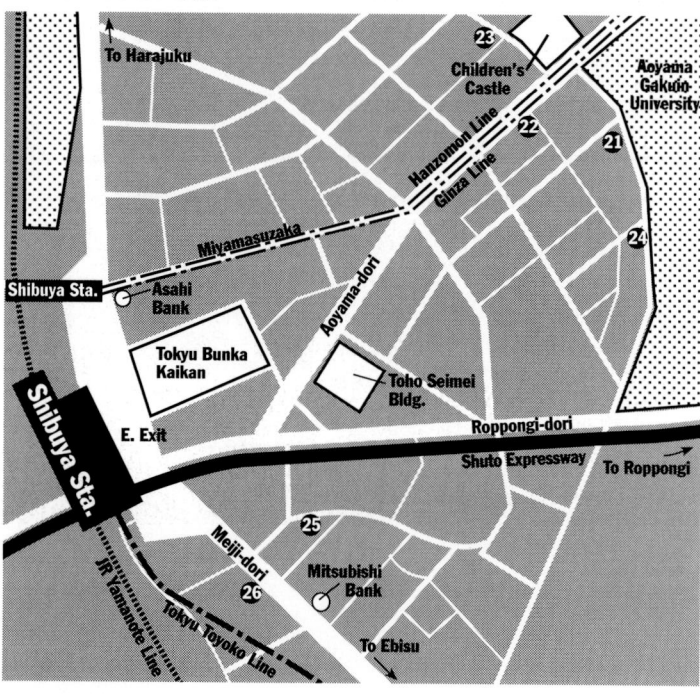

21 SHIMO-KITAZAWA 下北沢

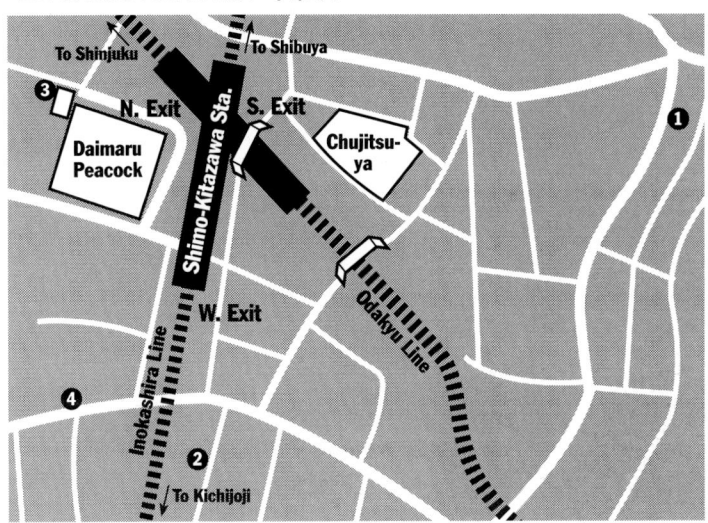

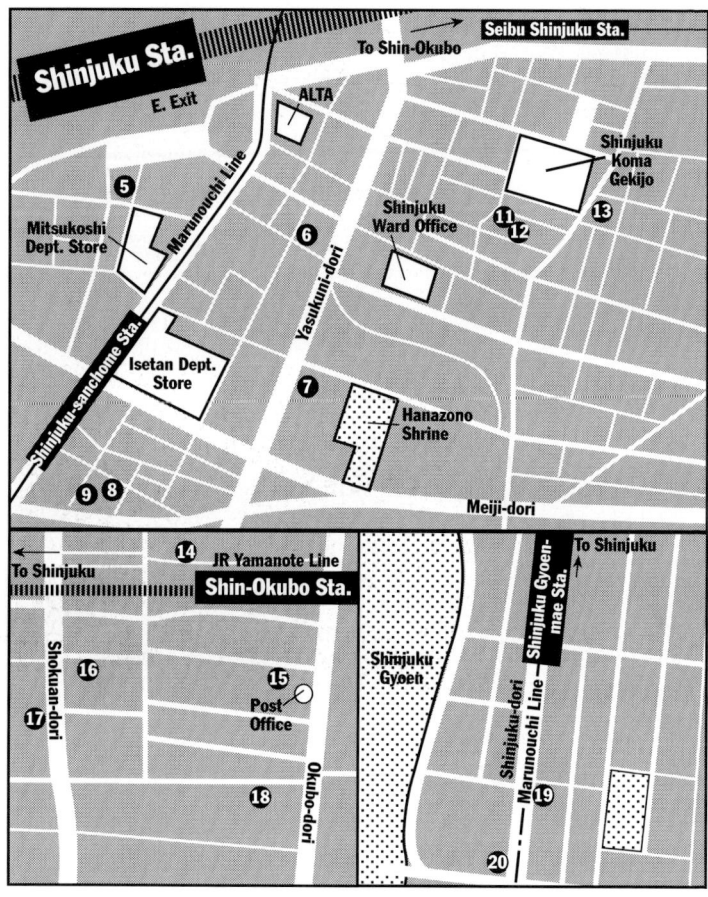

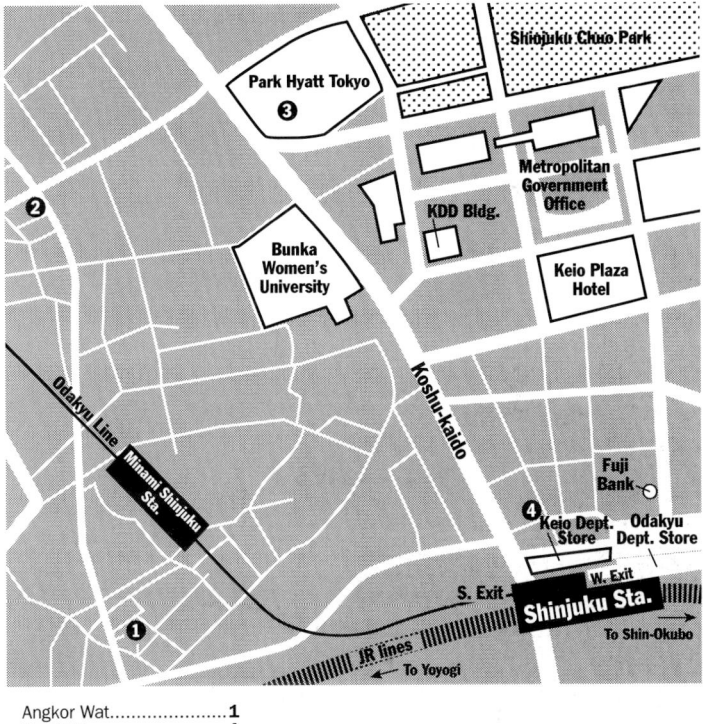

24 TAKADANOBABA/WASEDA 高田馬場／早稲田

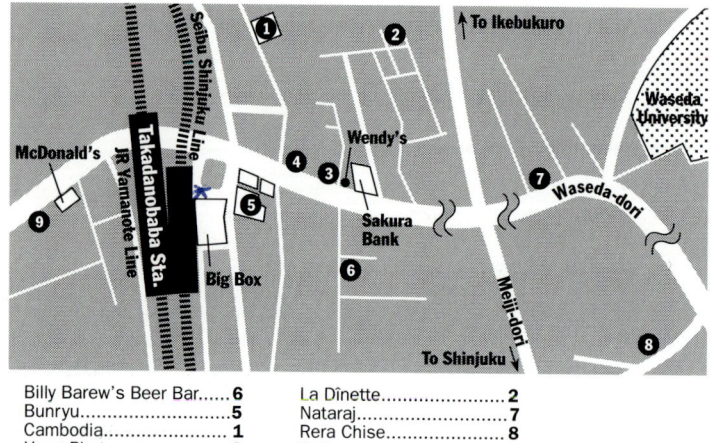

＊＝ Exit 3

25 TORITSU DAIGAKU 都立大学

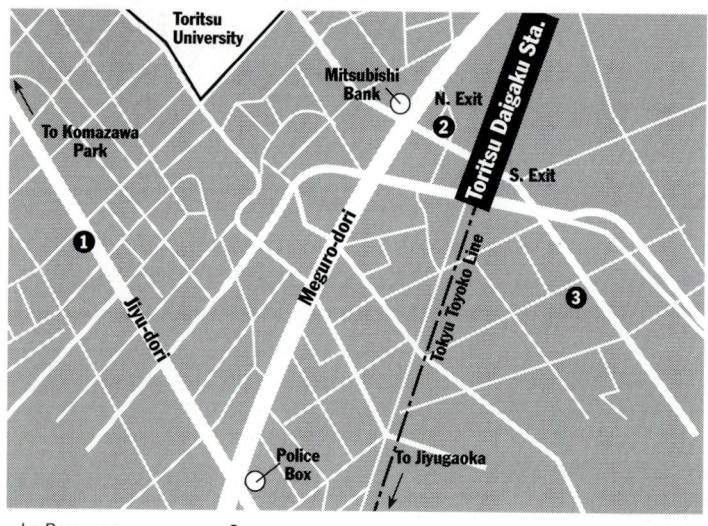

26

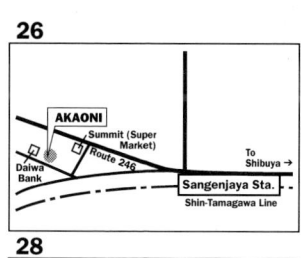

AKAONI

Summit (Super Market)
Route 246
Daiwa Bank
To Shibuya →
Sangenjaya Sta.
Shin-Tamagawa Line

27

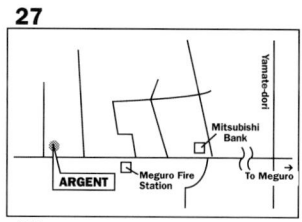

Yamate-dori
Mitsubishi Bank
ARGENT
Meguro Fire Station
To Meguro →

28

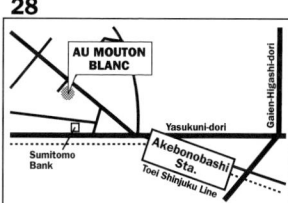

AU MOUTON BLANC
Gaien-Higashi-dori
Yasukuni-dori
Sumitomo Bank
Akebonobashi Sta.
Toei Shinjuku Line

29

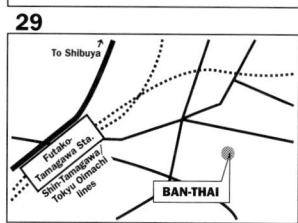

To Shibuya ↑
Futako-Tamagawa Sta.
Shin-Tamagawa/ Tokyu Oimachi lines
BAN-THAI

30

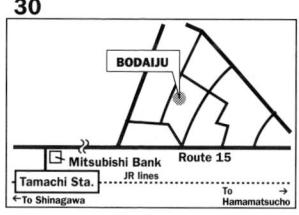

BODAIJU
Mitsubishi Bank
Route 15
Tamachi Sta.
JR lines
← To Shinagawa
To Hamamatsucho →

31

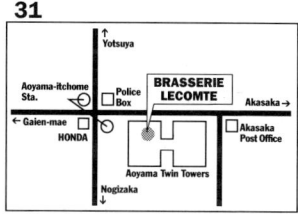

Yotsuya ↑
Aoyama-itchome Sta.
Police Box
BRASSERIE LECOMTE
Akasaka →
← Gaien-mae
HONDA
Akasaka Post Office
Aoyama Twin Towers
Nogizaka

32

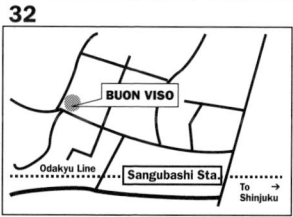

BUON VISO
Odakyu Line
Sangubashi Sta.
To Shinjuku →

33

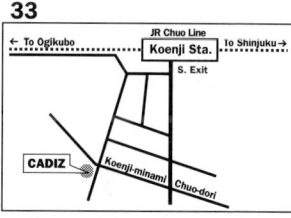

JR Chuo Line
← To Ogikubo
Koenji Sta.
To Shinjuku →
S. Exit
CADIZ
Koenji-minami
Chuo-dori

34

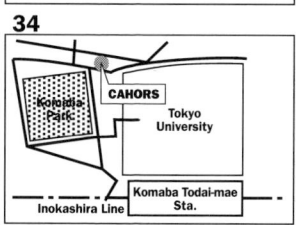

CAHORS
Komaba Park
Tokyo University
Komaba Todai-mae Sta.
Inokashira Line

35

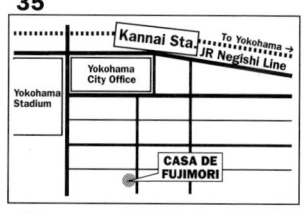

Kannai Sta.
To Yokohama →
JR Negishi Line
Yokohama City Office
Yokohama Stadium
CASA DE FUJIMORI

36

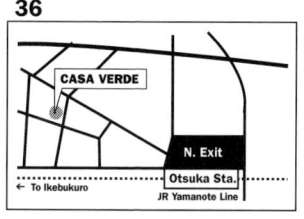

CASA VERDE
N. Exit
Otsuka Sta.
← To Ikebukuro
JR Yamanote Line

37

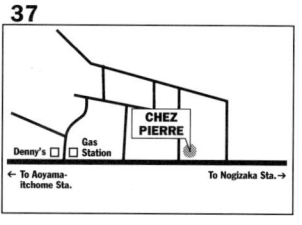

CHEZ PIERRE
Denny's
Gas Station
← To Aoyama-itchome Sta.
To Nogizaka Sta. →

38

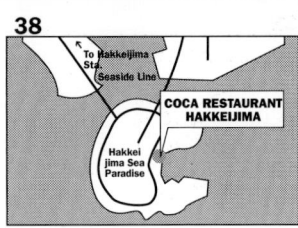

39

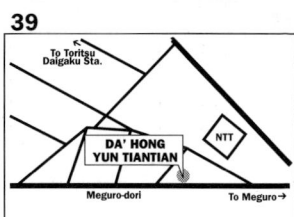

40

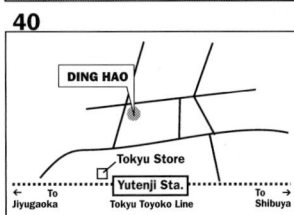

41

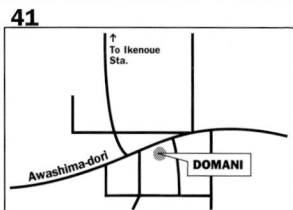

42

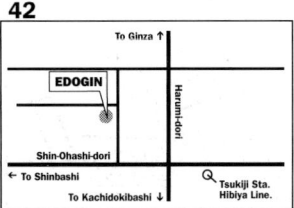

43

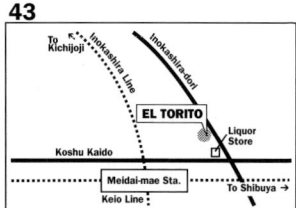

44

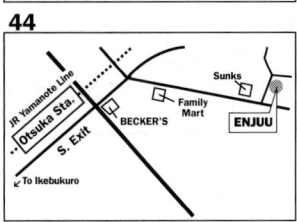

45

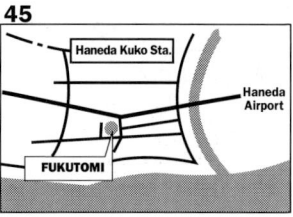

46

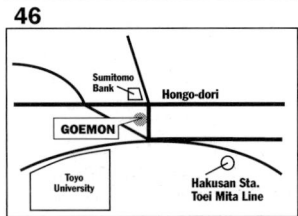

47

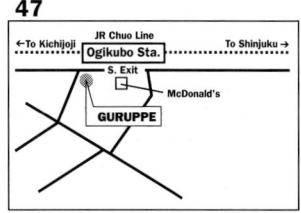

48

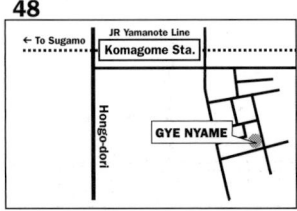

49

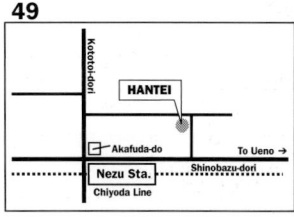

50

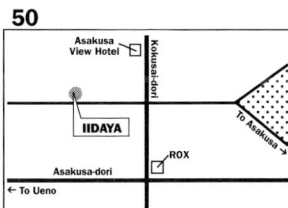

Asakusa
View Hotel

Kokusai-dori

IIDAYA

ROX

Asakusa-dori

← To Ueno

To Asakusa →

51

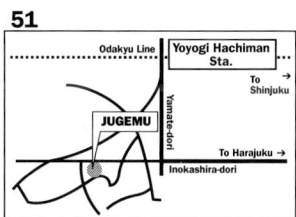

Odakyu Line

Yoyogi Hachiman
Sta.

To
Shinjuku

Yamate-dori

JUGEMU

To Harajuku →

Inokashira-dori

52

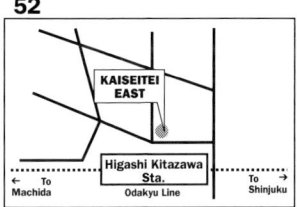

KAISEITEI
EAST

Higashi Kitazawa
Sta.

← To
Machida

Odakyu Line

To →
Shinjuku

53

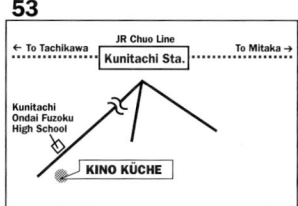

← To Tachikawa

JR Chuo Line

To Mitaka →

Kunitachi Sta.

Kunitachi
Ondai Fuzoku
High School

KINO KÜCHE

54

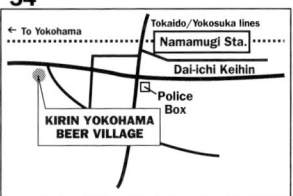

← To Yokohama

Tokaido/Yokosuka lines

Namamugi Sta.

Dai-ichi Keihin

Police
Box

KIRIN YOKOHAMA
BEER VILLAGE

55

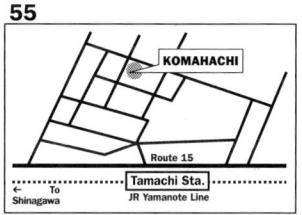

KOMAHACHI

Route 15

← To
Shinagawa

Tamachi Sta.

JR Yamanote Line

56

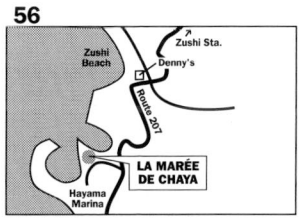

Zushi
Beach

Zushi Sta.

Denny's

Route 207

LA MARÉE
DE CHAYA

Hayama
Marina

57

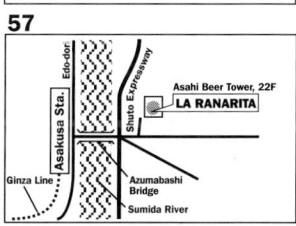

Edo-dori

Asakusa Sta.

Shuto Expressway

Asahi Beer Tower, 22F
LA RANARITA

Ginza Line

Azumabashi
Bridge

Sumida River

58

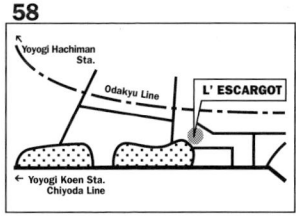

Yoyogi Hachiman
Sta.

Odakyu Line

L' ESCARGOT

← Yoyogi Koen Sta.
Chiyoda Line

59

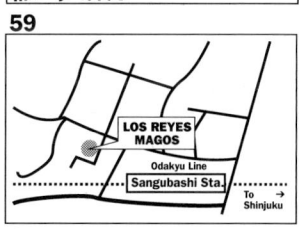

LOS REYES
MAGOS

Odakyu Line

Sangubashi Sta.

To →
Shinjuku

60

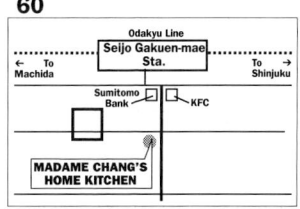

Odakyu Line

Seijo Gakuen-mae
Sta.

← To
Machida

To →
Shinjuku

Sumitomo
Bank

KFC

MADAME CHANG'S
HOME KITCHEN

61

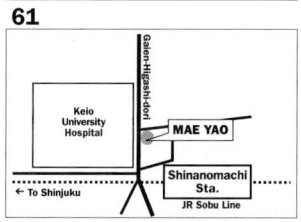

Gaien-Higashi-dori

Keio
University
Hospital

MAE YAO

Shinanomachi
Sta.

← To Shinjuku

JR Sobu Line

62

63

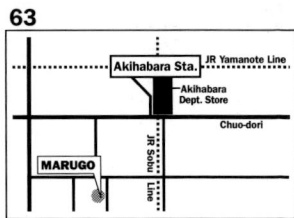

64

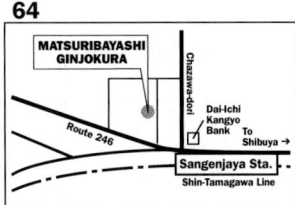

65

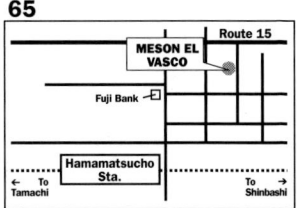

66

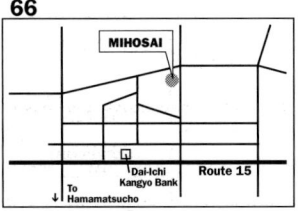

67

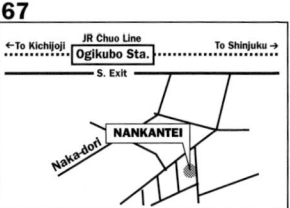

68

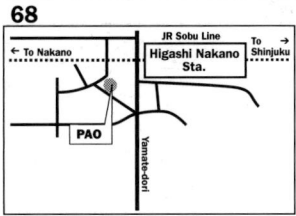

69

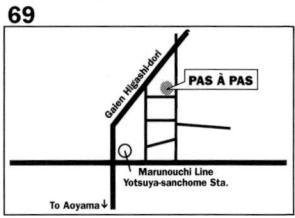

70

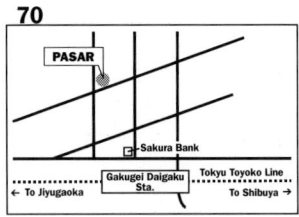

71

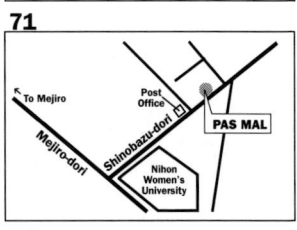

72

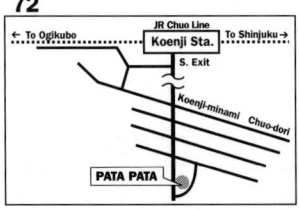

73

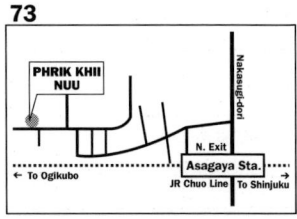

74
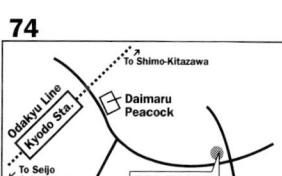

To Shimo-Kitazawa
Odakyu Line
Kyodo Sta.
Daimaru Peacock
To Seijo Gakuen-mae
ROS MARINO

75
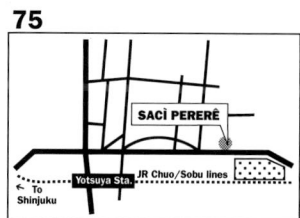

SACÌ PERERÈ
Yotsuya Sta.
JR Chuo/Sobu lines
To Shinjuku

76

← To Mejiro
Ikebukuro Sta.
To Otsuka →
JR Yamanote Line
Seibu Dept. Store
E. Exit
Mitsukoshi Dept. Store
Meiji-dori
SAIGON

77
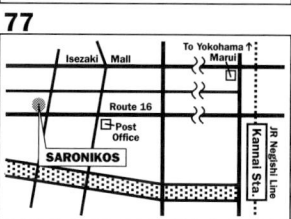

Isezaki Mall
To Yokohama ↑
Marui
Route 16
Post Office
SARONIKOS
JR Negishi Line
Kannai Sta.

78
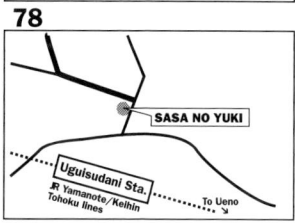

SASA NO YUKI
Uguisudani Sta.
JR Yamanote/Keihin Tohoku lines
To Ueno

79
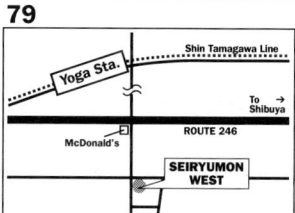

Shin Tamagawa Line
Yoga Sta.
To Shibuya →
McDonald's
ROUTE 246
SEIRYUMON WEST

80
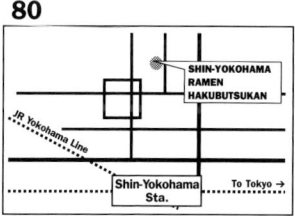

SHIN-YOKOHAMA RAMEN HAKUBUTSUKAN
JR Yokohama Line
Shin-Yokohama Sta.
To Tokyo →

81
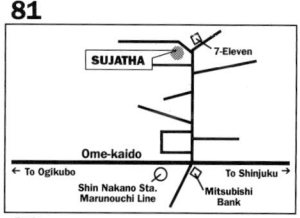

SUJATHA
7-Eleven
Ome-kaido
← To Ogikubo
Shin Nakano Sta.
Marunouchi Line
To Shinjuku →
Mitsubishi Bank

82
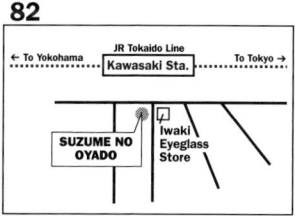

← To Yokohama
JR Tokaido Line
To Tokyo →
Kawasaki Sta.
SUZUME NO OYADO
Iwaki Eyeglass Store

83
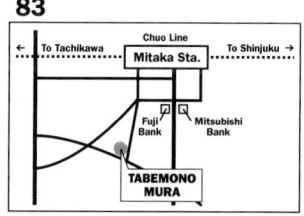

← To Tachikawa
Chuo Line
To Shinjuku →
Mitaka Sta.
Fuji Bank
Mitsubishi Bank
TABEMONO MURA

84
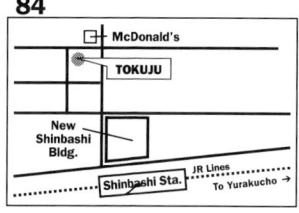

McDonald's
TOKUJU
New Shinbashi Bldg.
JR Lines
Shinbashi Sta.
To Yurakucho →

85
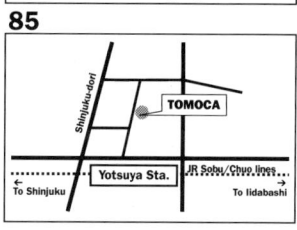

Shinjuku-dori
TOMOCA
Yotsuya Sta.
JR Sobu/Chuo lines
To Shinjuku
To Iidabashi

86

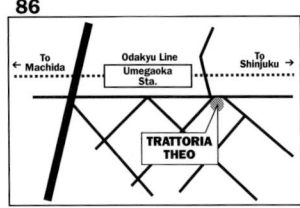

To ← Machida
Odakyu Line
Umegaoka Sta.
To Shinjuku →

TRATTORIA THEO

87

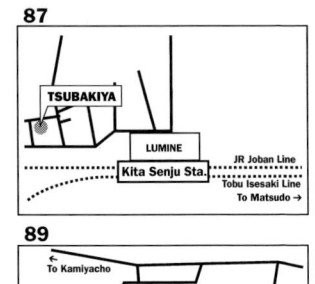

TSUBAKIYA

LUMINE

Kita Senju Sta.

JR Joban Line

Tobu Isesaki Line
To Matsudo →

88

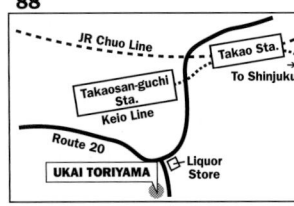

JR Chuo Line

Takao Sta.

To Shinjuku

Takaosan-guchi Sta.
Keio Line

Route 20

Liquor Store

UKAI TORIYAMA

89

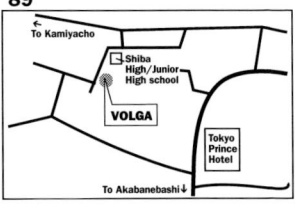

← To Kamiyacho

Shiba High/Junior High school

VOLGA

Tokyo Prince Hotel

To Akabanebashi ↓

90

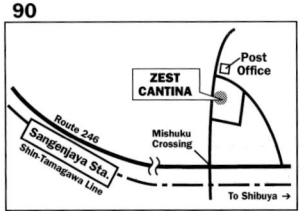

Post Office

ZEST CANTINA

Route 246

Sangenjaya Sta.
Shin-Tamagawa Line

Mishuku Crossing

To Shibuya →

INDEX

インデックス

Ikebukuro/Otsuka
池袋／大塚

Casa Verde
Enjuu
Goemon
Gye Nyame
Mareichan
Pas Mal
Saigon

Jiyugaoka/Toyoko Line
自由が丘／東横線沿線

Argent
Chianti
Da Hong Yun Tiantian
Ding Hao
Gold Leaf
La Baracca
La Pineta
Pasar
Petit Marché
Shanfon
Top Dog
Vegetable Magic II

Kanda/Ochanomizu
神田／お茶ノ水

Botan
Ichinochaya
Maenam no Hotori
Mandala
Matsuya
Muan Thai Nabe
Muito Bom
Tainan Taami
Toya

Kawasaki/Yokohama/
South
川崎／横浜／南部

Casa de Fujimori
Coca Restaurant
  Hakkeijima
Kirin Yokohama Beer
  Village
La Marée de Chaya
Saronikos
Shin-Yokohama Ramen
  Hakubutsukan
Suzume no Oyado

Meguro/Gotanda
目黒／五反田

Bistro Campagnard
Bistro d'Arbre
Blue Point
Brasserie Pierrot
7025 Franklin Ave.
Keawjai
Mekong Gawa
Sabado Sabadete
Tonki

Nakano/Chuo Line
中野／中央線沿線

Cadiz
Carthago
El Torito
Guruppe
Il Primo
Kino Küche
Korinbo
Nankantei
PAO
Pata Pata
Phrik Khii Nuu
Ryukyu Shukan
Sujatha
Tabemono Mura
Ukai Toriyama

Nihonbashi/Shiba/
Waterfront
日本橋／芝／
ウォーターフロント

Al Ponte
Bodaiju
Edogin
Fukutomi
Komahachi
Meson el Vasco
Mihosai
Royal Bengal
Sasashin
Torigin
Volga

Nishi Azabu
西麻布

Ari's Lamplight
Bindi
Bistro de la Cité
Casa Monnon
El Mocambo
Hokkaien
Itcho
Jungle
Kaotan Ramen
Kenbokke
La Escondida
Le Soufflé
Monsoon Café
Oz Café
Rice Terrace

Roppongi
六本木

Bellini's Pizza Kitchen
Bengawan Solo
Bernd's Bar German
  Restaurant
Cerveza
Chicken's
DJ's Pizzeria
Erawan
Ex
Fukuzushi
Gokoku
The Hamburger Inn
Hard Rock Cafe
Ichioku
Il Bianco
Il Forno
Inakaya
Kantipur
Kobe 77
Kuimonoya Raku
La Gola
La Terrasse
La Terre
Le Récamier
Lilla Dalarna
Maenam
Moti Darbar
Nanbantei
Panic Café

Gaia
The Hamburger Inn
Hanezawa Gardens
Hard Rock Cafe
Jungle
Kaiseitei East
Kirin Yokohama Beer
  Village
La Bodeguita
La Bohème
La Marée de Chaya
Las Chicas
Les Deux Magots
Le Soufflé
Oz Café
Pastis
Sankt Gallen
Selan
Spiral Café
Vino Hirata
Warung I
Wedgwood Tea Room
Zest Cantina

Chinese
中華料理

Aux Sept Bonheurs
Be-Mi
Bodaiju
Bunlin
Charlie House
Da Hong Yun Tiantian
Ding Hao
Hokkaien
Jigoku Ramen Hyottoko
Kaotan Ramen
Korinbo
Madame Chang's Home
  Kitchen
Mihosai
Reikyo
Rosokanabejo
Ryunohige
Ryunoko
Sankt Gallen
Seiryumon West
Shanfon
Shinsekai
Shin-Yokohama Ramen
  Hakubutsukan

Sodoten
Tainan Taami
Tohkalin
Tohryu
Tokyo Daihanten
Zuien Bekkan

French
フランス料理

Argent
Au Mouton Blanc
Bistro d'Arbre
Bistrot de la Cité
Bordeaux Cellar
Brasserie Bernard
Brasserie Flo
Brasserie Lecomte
Brasserie Pierrot
Café des près
Cahors
Chez Pierre
Enoteca
Gorger Jackpot
Ile de France
La Blanche
La Dînette
La Marée de Chaya
L'Amphore
La Terre
Le Mange-Tout
Le Récamier
L'Escargot
Les Deux Magots
Le Soufflé
L'Orangerie de Paris
Lyon
Mikasa Continental Hiroo
Pas à Pas
Pas Mal
Pastis
Petit Marché
Pomme de Terre
Requiem
Taillevent Robuchon
Tokyo Paris Shokudo

German/Other European
ドイツ料理／その他
ヨーロッパ料理

Bernd's Bar
Bois Celeste
Brussels
Chez Prisi
Club Kreisel
Ex
Keyaki Grill
Kino Küche
Kleines Wien
Lilla Dalarna
Pauke
Pilsen
Rogovski
Stockholm
Volga

Indian/Sri Lankan/
Nepalese
インド料理／スリラン
カ料理／ネパール料理

Ajanta
Ashoka
Bindi
Bombay
Café Tandoor
Ceylon Inn
Kantipur
Kenbokke
Maharao
Mandala
Mela
Moti Darbar
Nataraj
Palette
PAO
Raj Mahal
Royal Bengal
Samrat
Sujatha
The Taj
Tomoca
Yeti

Italian
イタリア料理
Alloro
Al Ponte
Bellini's Pizza Kitchen
Bistro Campagnard
Bunryu
Buono Buono
Buon Viso
Carmine
Chianti
DJ's Pizzeria
Domani
Il Bianco
Il Forno
Il Primo
La Baracca
L'Affresco
La Gola
La Granata
La Patata
La Pineta
La Ranarita
La Terazza
La Verde
Marumo
Pain Panico
Pasar
Pata Pata
Pizzeria Sabatini
Ponte Vecchio
Ros Marino
Sicilia
Sin
Sorriso
Tanto
Taverna Azzurra
Trattoria Theo
Un Quinto
Vino Hirata

Japanese
和食
Akaoni
Akimoto
Botan
Chablis-An
Donchaca

Edogin
Enjuu
Fukutomi
Fukuzushi
Fujii
Goemon
Gokoku
Gu
Guruppe
Hantei
Healthy-kan
Ichi
Ichinochaya
Iidaya
Inakaya
Itcho
Iwashiya
Jugemu
Kaiseitei East
Kobe 77
Komahachi
Kuimonoya Raku
Marugo
Matsuribayashi Ginjokura
Matsuya
Mokichi
Mominoki House
Mr. Garlic
Nanbantei
Nanpu
Panic Café
Rera Chise
Robata
Ryukyu Shukan
Sakana-tei
Sasa no Yuki
Sasashin
Sashimiya
Shabuzen
Shin-Yokohama Ramen
  Hakubutsukan
Shizenkan II
Shunju
Sushisei
Suzume no Oyado
Tabemono Mura
Tamakyu
Tenmi
Tofuya

Tonki
Tops
Torifuji
Torigin
Toriyoshi
Toya
Tsubakiya
Tsunahachi Tsunohazuan
Ukai Toriyama
Yurakucho Yakitori Alley

Korean
韓国料理
Grace
Hallelujah Bussan
Hosenka
Kotchan
Mugyodon
Nankantei
Tokuju

Mexican/Latin American
メキシコ料理／ラテン・アメリカ料理
Casa Monnon
Casa Verde
El Mocambo
El Torito
Jungle
La Bodeguita
La Casita
La Escondida
La Jolla
Muito Bom
Sacì Pererê
Zia
Zest Cantina

Mukokuseki
無国籍料理
(Eclectic and/or Japanese Contemporary)
An An
Cadiz
Chablis-An
Chicken's
Gaia
Gokoku
Ichi

Ichioku
Itcho
Kri-Kri
Kuimonoya Raku
Ninniku Mura
Panic Café
Pao
Robata
Tokyo Kaisen Market
Waigaya

Natural/Vegetarian
自然食／ベジタリアン料理
Bodaiju
Chicken's
Ding Hao
Goemon
Gu
Guruppe
Healthy-kan
Ichioku
Jugemu
Korinbo
Mominoki House
Nataraj
Natural House
Pata Pata
Sasa no Yuki
Shizenkan II
Tabemono Mura
Tsubakiya
Vegetable Magic II

Spanish/Mediterranean
スペイン料理／地中海料理
Cadiz
Casa Bella
Casa de Fujimori
El Castellano
Flags Annex
Los Reyes Magos
Meson el Vasco
Sabado Sabadete
Vegetable Magic II
Venencia

Thai/Southeast Asian
タイ料理／東南アジア料理
Angkor Wat
Ban-Thai
Bengawan Solo
Bougainvillea
Cambodia
Coca Restaurant
 Hakkeijima
 Erawan
Gold Leaf
Hong Phat
Jembatan Merah
Kao Tai
Keawjai
Maenam
Maenam no Hotori
Mae Yao
Mai-Thai
Mareichan
Mekong Gawa
Monsoon Café
Muan Thai Nabe
Myun
Only Malaysia
Phrik Khii Nuu
Rice Terrace
Saigon
Secca
Shinsekai
Siam
Yatana

Turkish/Middle Eastern
トルコ料理／中東料理
Apadana
Arabia
Asena
Carthago
Istanbul
Kri-Kri
Saronikos
Topkapi

CHEAP EATS
(¥2000 or less)
格安

Apetito
Bamboo
Bellini's Pizza Kitchen
Bindi
Bombay
Brasserie Lecomte
Cadiz
Café de Ropé
Café Tandoor
Casa Verde
Cerveza
Ceylon Inn
Chablis-An
Charlie House
Chicken's
Ding Hao
DJ's Pizzeria
Donchaca
El Torito
7025 Franklin Ave.
Fujii
Gaia
Gu
Guruppe
Hallelujah Bussan
The Hamburger Inn
Hard Rock Cafe
Healthy-kan
Homework's
Hong Phat
Jigoku Ramen Hyottoko
Jungle
Kao Tai
Kaotan Ramen
Kenbokke
Kirin Yokohama Beer
 Village
Korinbo
La Jolla
Les Deux Magots
Mae Yao
Mandala
Mareichan
Marugo
Matsuya

Mela
Mominoki House
Moti Darbar
Mr. Garlic
Nataraj
Natural House
Raj Mahal
Rera Chise
Ros Marino
Royal Bengal
Samrat
Seiryumon West
Shin-Yokohama Ramen
  Hakubutsukan
Shizenkan II
Sicilia
Suzume no Oyado
Tabemono Mura
Tainan Taami
Tanto
Tenmi
Tonki
Tony Roma's
Top Dog
Torigin
Tsubakiya
Valençay
Yurakucho Yakitori Alley

Ajanta
Ari's Lamplight
Billy Barew's Beer Bar
Bois Celeste
Brussels
DJ's Pizzeria
Donchaca
El Torito
Gu
Hallelujah Bussan
The Hamburger Inn
Hard Rock Cafe
Hosenka
Kaiseitei East

Kleines Wien
La Bohème
Maenam
Matsuribayashi Ginjokura
Moti
Nanpu
Oz Café
Panic Café
Pauke
Royal Bengal
Seiryumon West
Shinsekai
Sicilia
Tokuju
Zest Cantina

Akaoni
Angkor Wat
Chicken's
El Torito
Fukuzushi
Guruppe
La Bohème
La Jolla
Le Mange-Tout
Lunchan Aoyama
Mela
Natural House
New York Grill
Raj Mahal
Sakana-tei
Samrat
Shizenkan II
Sujatha
Tabemono Mura
Tenmi
Tohkalin
Victoria Station
Wedgwood Tea Room

Alloro
Apetito
Argent
Bamboo
Ban-Thai
Bellini's Pizza Kitchen
Billy Barew's Beer Bar
Bistro d'Arbre
Blue Point
Bordeaux Cellar
Brasserie Bernard
Brasserie Pierrot
Café de Ropé
Café des près
Café Tandoor
Chez Pierre
Club Kreisel
Coca Restaurant
  Hakkeijima
DJ's Pizzeria
El Mocambo
Enoteca
7025 Franklin Ave.
Goemon
Hanezawa Gardens
Homework's
Il Forno
Jungle
Kirin Yokohama Beer
  Village
La Bohème
La Casita
La Marée de Chaya
La Pineta
Las Chicas
La Terazza
La Terrasse
La Terre
Le Récamier
L'Escargot
Les Deux Magots
Le Soufflé

Lunchan Aoyama
Meson el Vasco
Mikasa Continental Hiroo
Mokichi
Monsoon Café
Oz Café
Pomme de Terre
Selan
Top Dog
Ukai Toriyama
Un Quinto
Yurakucho Yakitori Alley
Zest Cantina

SPLURGES
(¥10,000 up)
見栄張り

Aux Sept Bonheurs
Chez Pierre
Fukuzushi
Inakaya
Keyaki Grill
La Baracca
La Marée de Chaya
L'Amphore
L'Orangerie de Paris
Shunju
Spago
Taillevent Robuchon
Tohkalin

SUNDAY BRUNCH
日曜日のブランチ

L'Orangerie de Paris
Lunchan Aoyama
New York Grill
Selan
Spiral Café
Tokyo Daihanten
Trader Vic's

Garlic Restaurant 3446 5887
Ninnikuya

トーキョージャーナル・レストランガイド

1994 年 12 月 20 日　第 1 刷発行

著者　　ジョン・ケネデル
発行者　渡辺　正憲
発行所　洋販出版株式会社
　　　　〒169　東京都新宿区大久保3丁目14-9
　　　　電話　03-3204-1758

発売元　洋販（日本洋書販売配給株式会社）
　　　　〒169　東京都新宿区大久保3丁目14-9
　　　　電話　03-3208-0181

印刷　　小宮山印刷工業株式会社